P9-DGT-765

The Boulanger Affair

Political Crossroad of France
1886–1889

The Boulanger Affair

Political Crossroad of France

1886-1889

FREDERIC H. SEAGER

Cornell University Press

ITHACA, NEW YORK

Copyright © 1969 by Cornell University

All rights reserved. Except for brief quotations in a review, this book, or parts thereof, must not be reproduced in any form without permission in writing from the publisher. For information address Cornell University Press, 124 Roberts Place, Ithaca, New York 14850.

First published 1969

Library of Congress Catalog Card Number: 68–9753

PRINTED IN THE UNITED STATES OF AMERICA
BY VAIL-BALLOU PRESS, INC.

To the memory of my father

Preface

Whenever a new work appears on a familiar subject, the author owes his readers a word of explanation. In the case of the Boulanger affair, the subject is not only familiar but, as treated by several writers, positively entertaining. History books abound with accounts of the general on horseback who nearly overthrew the Third Republic and, failing in the effort, shot himself on the grave of his mistress. Anyone who attempts a new treatment of the affair must, therefore, first ask himself what questions, if any, these accounts leave unanswered.

To English-speaking readers, the best-known version is probably that found in *The Development of Modern France, 1870–1939,* published in 1940 by Denis W. Brogan. The French, it is claimed, were tired of the Republic by 1886 and rushed to join a movement called Boulangism, which in this account is indistinguishable from the personal popularity of Boulanger. The General was indeed so popular that all the malcontents of France—apparently the vast majority of the population—wished to see him overthrow the regime. Only his personal indecision kept him from seizing supreme power after his election victory in Paris on January 27, 1889. By fleeing to Belgium several weeks later, Boulanger destroyed the movement which had sprung up around him. The Republic, concludes Brogan, was "saved." What the author fails to explain is why the French, who were apparently so hostile to the regime at one moment, overwhelmingly rallied to it the next.

Professor Brogan's views on the affair are apparently inspired by *Le boulangisme,* written by Adrien Dansette in 1938. At the heart of the problem is what Dansette calls "latent Caesarism" in France. According to this theory, it was nostalgia for the Second Empire that drove the French to support a dashing general's bid for power. This support is called Boulangism; but Boulanger's following was so varied, and the aims of his partisans so often contradictory, that Dansette resorts to the expression, "the multiplication of Boulangisms" in order to include everyone. This awkward terminology leaves the reader with little understanding of the movement's political content.

Jacques Chastenet, author of a popular multivolume *Histoire de la Troisième République* of recent vintage, solves the problem of content simply by not discussing it. Once we are informed that Boulangism was "launched" by a popular song, the whole affair is reduced to the proportions of a tragi-comic opera. Boulanger, the lead tenor, leaps to stage center, is seconded by a discordant chorus of royalists, Bonapartists, and militants of the Left, and is cheered wildly by the populace. At the critical moment, however, he retreats to the wings, where his mistress detains him. Enter now the villain, Interior Minister Ernest Constans, who forces our hero to flee. The curtain falls amid a barrage of insults exchanged by members of the chorus.

Inasmuch as the anecdotal approach of the three foregoing writers is typical of conservative historians, one might expect a thoroughly political analysis of the affair from a socialist. On that score, however, Alexandre Zévaès has little to offer in his

1931 work, *Au temps du boulangisme.* Although the author does see Boulangism as a genuinely popular movement directed against the bourgeois Republic, his narrative revolves almost exclusively around Boulanger, the man. The political significance of the affair is unclear.

One historian who manages to discuss the question without referring constantly to the General is a former member of *Action Française,* a kind of Marxist monarchist named Emmanuel Beau de Loménie. In the second volume of *Les responsabilités des dynasties bourgeoises,* which first appeared in 1947, Beau de Loménie relies mainly on the newspaper press to show how the Right was attracted to Boulangism. True to his thesis that the economic interests of the Orleanists and those of the moderate Republicans were mutual, he notes that the former had no vital reason to seek an alliance with Boulanger. The author largely avoids discussing the General's original leftist followers, however, and fails to explain their preoccupation with constitutional revision.

It remained to Jacques Néré to take up the constitutional question in an unpublished doctoral thesis of 1959 entitled "La crise industrielle de 1882 et le mouvement boulangiste." A student of Ernest Labrousse, Néré devotes the first half of his dissertation—about 500 pages—to showing that an economic crisis did exist prior to the Boulanger affair. In the second half he attempts to prove that the Boulangists favored revision of the constitution as the sole means of effecting social reforms. Unfortunately, he produces little evidence that they possessed such a coherent policy. His only published work on the subject, *Le boulangisme et la presse* (1964), contains a wealth of newspaper clippings on Boulanger but very little on his party's program.

As the foregoing works indicate, there is no lack of secondary material on the Boulanger affair. Yet none of the authors mentioned above has succeeded in explaining the place of this episode in the context of French political history. To arrive at such an explanation, the historian must at the very least try to define Boulangism. If, as Dansette and others claim, Boulangism was nothing more or less than the General's personal popularity, it was a phenomenon of short duration and minor importance. The Boulanger affair is then a mere anecdote, a passing shadow without any real influence on the evolution of the Third Republic.

If, on the other hand, Boulangism was a political philosophy, it should be studied both for its origins and its lasting effects on the political life of France. One must ascertain who the Boulangists were and why they were so eager to revise the constitution. The reaction of the established political parties to this new movement also requires explanation. Why did the Orleanists rush to abandon a constitution which they themselves had written, and how did the different republican groups try to deal with this new wave of revisionism? Their behavior may help explain the success of Boulangism as well as its crushing defeat.

The present study, then, proposes to analyze the Boulanger affair as a chapter in the political history of modern France. For this purpose, contemporary newspapers and periodicals were consulted extensively in order to gain an understanding of political issues. Police reports were also of help in examining the inner workings of the Boulangist organization and those of its allies. Personal diaries and memoirs yielded some information of value, but their importance was clearly secondary.

An inquiry of this kind presents several difficulties, among which the greatest is probably the evaluation of party labels in French politics of the time. The left-center-right spectrum has been respected because this is the way Frenchmen categorized their political formations. On the other hand, a real attempt

Preface

was made to get behind the party labels and to explain in what sense a given politician was leftist, centrist, or rightist. In most cases, ideology rather than economic interests determined political classifications in the 1880's.

Perhaps the most challenging aspect of this work was to study a political disturbance and always to bear in mind that it took place in a country which, at the time, was the only major power in Europe to have a republican form of government.

The author wishes to thank Professor Shepard B. Clough of Columbia University, whose counsel has been of inestimable value. Professor John H. Wuorinen also offered many helpful suggestions. Finally, to Professor Edward W. Fox of Cornell University goes a heartfelt expression of gratitude for having suggested this topic and given initial orientation to its research.

Frederic H. Seager

Montreal
May 1968

Contents

Contents

The Boulanger Affair

Political Crossroad of France
1886–1889

1

Defeat for the Center
1885

Behind the many cabinet crises and political scandals which dot the history of France's Third Republic, there can be discerned a distinct political evolution: whereas ideological issues were prominent in the regime's early years, economic questions came to the fore by the twentieth century.[1] It is this evolution which perhaps best explains the gradual shift in the political center of gravity from right to left during the Republic's first four decades. The only essential difference of views between the monarchists who dominated the National Assembly of 1871 and their Republican successors was over the form of government. In the 1880's, however, these moderate Republicans were challenged by Radicals, who pressed for what they called a more militantly republican policy, especially toward the Church. The Radicals, in turn, were pushed into the center by the election, in 1893, of a large bloc of Socialists.

In retrospect, one might almost say that each party group which held power in the early years of the Third Republic had been elected to accomplish a particular task. Once its task was

[1] David Thomson, *Democracy in France: The Third and Fourth Republics* (London: Oxford University Press, 1958), pp. 72–74.

1

accomplished, that party had to yield to another, further to the left, which had a new task to perform, and so on. Thus, the monarchist assembly of 1871 was elected primarily to make peace with Germany and give the new regime a certain measure of financial stability.[2] Having fulfilled their mandate, the monarchists were replaced in government by moderate Republicans, whose main purpose was to establish the Republic on a permanent constitutional basis. Once the Republic was no longer seriously questioned, the Radicals assumed the reins of government after 1900 and severed the connection between Church and state.[3]

Simple as this procedure may seem to historians of the twentieth century, it was riddled with complications while it was taking place. For one thing, the party being displaced did not accept its defeat gracefully, but, as is only natural in politics, tried to regain its former position. At the same time, the challengers on the left raised new issues in order to embarrass the party in power and eventually to replace it. In the course of this evolution, economic and social issues, particularly those relating to industry, came into prominence only gradually. Unlike Germany and England, France experienced only slow and inefficient economic growth in the 1871–1914 period.[4] Since industrialization made only slight advances, the number of voters engaged in factory work remained a minority. Their problems, though persistent, were therefore of only secondary importance on the scale of national politics. At the

[2] Jacques Chastenet, *Histoire de la Troisième République*, Vol. I: *L'enfance de la Troisième, 1870–1879* (Paris: Hachette, 1952), p. 52.

[3] François Goguel, *La politique des partis sous la IIIe République* (Paris: Editions du Seuil, 1958), pp. 124–128.

[4] John H. Clapham, *The Economic Development of France and Germany, 1815–1914* (Cambridge: The University Press, 1955), p. 159.

same time, the low level of productivity in France allowed an artisan class to survive, albeit with some difficulty. General indifference to workers' problems allowed chronic discontent to smolder among France's artisans and industrial proletariat, most of which were concentrated in or near Paris.

Chronic discontent bred a chronic protest vote, which was the bane of Third Republic politics. The chief target of such protest was immobilism in government, which resulted from a parliamentary incapacity to form stable coalitions. Governments were often preoccupied with defending their parliamentary majorities and had little opportunity to enact legislation on vital issues. The resulting stalemate left the hardcore opposition no free expression within the system; its only outlet was protest.[5] As long as the government was not completely bogged down and could manage the affairs of state with relative smoothness, the protest vote was only a minor irritant. Should the government be faced with systematic opposition on both sides of the Chamber, however, it might easily retreat into a position of self-defense and virtually cease to govern. At that point the smoldering protest could ignite a full-scale crisis. One such crisis was the Boulanger affair, which reached its tortured climax in 1889, at a time when the French government was caught in just such a stalemate. The political expression which was then assumed by the chronic urban protest was known as Boulangism.

The Boulanger affair is generally pictured as a vast, spontaneous popular movement toward Caesarism. This explanation is based on the theory that the French people were dissatisfied with the Republic and returned, if only briefly, to

---

[5] Stanley Hoffman, "Protest in Modern France," *The Revolution in World Politics,* ed. Morton A. Kaplan (New York: Wiley, 1962), pp. 76–79.

their supposedly deep-seated preference for a general on horseback.[6] Yet Boulanger himself was a mediocre personality; he was no Napoleon and still less a Hitler. It is doubtful that more than a small minority of those who voted for him were seeking a Boulangist empire. The bulk of the General's votes in by-elections came not from Boulangists, who were in fact latter-day Jacobins, but from embittered royalists and Bonapartists. Inasmuch as the royalist and Bonapartist groups had deliberately avoided presenting candidates against Boulanger, the rightist voters really had no one else to support. But they were not Boulangists, and they did not vote for Boulangist candidates against royalists or Bonapartists in the general elections of 1889. The General's hard-core support, in the by-elections as in 1889, was drawn from artisans and industrial workers, who were not seeking a dictatorship, but rather a better sort of Republic, more responsive to their needs.

Even the common denominator under which were grouped the very disparate forces of the Right and the far Left was not the General himself, but a vague promise to revise the constitution of 1875. Since the Third Republic's basic laws had been drafted and passed by a monarchist assembly, they did not enjoy official Republican sanction. When, in 1887, the royalist pretender formally rejected the document which was to have served as his own charter, his party also abandoned the regime. Now that the constitution was left without avowed defenders, its revision became a convenient issue for any revolutionary group or coalition.

Yet it was, at bottom, an artificial issue. If Frenchmen of the late 1880's lacked a fervent loyalty to their constitution, they nonetheless preferred the regime to unknown experi-

[6] This thesis is best expressed by Adrien Dansette, *Le boulangisme* (Paris: Fayard, 1946), pp. 143–146 *et passim*.

4

ments. With the defeat of Boulanger and his allies in the general elections of 1889, the constitution quickly ceased to be questioned. Stripped of its melodramatic aspects, then, the Boulanger affair is revealed as one of the great turning points in the history of the Third Republic. It was at this juncture that the government met and eliminated a bothersome ideological question—that of the Republic's monarchist origins—before taking up more practical tasks. Thus relieved of its ideological handicap, the regime emerged from the affair greatly strengthened.

In reality, the basic problem raised by the Boulanger affair was less the regime itself than the difficulty of a center coalition to govern without a responsible opposition. The General became the figurehead of the Right, which had refused to yield to the Center, and of the far Left, which chafed at the slowness with which the Center considered reforms. Opposition to the Center was the only real factor which united the two components of the Conservative-Boulangist alliance, and this opposition had existed long before the affair itself. Its origins lie in the evolution of the Third Republic prior to the general elections of 1885.

REPUBLICAN POLITICS BEFORE 1885

The Third Republic, France's longest-lived regime since 1789, was founded as a republic only in name. Its constitutional laws were passed in 1875 by an assembly whose Orleanist leaders hoped eventually to restore the monarchy by substituting their pretender for the current President of the Republic.[7] Following the general elections of 1876, however, a Republican majority entered the Chamber. In a famous test of strength on May 16, 1877, these Republicans succeeded in

[7] J.-L. de Lanessan, *La république démocratique* (Paris: Colin, 1897), p. ii.

5

imposing their will on Marshal MacMahon, whom the Orleanists had installed as chief of state.[8] MacMahon's resignation in 1879 and his replacement by Jules Grévy, an avowed Republican, marked the final step in the regime's transition from monarchist to Republican control.[9] Confused and disorganized, the forces of the Right lost still more ground to the Republicans in the general elections of 1881.[10]

By far the greatest number of Republicans in the overwhelmingly Republican Chamber of 1881 were moderates, whose conservative economic views reflected those of their constituents. Most French peasants were firmly attached to the Republic if only because they owned their land by virtue of the Revolutionary land settlement. At the same time, they shared with the bourgeoisie a deep-seated conviction in the sanctity of private property.[11] It was to these unadventurous elements in French society that the Republican Deputies elected in 1881 owed most of their success.

Another important factor in the great Republican victory of 1881 was the profound disunity on the Right. Most divided were the royalists, who were split into two factions. The Legitimists supported the Comte de Chambord, while the Orleanists gave their formal allegiance to the Comte de Paris, grandson of Louis-Philippe. Among the Bonapartists there were also divided loyalties. Despite the general disrepute into which the Second Empire had fallen, this party still retained some of its popular appeal in the countryside, particularly in the department of the Charente. But the death in 1879 of the Prince Imperial forced its members to choose between Jérôme Bona-

[8] J.-J. Chevalier, *Histoire des institutions politiques de la France moderne, 1789–1945* (Paris: Dalloz, 1958), pp. 321–324.

[9] *Ibid.*, pp. 335–338.

[10] Goguel, *op. cit.*, pp. 55–56.

[11] James Bryce, *Modern Democracies* (2 vols.; New York: Macmillan, 1921), I, 220.

parte, cousin of the late Emperor, and Jérôme's son, Prince Victor. The former was an idle schemer who had virtually accepted the Republic, while the latter, although a professed "pure" Bonapartist, was too young to lead a political movement effectively.[12]

At the other end of the political spectrum stood the small band of Radical Deputies, who had seceded from the moderate Republicans following the *seize mai* incident.[13] This new party party resolved to be militantly Republican, as indicated by its official program, presented by Georges Clemenceau in a speech in Marseilles on October 28, 1880. Chief among the Radicals' demands were these: (1) complete amnesty for the Communards; (2) separation of church and state; (3) vastly expanded secular public education; (4) freedom of association, especially for trade unions; and (5) reform of the 1875 constitution. Economic and social reforms—such as the graduated income tax, a shorter work week, and the prohibition of child labor—were also mentioned, but rather as an afterthought.[14] Nor was the labor problem alluded to by Clodomir Dutilh, a positivist schoolteacher who attempted to summarize the Radicals' position in a hundred-page opuscule two years later. The only points which he added to Clemenceau's program were universal military service and a divorce law.[15]

In Europe of the 1880's, dominated as it was by monarchies, the very existence of a radical party appeared to the established classes as a fearsome novelty. But not even the

[12] France, Archives de la Préfecture de Police, B a/976, May 17, 1888; hereinafter cited as A.P.P.; Cf. René Rémond, *La droite en France de 1815 à nos jours* (Paris: Aubier, 1954), pp. 145–146.

[13] Lanessan, *op. cit.*, pp. 93–94.

[14] *La Justice,* Nov. 10, 1880.

[15] Clodomir Dutilh, *Opportunistes et radicaux* (Bordeaux: Bellier, 1882), pp. 19–20.

Radicals were to monopolize the French Left for long. On July 11, 1880, a law granting virtually total amnesty to the Communards was passed, so that Clemenceau's first demand had in effect already been met. The immediate result of the new law was to help its moderate Republican sponsors win a tremendous majority of seats in the Chamber of 1881.[16]

The long-term effect of the amnesty was, however, to increase pressure on the Center by the Left. Among the returning exiles the most important—or at least the most conspicuous—was Henri Rochefort, a self-styled intransigent, whose views were similar to those of the Radicals, but more extravagantly stated. Thanks in part to a severe split among the renascent Socialists in 1881, Rochefort enjoyed a large following among the workers of Paris.[17] The Radicals responded to this new force on the Left by reaffirming their desire to continue the work of the Revolution of 1789.[18] Now that the amnesty question was a dead letter, they had to redouble their efforts in other areas so as not to be outdone by the newly arrived Communards.

While the oppositions of Right and Left sought ways to increase their respective electoral followings, the government from 1881 to 1885 was firmly controlled by the Center parties. Chief among these was Gambetta's *Union républicaine,* dubbed the "Opportunists" by Rochefort because its members favored reforms only "when the time is opportune." [19] Since

[16] Jean T. Joughin, *The Paris Commune in French Politics, 1871–1880* (2 vols.; Baltimore: Johns Hopkins University Press, 1955), II, 478.

[17] Charles Seignobos, *L'évolution de la Troisième République, 1875–1914,* Vol. VIII of *Histoire de France contemporaine,* ed. Ernest Lavisse (10 vols.; Paris: Hachette, 1921), pp. 97–98.

[18] Dutilh, *op. cit.,* p. 15.

[19] J. Hampden Jackson, *Clemenceau and the Third Republic* (New York: Collier, 1962), p. 45.

the death of its founder in 1882, the party was led by Jules Ferry, who became known to his friends and enemies alike as the very incarnation of Opportunism. While the word "Republic" meant continuing revolution to the Left, Ferry understood it to mean a stable, bourgeois regime—just as legitimate in practice as any monarchy.[20] "To temper and moderate democracy is a noble role," he once remarked.[21] He wished to domesticate the Republic, making it acceptable to both the royalty of Europe and the bourgeoisie of France. Given that nation's diplomatic isolation and its need for orderly economic progress, such a policy seemed on its face quite reasonable.

Government by the Center did, however, have one serious defect: it operated without a loyal opposition on either the Right or the Left.[22] Although this defect was not immediately apparent in the wake of the Opportunists' success of 1881, it did make itself felt as the party tried to implement its program. On the domestic scene, state aid was allocated to the growing railroads and created vast new public works projects, especially in school construction. As a means of cultivating national patriotism, which had been too seldom in evidence during the Franco-Prussian War, state education was made secular, free, and compulsory throughout elementary school.[23] The Opportunists' foreign policy was dominated by a concern to get France out of its diplomatic isolation. Since this normally precluded any revolutionary expansion in

[20] Jules Ferry, *Discours et opinions*, ed. Paul Robiquet (7 vols.; Paris: Colin, 1893–1901), VII, 120–121.

[21] Charles de Mazade, "Chronique de la quinzaine," *Revue des Deux Mondes*, LXXVII (Sept. 1, 1886), 228.

[22] Cf. Edward Whiting Fox, "The Third Force, 1897–1939," *Modern France*, ed. Edward Mead Earle (Princeton: Princeton University Press, 1951), p. 127.

[23] Evelyn Martha Acomb, *The French Laic Laws, 1879–1889: The First Anti-clerical Campaign of the Third French Republic* (New York: Columbia University Press, 1941), pp. 98–99.

Europe, French territorial aggrandizement was limited to rather costly and not immediately popular colonial acquisitions in North Africa and the Far East.

Certain aspects of this program, such as state aid to railroad construction, pleased the French Right. Others, such as the laic school project, were favorably received by the Left. In order to oppose the Opportunists politically, however, both the Right and the Left repeatedly drew attention to the program's shortcomings. From 1881 to 1885, opportunities for such partisan criticism were rarely lacking. Railway expansion and school construction necessitated higher taxes, just as France entered a period of economic crisis in 1882.[24] Ferry won the enmity of the Paris proletariat by refusing to take more than token measures against growing unemployment. He blamed the recession on excessively high (!) wages, which, he claimed, left factory owners with hardly any funds to invest in new and more productive machines. Despite mounting demands, he steadfastly refused to raise tariffs or restrict the immigration of foreign workers.[25] In the election campaign of 1885, the Opportunists' economic policy became a convenient target for both the Left and the Right.[26]

Concerning the relationship between church and state, the Opportunists were similarly under fire from both sides. Inasmuch as Ferry's laic school program was inevitably anticlerical, many practicing Catholics were drawn into support for the Right, not because they were necessarily royalist or Bonapartist, but because the Republic seemed to them to be anti-Catholic as a matter of principle.[27] The Radicals, on the

[24] Shepard B. Clough, *France: A History of National Economics, 1789–1939* (New York: Scribner's, 1939), pp. 217–219.

[25] Jean Dietz, "Jules Ferry: Sa seconde présidence du Conseil, III," *Revue Politique et Parlementaire*, CLXIV (Dec. 10, 1935), 509–510.

[26] Cf. *infra*, pp. 12–13.

[27] Gabriel Monod, "The Political Situation in France," *Contemporary Review*, LV (April, 1889), 489.

other hand, accused Ferry of excessive timidity in not pressing for the immediate disestablishment of the Catholic church. To this he replied candidly that the abrogation of France's Concordat of 1801 with the Vatican would indeed be the logical outcome of the nation's current evolution in that field. But to effect it now, he argued, would rob the government of the vital power it still exercised over the French Church through its right to nominate bishops and pay clerical salaries.[28] Logical as such reasoning may have been, it does not appear to have satisfied anyone on the Left.

In similar fashion, Ferry tried to evade another chief Radical demand: revision of the constitution. The elections of 1881 had generally been interpreted as giving the Chamber a mandate to amend France's basic laws; but until becoming leader of the *Union républicaine,* Ferry had openly opposed revision. On being installed as Premier for a second time, he claimed to favor it, but in practice he sought to restrict any constitutional change as much as possible. He also tried to postpone enactment of such changes until shortly before the general elections of 1885, in order to remind the public of his party's role in promoting reforms.[29]

When Ferry summoned both Chambers to meet at Versailles from August 4 to 14, 1884, in order to discuss proposed amendments, he had the support of all factions of the Center. The moderate Republicans were not dissatisfied with the existing constitution, but they believed that not to act at once would invite more extreme changes later. The changes agreed upon at Versailles were modest enough: only one, which suppressed the seventy-five life senators and altered the electoral law for the Senate to make that body more represen-

[28] Ferry, *Discours et opinions,* III, 22–23.

[29] Jean Dietz, "Jules Ferry: La révision de la Constitution et le scrutin de liste, I," *Revue Politique et Parlementaire,* CLXVI (March 10, 1936), 520–522.

tative of urban areas, was at all significant. Such slim results were achieved after a session that was so disorderly as to leave even the most dedicated proponents of revision disillusioned with the procedure necessary to accomplish it.

It was these Deputies—Radicals for the most part—who were the real victims of Ferry's maneuver. To be sure, they could never agree on just what kind of revision they wanted. The recent creation of the *Ligue révisionniste* by the Radical leaders Barodet, Clemenceau, and Pelletan revealed the lamentable confusion of its members' ideas. Some wanted to call a constituent assembly to draft an entirely new constitution. Some wished to abolish the Senate; others, the office of President of the Republic. A few even wanted to abolish the Republic itself. All they could agree upon was that Ferry's halfway revision scheme had deprived them of a fruitful issue for the coming general elections.[30]

THE ELECTION CAMPAIGN

As the elections of 1885 approached, it became increasingly clear that the Opportunists were losing strength. On March 31 of that year, the second ministry of Jules Ferry was overthrown, ostensibly because of colonial difficulties. In reality, a temporary coalition of Right and Left defeated the Premier out of dissatisfaction with his domestic program, particularly the anticlerical measures and the vast expenditures for public works. French military reversals in Tonkin were simply a pretext, but one with such popular appeal that Ferry's own party largely abandoned him on a vote of confidence.[31] Seldom was the Opportunists' unofficial title so well deserved.

[30] Gabriel Monod, "Contemporary Life and Thought in France," *Contemporary Review*, XLVII (Jan., 1885), 120–123.

[31] Thomas F. Power, Jr., *Jules Ferry and the Renaissance of French Imperialism* (New York: King's Crown, 1944), p. 188.

The fall of the Ferry cabinet removed whatever centralizing influence the Opportunist party still retained. Always content to follow public opinion rather than lead it, the Opportunists avoided questions of principle and hoped to stay in power through the adroit use of political patronage. By 1885, however, such use was widely considered abuse. In the first years of the Third Republic, public officials had been chosen primarily on the basis of ability. Even capable civil servants who had served under the Second Empire were allowed to keep their posts. After 1879, however, the public services were carefully combed, with the result that all administrators suspected of rightist leanings were dismissed and replaced by loyal Republicans. The hiring policy of the Opportunists became increasingly circumscribed until favoritism began to exclude even qualified personnel who held opinions differing from those of the government. As a result, virtually all institutions of the Republic, including the magistracy, were in Opportunist control by 1885.[32]

In defense of the Opportunists it may be noted that some of the judges who were removed had been openly hostile to the government after 1877, and that the Opportunist "purge" was somewhat more moderate than what the Radicals demanded.[33] Yet the Opportunists' exclusiveness did leave them open to the charge of government by coterie, a charge frequently leveled at them in 1888 and 1889 by the followers of General Boulanger. It also helped postpone a solution to one of the regime's most urgent problems: that of incorporating the Right, especially the Orleanists, into the Republic. Outside the Republic, the Right continued to be a disloyal opposition,

[32] Monod, "Political Situation in France," p. 483.
[33] Jacques Chastenet, *Histoire de la Troisième République*, Vol. II: *La République des républicains, 1879–1893* (Paris: Hachette, 1954), p. 55.

which later provided Boulanger with most of his votes and almost all his campaign funds.

If the parties of the Right still refused to join the Republic, they at least knew how to adapt to it for electoral purposes. The death of the Comte de Chambord, France's last surviving Bourbon pretender, in August, 1883, had helped reduce differences among the royalists. In a show of unity that contrasted sharply with the Right's disorganized spectacle of 1881, they now joined forces with the Bonapartists and some conservative Republicans under a single label: Conservative. The Conservative party wisely avoided any talk of a restoration (which would only have split its ranks again) and instead concentrated its attacks less on the regime itself than on bad government. A pre-election appeal in the nation's leading royalist newspaper reflected the new strategy.

Persecuted Catholics, hard-pressed taxpayers, humiliated heads of families, peasants crushed by taxes and high interest, businessmen hard hit by [foreign] competition, shopkeepers affected by recessions, royalists, Bonapartists, Imperialists, Solutionists, and honest, disillusioned Republicans!

Vote for the Conservative lists—that is, against waste, against faraway expeditions, against violence, against infamy, against Republican turpitude! Vote for God, for Order, and for *La Patrie!* [34]

The Bonapartists were, if anything, even more conciliatory. Paul de Léoni, one of their most widely read journalists, wrote shortly before the elections: "The Republican regime is no longer questioned. In the last elections the issue was one of *establishing* the Republic. Today what matters is to *organize* it." As both Opportunists and Radicals sought to discredit the Conservatives by calling them reactionary, de Léoni objected,

[34] *Le Gaulois,* Oct. 2, 1885.

saying: "The 'reaction' does not threaten the Republic; it threatens only the Opportunists. . . . There are no reactionaries; there are only the discontented." [35] Having had power all to themselves for four years, the Opportunists now had to face partisan attacks from an opposition whose only unifying factor was anti-Opportunism. A similar kind of opposition later made Boulanger a threat to the regime.

In the campaign against the incumbent party, the Radicals were every bit as active as the Conservatives. Three years earlier, Dutilh had written: "In my view, the struggle since the last elections has been between Opportunists and Radicals." [36] The Radicals apparently accepted this view in 1885; paying little attention to the Right, they concentrated their greatest fury on the moderate Republicans. A pre-election manifesto by the Radical committee of the Seine-et-Oise bitterly criticized the Opportunists for waste and monopoly of power. That the tone and even the wording of this notice were markedly similar to those published by the Conservatives apparently did not trouble its authors.[37] In similar fashion, the official electoral program of the national Radical committee reflected Conservative criticism by calling for an end to the Opportunist "policy of adventures and conquests." [38]

Radical attacks on the Opportunists were motivated by a further consideration: that of having no enemies on the left. A few weeks before the elections, the principal Radical newspapers of Paris (the capital then had some fifty dailies) banded together in a so-called *Union de la presse radicale et socialiste* to support a common list of candidates. There was, in fact, nothing socialistic about this group except the adjec-

[35] *Le Pays,* Sept. 25, 1885.   [36] Dutilh, *op. cit.,* p. 23.
[37] André Daniel, *L'année politique,* Vol. XII (1885) (Paris: Charpentier, 1886), p. 194.
[38] *Ibid.,* p. 181.

tive itself, which had apparently been appended in an attempt to win votes from Paris workers. In those days of economic distress, the very word "socialism" had much appeal for the struggling urban masses, most of whom understood socialist theories only slightly, if at all. Despite its label, however, the *Union* failed to win the membership of *La Lanterne* and Rochefort's *L'Intransigeant,* two extreme Jacobin but non-Marxist papers. Although they actually supported the same list of candidates, their editors wished to remain conspicuously apart from the Radical party. The effect of this move was to embarrass the Radical leaders by making them realize that they had been overtaken at the vanguard of the left.[39]

In a vain attempt to catch up, the Radical party issued a new pre-election manifesto, proclaiming its allegiance to socialism—albeit in the vaguest possible terms. "Whoever is not a socialist today is not a Republican," it cried. Yet the Radicals themselves were far too firmly attached to the institution of private property ever to espouse true socialist doctrine.[40] Other than some very general criticism of the country's existing tax structure, the manifesto raised no economic issues. It was largely a repetition of older themes, coupled with increased attacks on the Opportunists, who were accused of betraying "the spirit of the Revolution." [41] Thus in order to prove their loyalty to the Left, the Radicals were reduced to the expedient of exaggerating their differences—which in many cases were only of degree—with the Center.

Caught in a brutal crossfire, the Opportunists did precious little to defend themselves. The party's leaders drew up no electoral manifesto because they could not agree on one.

[39] *La Justice,* Sept. 27, 1885.
[40] Mermeix [Gabriel Terrail], *La France socialiste: Notes d'histoire contemporaine* (Paris: Fetscherin et Chuit, 1886), p. 5.
[41] *La Justice,* Oct. 1, 1885.

Throughout the country, Opportunist candidates appeared before the voters as penitents who denounced Ferry openly, hoping thereby to shift all discredit on to him.[42] In the end, however, they seem to have succeeded only in projecting Ferry's mistakes on the whole party. Like most other Opportunists, Ferry addressed himself mainly to the peasants, for whom he professed to have great respect.[43] Yet his government had done little to combat the phylloxera epidemic which ravaged most of France's vineyards. At the same time, the Tonkin expedition had aroused deep suspicion among the peasants, who could see no practical compensation for the cost involved.[44] Sensing the growing criticism of his policies, Ferry himself assumed an apologetic attitude during the 1885 election campaign. In a speech before a largely Radical audience in Lyons, he asked plaintively: "Do you really think that we liked colonial adventures any more than you do?"[45]

The Opportunists' lack of unity on both the program and the campaign levels might have been less dangerous if not for a recently enacted change in voting procedure. Under the *scrutin d'arrondissement,* which had been in effect since 1871, the Chamber's electoral base had been the single-member constituency. Beginning with Gambetta, however, the French Left favored the *scrutin de liste,* by which voters chose an entire slate of candidates for each department. Camille Pelletan spoke for his fellow Radicals by calling it "the only voting procedure compatible with Republican doctrine." His party contended that the single-member constituency filled the

[42] Gabriel Monod, "Contemporary Life and Thought in France," *Contemporary Review,* XLVII (Dec., 1885), 888–890.

[43] Maurice Pottecher, *Jules Ferry* (Paris: Gallimard, 1930), pp. 172–173.

[44] E. Masseras, "La leçon des faits sous la République," *La Nouvelle Revue,* XXXVIII (Feb. 1, 1886), 506, 513.

[45] *Année politique,* XII (1885), 161.

Chamber with local worthies representing bourgeois or aristocratic interests. "The *scrutin d'arrondissement,*" Pelletan asserted, "is the vote for a man; the *scrutin de liste* is the vote for a program." [46]

While Gambetta was still alive, no change in voting procedure was approved by the Chamber out of fear that his personality would dominate the next elections. Since this possibility no longer existed in 1885, the Opportunist Deputy, René Waldeck-Rousseau, proposed the adoption of the *scrutin de liste* early that year. He casually dismissed as unfounded the objection of a colleague that such a change might result in losses for the Republicans. So strong was the reform current that even Ferry, who had previously opposed any electoral modifications, now had to follow it.[47] After only token debate, Waldeck's proposal won in the Chamber on March 24, 1885, by the lopsided vote of 402 to 91.[48] What had happened was that Republicans of all shades allowed themselves to be swayed by an ideological commitment to allow the main currents of public opinion to be faithfully reflected in the Chamber. An argument expressed earlier that such currents should be restrained in the interests of political stability[49] now went unheeded. In political terms, this proved to be a grievous error, for by 1885 the tide was running heavily against the Opportunists.

DEFEAT, BUT NOT DISASTER

The extent to which the incumbent party had lost popular favor was indicated by a remarkable advance of the Right on

[46] *La Justice,* March 20, 1885.

[47] *Année politique,* XII (1885), 45–47.

[48] France, *Journal Officiel,* Chambre des Députés, Débats Parlementaires (1885), 648–657; hereinafter cited as *J.O.C.*

[49] E. Masseras, "Le scrutin de liste et le scrutin d'arrondissement," *La Nouvelle Revue,* IX (March 1, 1881), 46–47.

the first ballot, which took place on October 4. By law and custom, French elections were held on the two-ballot system, by which candidates had to win an absolute majority to be elected on the first ballot. Those who did not remained in a runoff election called *ballotage*. On the second ballot, which took place two weeks after the first, a simple plurality sufficed for election. The ballot of October 4 gave 176 seats in the Chamber to the Conservatives, as against only 127 for Republicans of all persuasions. Symbolizing Opportunist ill fortune, Jules Ferry failed to win in clear majority in his home department of the Vosges. He won on the second ballot only after a Radical desisted in his favor.[50]

Admittedly, the Conservatives had used clever campaign tactics: they avoided calling the regime into question and instead concentrated on specific grievances. Everywhere, they anticipated the voters' wishes and promised to satisfy them. In wheatgrowing regions they promised to raise the price of wheat, while in industrial areas they agreed to lower the cost of life's necessities. Conservative candidates adopted a protectionist program in the North; in the Midi they were thoroughgoing free-traders. Ordinary citizens were promised lower taxes at the same time that civil servants were offered visions of higher salaries.[51] This may explain why in the normally Republican departments of the Nord and the Pas-de-Calais the Conservatives scored a brilliant victory over unified Republican lists.[52]

In general, however, the Republican candidates rarely appeared in unified lists for the first ballot. Except in Paris, where the Opportunists allowed the more popular Radicals to

[50] Auguste Soulier, *L'instabilité ministérielle sous la Troisième République, 1871–1938* (Paris: Sirey, 1939), p. 80.

[51] *Le Temps*, Oct. 15, 1885.

[52] Charles de Mazade, "Chronique de la quinzaine," *Revue des Deux Mondes*, LXXI (Oct. 15, 1885), 946.

win most of the seats as the only Republican candidates present, the two parties fought a vicious duel. Wherever possible, the Radicals drew up a separate slate, which was directed not against the Conservatives, but against the Opportunists alone.[53] Surveying the results of the first ballot, a leading Opportunist newspaper blamed Republican lack of unity for the defeat. "Out of ninety departments (including Algeria), there are fifty-one in which the Republicans have presented two or more lists. With a very few exceptions, neither of these lists will win an absolute majority of the votes cast." [54] The Opportunists then called on their Radical colleagues to join them in forming unified lists for the second ballot.

The Radicals' initial reaction after the first ballot, in which their position had improved markedly over that of 1881, was one of undisguised satisfaction. The election results, crowed Pelletan, "are the condemnation of Opportunism." [55] Yet only a day later, the same Pelletan was asking his fellow Radicals to make common cause with the condemned party. "One feeling emerges from the entire Republican press," he noted. "We must unite; we must band together; we must stand and face the enemy." The enemy was none other than the Conservatives, who were already making discreet overtures to the Opportunists for collaboration on the second ballot. To foil such plans, the Radicals now had to bury their differences with their erstwhile opponents—at least for the time being.[56] After much hesitation, even Rochefort, who prided himself on being in the very vanguard on the Left, urged reconciliation with the Center.[57]

[53] *Année politique*, XII (1885), 173–176.
[54] *La République Française*, Oct. 6, 1885.
[55] *La Justice*, Oct. 7, 1885.   [56] *La Justice*, Oct. 7, 1885.
[57] *L'Intransigeant*, Oct. 15, 1885.

Thus was begun the process of "Republican discipline," by which the Republican groups combined to win on the second ballot most of the seats not decided on the first. The fact that a simple plurality now sufficed for election was an obvious invitation for two parties, both of whose candidates were trailing in a three-sided contest, to present a combined list. Unless a substantial number of voters changed sides, the coalition was almost certain to win. So Opportunists and Radicals agreed that wherever both parties were present, the weaker candidates would withdraw in favor of the stronger. Such arrangements were to become established practice during the course of the Third Republic's history.[58] The effect of this particular agreement was to preserve Center government, while making it dependent on support from the Left.

Impressive as it was, the reconciliation of Opportunists and Radicals was not the only reason for their success on the second ballot. Another important factor was the overly hasty revelation by some Conservatives of their ultimate intentions. All moderate observers in France, including correspondents of foreign newspapers, agreed that the election results of October 4 in no way indicated dissatisfaction with France's republican form of government.[59] Yet as soon as the results became known, the nation's leading royalist newspaper erected outside its building an illuminated sign, which read as follows:

LE GAULOIS

172 MONARCHIST DEPUTIES

LONG LIVE FRANCE!

The sign attracted many passers-by, who soon began to fight according to their political convictions. Many arrests were made by the police, but the paper denied any provocation to violence. "On our side we cried: 'Long live France!' and

---

[58] Soulier, *loc. cit.*   [59] *Le Temps,* Oct. 8, 1885.

'Long live *Le Gaulois!*" it explained. "The cry of 'Long live the King!' remained in our hearts." [60]

Whatever one may think about the nuances of such an explanation, the secret was out: many Conservatives did want a restoration after all. Some Bonapartists went even further than the royalists in revealing their true aims. Subtlety was surely not the forte of Paul de Cassagnac, who was perhaps the most outspoken Bonapartist in the Chamber. Cassagnac was what was then known as a Solutionist: that is, he was willing to accept an Orleanist restoration if neither of the two Bonapartist claimants obtained the necessary following. On learning of the first ballot results, he gleefully announced: "The Republic is dying!" [61] A week later, he urged all Conservatives to show their true colors. "It would be perfectly childish for the Conservatives to keep a mask on their faces. We have been elected to overthrow the Republic. And we shall try to overthrow it." [62] Both Opportunists and Radicals were quick to draw public attention to such indiscretions.[63]

On the second ballot, the Republican coalition won an overall majority of seats in the Chamber, but remained far short of even the Center's undisputed hold on the legislature from 1881 to 1885. Further Conservative gains on October 18 were held to a mere 25 seats, while the combined Republican groups registered an advance of 254. Most of the Conservative candidates in *ballotage* had, moreover, refused to "unmask" and still avoided any attacks on the regime.[64] They thus largely confirmed Jules Simon's analysis of the elections. "It may be taken for certain," he reassured English readers,

[60] *Le Gaulois,* Oct. 6, 1885.   [61] *Le Pays,* Oct. 7, 1885.
[62] *Ibid.,* Oct. 14, 1885.
[63] Cf. *La République Française,* Oct. 10, 1885; *La Justice,* Oct. 20, 1885.
[64] *Année politique,* XII (1885), 224.

"that if the two hundred [Conservative] candidates who have just been elected had said to their constituents: 'Vote for me, that I may go to Paris and overthrow the Republic,' not one of them would have been returned." [65]

The new Chamber numbered some 201 Opportunists, about 180 Radicals and members of the far Left, plus some 203 Conservatives. Of the last, an estimated 100 belonged to one or another royalist tradition; approximately 50 were Bonapartist; and the rest were simply Conservative, without regard to faction.[66] In these days before formal party labels, such figures are necessarily approximate. The overall result of the elections, however, was self-evident: the Opportunists could no longer govern alone. In a message to the incoming Chamber, President Grévy expressed the wish that Republicans of all tendencies would cooperate in the interests of stable government.[67] He thereby recognized that, in order to form a new cabinet, the Opportunists would need Radical support.

Although Conservatives and Republicans apparently did not realize it at the time, the elections of 1885 had led them to a crossroad in French political history. Which road the country would now take depended chiefly on the attitude of the Right. With over one-third of the seats in the Chamber, the Conservatives were strong enough to become a loyal opposition within the Republic, but too weak to attempt a restoration of any kind by parliamentary means. As a loyal opposition, they could reasonably hope to join with the more conservative Republicans in the formation of a Republican Right.

[65] Jules Simon, "The General Election in France," *Contemporary Review,* LXVIII (Nov., 1885), 613.

[66] Gabriel Monod, "Contemporary Life and Thought in France," *Contemporary Review,* LXVIII (Dec., 1885), 892.

[67] Maxime Lecomte, *Les ralliés: Histoire d'un parti, 1886–1898* (Paris: Flammarion, 1898), p. 53.

If they continued to oppose the government as a matter of principle, however, they would make the existence of future cabinets depend solely on agreement between Opportunists and Radicals. In that eventuality, the two Republican factions would need a far greater spirit of cooperation than they had shown heretofore. But should neither condition be fulfilled, parliamentary government could well become unworkable.

It was at precisely this delicate moment that an ambitious general named Boulanger arrived on the political scene.

2

Boulanger Makes His Debut

1886

General Boulanger made his political debut as a direct result of the general elections of 1885. The new Freycinet ministry, installed on January 7, 1886, required Radical as well as Opportunist support in order to survive. To obtain cooperation from the Radicals, the Premier had to include several of their number in his cabinet. Chief among these were Granet, who was put in charge of Posts and Telegraphs, and Lockroy, who became Minister of Commerce—now called Commerce and Industry in order to indicate a concern for labor. These appointees excited the most attention in Radical circles, not the new War Minister.[1] In keeping with established tradition, he was a general, who at the age of forty-nine was the youngest in the French army. He was of Anglo-Breton descent, and his name was Georges Ernest Jean-Marie Boulanger.

Little was known about Boulanger at the time, except that he had been a schoolmate of Clemenceau at the Lycée of Nantes and was supposedly a Republican. His father, a lawyer during the Second Empire, had reportedly been persecuted by the government because of his Republican sympathies.[2] With-

[1] *La Justice,* Jan. 8, 1886.
[2] Alexandre, Zévaès, *Au temps du boulangisme* (Paris: Gallimard, 1930), p. 26.

in a few years Boulanger was to become known to those who met him personally as a man of few principles but of considerable ambition. His overriding aim was less to lead men than to win their sympathy. When asked to give his viewpoint to a parliamentary committee on a technical question, for example, he reversed himself in mid-course on realizing that the Deputies present disagreed with his first proposals.[3] Although he once tried to steer France into a conflict with Germany, he could successfully reassure an English pacifist a few months later that the cause of peace was his greatest concern.[4] The young Maurice Barrès was later to support Boulanger as a friend of artists and intellectuals, even though the General had said nothing about the arts publicly.[5] Indeed, of all those who later called themselves Boulangists, Barrès seems to have been the only one who ever expressed personal praise for the General. The others apparently had little regard for him, save as a means to further their own projects.

As the new government took office, it was generally agreed that Boulanger owed his portfolio to the personal intervention of Clemenceau.[6] Yet it does not appear that the Radicals as a party originally had any clearly defined plans for the new War Minister. Their main interest lay in domestic affairs. Such ideas as they did have on military and foreign policy were seldom carefully thought out. Admiral Aube, the Naval Minister in the Freycinet cabinet, found favor among the Radi-

[3] Gabriel Hanotaux, *Mon temps* (4 vols.; Paris, Plon, 1947), IV, 273–274.

[4] Wilfred S. Blunt, *My Diaries* (2 vols.; New York: Knopf, 1921), I, 4–5.

[5] Maurice Barrès, "M. le général Boulanger et la nouvelle génération," *Revue Indépendante*, VII (April, 1888), 58–59.

[6] Georges Grison, *Le général Boulanger jugé par ses partisans et ses adversaires* (Paris: Librairie Illustrée, 1889), pp. 14–16.

cals because he preferred small ships over large ones.[7] In any case, the cabinet posts of War and the Navy were considered by almost all Republicans to be nonpolitical.

A NEW KIND OF WAR MINISTER

Once installed in the War Minister's office on the rue Saint-Dominique, however, Boulanger conducted himself in a most political manner. Within twenty-four hours he had dismissed all upper-echelon personnel in the various bureaus without regard to ability or years of service and replaced them with his own acquaintances. This was the first in a series of acts designed to increase his authority as a man of the Left. The General's decisiveness won praise even from the Opportunists,[8] but growing suspicion from Conservatives. Boulanger's own explanation that "in a new situation we need new men" did little to relieve their fears. One royalist observer complained: "General Boulanger has been behaving in the offices of the War Ministry like a revolutionist in a city hall." [9]

As part of his wholesale reorganization of the War Ministry, Boulanger created a press office, from which was to pour a steady flow of orders and proclamations for release to the newspapers. The first of these, issued on January 9, was an order of the day to all officers and enlisted men of the army, in which the new War Minister called for discipline and promised to continue the work of military renovation begun fifteen years earlier. Noble intentions of this sort had been shared by Boulanger's predecessors, but their publication in the form of an order of the day was altogether new. It left many observers

[7] *La Justice,* Jan. 8, 1886; *La République Française,* Jan. 11, 1886.
[8] *La République Française,* Jan. 11, 1886.
[9] Auguste Boucher, "Chronique politique," *Le Correspondant,* CXLII (Jan. 25, 1886), 308–381.

with the impression that the War Minister wished simply to draw attention to himself.[10]

This was not the first time that Boulanger exceeded his normal responsibility in order to seek public attention. As French military commander in Tunisia in 1884, he had made an extensive tour of the country, visiting not only army bases, but tribal chiefs as well. By acting like his country's chief representative, Boulanger came into direct conflict with Paul Cambon, then French governor of Tunisia, who wished to maintain civil control there. Once, after a theatre brawl between French and Italian officers in Tunis, Boulanger authorized all officers under his command to use their weapons if so "provoked" in the future. Cambon then complained to Paris that such conduct could seriously harm Franco-Italian relations. Cambon soon received the title of resident-general and commander of all French troops in Tunisia.[11]

Boulanger, however, refused to recognize Cambon's new authority and left for Paris late in July, 1885, in order to direct a propaganda campaign against him. Shortly after the General's arrival, *La Lanterne* and other leftist papers in the capital began to accuse Cambon of having betrayed France's national honor. In this period when the French Left was most aggressively nationalistic, it is natural that Boulanger's allies came from that quarter. Cambon also had allies—in the government; he had, in fact, gone to Paris earlier that month in order to reinforce his position. For six months, the two protagonists continued their feud in the capital, leaving the actual management of French affairs in Tunisia to subordinates.

[10] *Le Temps*, Jan. 10, 1886.

[11] Alfred Ruhemann, *General Boulanger, "der Reformator des französischen Armee": Lebensbild des französischen Kriegsministers* (Berlin: Walther und Aplant, 1887), pp. 33–34.

Only Boulanger's accession to the post of War Minister allowed Cambon to return to Tunis with his authority intact.[12]

In his new position, Boulanger was determined to be known as a militant Republican. It was not long, therefore, before he introduced politics into military affairs. On January 26, for example, he ordered the ninth cavalry brigade, then stationed at Tours, to be transferred to Nantes and Pontivy, in exchange for the eleventh. A few days later, on February 1, a royalist Deputy interpellated the War Minister in the Chamber, asking him if the order was definitive and if so, whether it was of a military or a political nature. Eager to show his Republican loyalty, Boulanger sprang to the reply. Recalling that units whose commanders were politically suspect had been transferred under previous regimes, he implied that the officers of the ninth cavalry had been corrupted by the royalist atmosphere of Tours. He then taunted his questioner with the rhetorical query: "Are we, yes or no, in a Republic?" With no reply forthcoming, all Republicans in the Chamber united for a vote of confidence in the War Minister.[13]

By defending his actions on political rather than military grounds, Boulanger assured himself of a large audience. There was widespread apprehension among Republicans that the French officer corps was growing royalist. During the Second Empire, many sergeants had been granted commissions simply by virtue of length of service. The reforms begun under Thiers put an end to this practice, however, and required that all officers undergo special training in order to be commissioned. Inasmuch as young men of aristocratic background were usually the most capable of assimilating such training, the

[12] Paul Cambon, *Correspondance, 1870–1914* (2 vols.; Paris: Grasset, 1940) I, 244–245n.

[13] *J.O.C.* (1886), pp. 83–84.

social level of army officers had risen markedly since 1872.[14] While this fact alone did not prove their disloyalty to the regime (it was never proved), Boulanger's action with regard to the two cavalry brigades was warmly applauded by all segments of Republican opinion.[15] It was viewed with horror by the royalists, who accused him of turning over the entire army to the Radicals. One commentator predicted that the Republicans' "purge" of state institutions would now be extended to the nation's military establishments.[16]

No wholesale elimination of royalists from the army was, in fact, ever undertaken by Boulanger, but he did try to reduce some of the more glaring inequalities of military service. To this end, he fostered a series of rather superficial reforms, beginning with the permission for all soldiers to wear beards. This move was logical enough, since Boulanger himself had just begun to grow a beard. Other changes included an improvement in soldiers' food, the painting of sentry boxes red, white, and blue, and the elimination of the black satin collar for officers and adjutants. To improve morale still further, married noncommissioned officers were now allowed to live in town with their families, while all military personnel could henceforth list illegitimate children as dependents. Finally, new conscripts were to be greeted at the railway station by a military band.[17]

In a more genuinely democratic vein, Boulanger extended student deferments, but favored the three-year military service bill, which would have required all students to serve in due

---

[14] Raoul Girardet, *La société militaire dans la France contemporaine, 1815–1939* (Paris: Plon, 1953), pp. 187–188.

[15] *La République Française*, Feb. 3, 1886.

[16] Auguste Boucher, "Chronique politique," *Le Correspondant*, CXLIV (Feb. 10, 1886), 576–577.

[17] "Le général Boulanger, Ministre de la Guerre," *Le Correspondant*, CXLIV (Sept. 25, 1886), 1048.

course. These were to include students preparing for the priesthood, a category which the anticlerical Radicals were most eager to see drafted. The bill was passed by the Chamber in 1887, but ran into opposition (on grounds of military strategy) in the Senate. Finally, on June 12, 1888, the Senate passed a slightly altered version, which was approved by the Chamber in 1889. Since Boulanger had already left the War Ministry by then, he was unable to take full credit for the measure, which in any case had not originated with him.[18]

Most important of all, from the standpoint of the General's subsequent career, were the reforms which never saw passage. The most radical was a proposal to abolish promotion in the army by seniority. "Successful passage of this measure," notes an American scholar, "would be a direct blow to the old officer group." [19] The Radicals were ideologically committed to oppose the high officers, who were suspected, with some justification, of royalist sympathies. Boulanger's plan to abolish promotion by seniority further endeared him to his Radical patrons and won him a large following among the lower ranks of the army. At the same time, it made him the nemesis of the older officers.[20] Their steadfast opposition to Boulanger precludes any theory that his political success of 1888 and 1889 might in some way resemble a South American-type coup.

Another stillborn reform inspired by leftist ideology was one to abolish Saint-Cyr and the Ecole Polytechnique as military academies. The former was to be eliminated entirely, while the latter would function as an engineering school only.

[18] Charles de Freycinet, *Souvenirs, 1878–1893* (Paris: Delagrave, 1913), pp. 409–411.

[19] Jess Gale Carnes, "The French Army Officers and the Establishment of the Republic" (unpub. Ph.D. diss., Cornell University, 1949), pp. 343–344.

[20] *Ibid.*, pp. 357–358.

Both would be replaced by a more democratic institution called the Ecole Normale Militaire, which would presumably be open to all qualified candidates regardless of social position. It would offer a one-year officer candidate program to all enlisted men and noncommissioned officers.[21]

Although frustrated in his attempt to create a new military academy, the new War Minister toured the existing ones extensively and let the cadets know where he stood politically. On May 8, 1886, he told those at Saint-Cyr: "Open your minds wide to the ideas of your century." [22] This admonition does not appear to have been well received by the cadets, who expressed slight regard for the "political general," whom they considered a *parvenu*.[23] At the Ecole Polytechnique two days later, he reminded the students that it was the National Convention which created their school during the Revolution. He called on them to be mindful of such a glorious heritage.[24] Since the cavalry was considered the most royalist of all the armed services, Boulanger gave special notice to the cadets at the Saumur cavalry school on June 15 that his circular of February 1 concerned them also. In it, he had summoned all military personnel to give their full support to the Republican regime.[25]

Whenever Boulanger got the opportunity, he expressed his views on matters still further removed from the military. Such an occasion arose during the bitter coal miners' strike at Decazeville. The miners had walked off their jobs on January 26, 1886, in protest over low pay and forced buying at the

[21] "Le général Boulanger, Ministre de la Guerre," p. 1067.

[22] Boulanger, *Les discours du général Boulanger depuis le 4 août 1881 jusqu'au 4 septembre 1887* (Paris: Périnet, 1888), p. 64.

[23] Maxime Weygand, *Mémoires,* Vol. I: *Idéal vécu* (Paris: Flammarion, 1953), p. 17.

[24] Boulanger, *Discours,* p. 67.   [25] *Ibid.,* p. 85.

company store. During one demonstration, an engineer named Watrin, who was especially hated by the miners, was killed. Nationwide shock at this act obliged the government to send in troops.[26] Only the Parisians seemed to have any real sympathy for the striking miners. The Paris city council, although lacking jurisdiction in this matter, voted nonetheless to send 10,000 francs to the strikers in order to alleviate their misery.[27]

The question came up for debate in the Chamber on March 11, amid great equivocation on the part of the government. The following day, an interpellation was presented by Georges Laguerre, one of the leftist Deputies elected from Paris in the recent elections and a future leader of the Boulangist movement. He asked specifically what, if anything, the government was doing to help the strikers and what the role of the army was at Decazeville. Boulanger immediately asked for the floor and replied that the army was sent to keep order, and that he had made sure personally that there would be no conflict between soldiers and miners. How could there be, he asked, when the army now represented the whole nation? "Could our workers, soldiers of yesterday, have anything to fear from our soldiers of today, workers of tomorrow?" Letting his imagination run free, the War Minister reassured his questioner that "perhaps, at this very moment, each soldier is sharing his soup and ration of bread with a miner." Wild applause from the Left followed this rhetorical gambit.[28]

By a series of speeches and some action, Boulanger soon

[26] E. Beau de Loménie, *Les responsabilités des dynasties bourgeoises,* Vol. II: *De Mac-Mahon à Poincaré* (Paris: Denoël, 1963), pp. 129–130.

[27] *L'Autorité,* March 12, 1886.

[28] *J.O.C.* (1886), pp. 440–441.

established his reputation as a progressive Republican. It is in this light that his personal success at the military review of July 14, 1886 should be viewed. This holiday was, in effect, the Republic's birthday, having been made an official national holiday only six years previously. Its original celebrations had been confined to a simple military formation in which the regiments stationed in Paris received their standards from the President of the Republic. Boulanger changed all this; he brought to the parade grounds at Longchamp units from all over France in order to stage a full-scale review, which he led himself.[29] Thanks also to a recent café song in his honor, entitled *En r'venant de la revue,* the War Minister was enthusiastically applauded by the Paris spectators, who acclaimed the troops with equal fervor. Republican observers present naturally attributed this applause to the Parisians' love for the Republic, while royalists considered it merely a personal triumph for Boulanger alone.[30]

THE EXPULSION OF THE PRINCES

Colorful as it was, Boulanger's entry into the War Ministry was far from being the only important political event of 1886. Even more important, at the time, was the enforced exile on June 21 of all pretenders to the throne of France. It all came about as a direct result of the uncompromising position into which the Conservatives had got themselves following the 1885 general elections. These elections, it will be recalled, had left the Opportunists and Radicals united on the question of regime, but very little else. In the new Chamber, therefore, they repeatedly emphasized their unity in the defense of the Republic as a means of concealing their differences on other

[29] *Le Temps,* July 13, 1886.
[30] *La Justice, July 15, 1886; L'Intransigeant,* July 16, 1886; *Le Gaulois,* July 15, 1886.

issues. Conversely, the Conservatives failed to remember the lesson of October 18, 1885, and made the Republic their principal target.[31]

Such tactics might not have frightened the Republicans in the Chamber had the Conservative deputation been small. But now that the Right occupied more than one-third of all the seats, many Deputies, particularly among the Radicals, believed that they had legitimate cause for alarm. It was rumored, for example, that the princes, encouraged by the recent success of their parties, had been making contacts with foreign diplomats and high French civil servants with a view to restoring their respective regimes.[32] The last straw came just after the reception preceding the marriage of the daughter of the Comte de Paris to the Crown Prince of Portugal. At the ceremony in Paris were present all the leading members of the Orleanist faction, thereby prompting a columnist from France's most respected Conservative newspaper to declare:

France, conservative and liberal, religious and monarchical, was found again last night fortified in its faith and its hopes. At arm's length could be seen the complete retinue of a great government with its princes, its lords, its deputies, its councillors of state, its civil servants, its intelligent youth—all social forces in their most lofty and popular form. It was like a powerful reserve, showing to all eyes what values and resources our country still possesses for future reparation.[33]

This was the signal for the Radicals, led by cabinet ministers Granet and Lockroy, to revive an old, long-abandoned project of expelling the royal family from French territory. The Opportunists were naturally hesitant. They realized that if

[31] Henri Germain, "L'état politique de la France en 1886," *Revue des Deux Mondes*, LXXV (June 15, 1886), 820–821.

[32] Freycinet, *Souvenirs*, pp. 337–338.

[33] *Le Figaro*, May 16, 1886.

the Comte de Paris had given a clandestine character to the ceremony, Portuguese feelings would have been hurt. Here again, republican France had to bend a principle or two in order to live in peace within a monarchical Europe. With these realities in mind, President Grévy sent a congratulatory note to the King of Portugal, as well as an ambassador extraordinary to represent France at the Lisbon wedding. The ambassador told the King "of the sympathy with which his government envisages a union which is to establish a further tie between the two nations." [34]

Meanwhile, the Deputies in the Chamber were busily debating whether or not to expel the princes. To those on the Left, the realities of European diplomacy mattered less than the prospect of a monarchical restoration. They presented a bill to exile the Comte de Paris and his immediate entourage. The Center countered with a proposal to banish Bonapartist pretenders as well, which the government, to avoid the appearance of partiality, had referred to an *ad hoc* committee. When that body voted six to five in favor of the Center's motion, the government was committed to it. After much debate, the Chamber voted on May 27 to exile from French soil the heads and heirs apparent of any of the families which had once ruled France. The Chamber majority in the 315 to 232 count was composed entirely of Republicans. With public opinion still rather indifferent, the Senate approved the measure on June 22 by a vote of 137 to 122.[35]

Once voted into law, the expulsion proceeded without a hitch. Liberal Catholic Deputies Jacques Piou and Albert de Mun had objected that it would deny to the Republic the

[34] Charles de Mazade, "Chronique de la quinzaine," *Revue des Deux Mondes,* LXXV (June 1, 1886), 707–709.

[35] André Daniel, *L'année politique,* vol. XIII (1886) (Paris: Charpentier, 1887), pp. 100–106, 163–165.

support of many Conservatives to whom the question of regime was of secondary importance. Premier Freycinet justified the measure by saying that the Republic now proved that it could make itself respected. Subsequent events were to bear him out; for whenever the regime seemed to be threatened, quick counteraction rather than compromise proved to be the best immediate remedy. In any event, Conservative protests at the expulsion never went beyond the verbal form. As the Radical Deputy, Madier de Montjau, wryly noted, most politicians of the Right were beginning to find the princes rather embarrassing.[36] The Comte de Paris might proclaim mightily that "the Republic is afraid" in exiling him, but no outburst of public sympathy followed him on his journey to England.[37]

Along with the Orleanist pretender were exiled not only his wife and children, but also his uncle, the Duc d'Aumale— even though the latter was not an heir apparent and played no political role. The Chamber, in voting the expulsion, had reserved the right to expel other princes should the need arise. Boulanger took advantage of this provision to strike from the army roster the names of the Duc d'Aumale, a major general, and the Duc de Chartres, a cavalry colonel. The former had been off active duty since 1882 and protested, in a strongly worded note to Grévy, that no one could take his rank from him. In parliament, Boulanger defended his action against royalist attacks by claiming that the Duc d'Aumale, who had become a major general at twenty-one, owed his rank to influence. By even wider margins than for the first expulsion, both houses voted to expel the two officers.[38]

The royalists now sought to humiliate the War Minister

---

[36] Charles de Mazade, "Chronique de la quinzaine," *Revue des Deux Mondes*, LXXV (June 15, 1886), 946–947.

[37] Beau de Loménie, *op. cit.,* pp. 139–140.

[38] *J.O.C.* (1886), pp. 1479–1481.

publicly. When Baron de Lareinty, a Conservative Senator, referred to Boulanger's statements about the Duc d'Aumale as terms of cowardice, a duel ensued. Its bloodless outcome seems to have had no adverse effect on the General's popularity.[39] In a further attempt to embarrass him, several royalists had a Belgian newspaper publish three sycophantic letters, which purported to be from Boulanger to the Duc d'Aumale in 1880, thanking the latter for having got him the rank of colonel. Boulanger flatly denied having written these letters and, in fact, he had not. They turned out to be adulterated versions, made to sound even more obsequious than those he had really written. Even when faced with the original, formally correct letters of thanks which he had sent to his former commanding officer, the War Minister continued to deny authorship for several days. Only after prodding from sections of the Republican press did his memory improve to the point where he recognized having written them.[40]

If this episode did Boulanger no credit, it appears to have profited the Conservatives even less. Local elections were held in half of France's departments on August 4 and 18. For several weeks previously, the royalist press had tried to represent the vote as a national plebiscite on the regime, even though only local questions were at issue.[41] Whether or not the electorate accepted this view is difficult to determine; it certainly did not rush headlong into the Conservative camp, as had been predicted. Out of 987 offices up for re-election, the Right made an overall gain of only fifteen. That devout royalist, Auguste Boucher, had to admit: "The elections of August 1 have dashed the Conservatives' hopes—if not en-

[39] Alfred Barbou, *Le Général Boulanger* (Paris: Perrin, 1887), pp. 176–178.

[40] Francis Laur, *L'époque boulangiste* (2 vols.; Paris: Le Livre à l'Auteur, 1912–1914), I, 130–134.

[41] *Année politique*, XIII (1886), 168–171.

tirely, at least in part." Interior Minister Sarrien claimed, not without some exaggeration, that they constituted "a great success" for the Republic.[42]

A PERIOD OF PARTY MANEUVER

Conservative disappointment in the local elections of August brought home to many Deputies of the Right what some of their more astute colleagues had realized since January: like the proverbial dude, they were all dressed up but had nowhere to go. Although the *Union des droites* was over two hundred strong in the Chamber, it had no way of influencing policy. Six months of systematic opposition in the legislature had succeeded only in forcing the Conservatives' nominal leaders into exile and causing the party to lose some of its popular support. Other than mounting a forceful overthrow of the government, the only way in which the Right could now enjoy some measure of power was to work within the Republic itself. This is precisely what Edgard Raoul-Duval and Auguste Lepoutre, two Conservative Deputies, were prepared to suggest to their colleagues.

As early as 1881, Raoul-Duval had written that the Republic was a *fait accompli* and that the role of his party should be to improve the regime, not destroy it. Although rejected by most Conservatives, this declaration was warmly welcomed by Gambetta, who had long hoped for a right and left party system within the Republic.[43] No considerations of altruism should be sought as an explanation for Raoul-Duval's position. He was, first of all, a Protestant and did not oppose the Republic on religious grounds. Economic, not constitutional,

---

[42] Auguste Boucher, "Chronique politique," *Le Correspondant,* CXLIV (Aug. 10, 1886), 572–573.

[43] Ernest Gay [Garennes], *Dernière défaite* (Paris: Savine, 1891), p. 15.

issues were uppermost in his mind; and on these issues he shared the essentially conservative attitude of the moderate Republicans. Nor was there anything coincidental in this common attitude. Raoul-Duval was a cousin of the leading moderate economist and politician, Léon Say, and sat with him on the boards of directors of several large companies, including the Decazeville mines. Many important Orleanists were similarly joined to the moderate Republicans by economic interests, but parted company over constitutional questions. In accepting the Republic, Raoul-Duval merely sought to bring these Orleanists' constitutional thinking into line with their economic position.[44]

Raoul-Duval's failure to create a Republican Right explains to a very great degree the political success of General Boulanger, indeed the entire Boulanger affair. Had the Conservatives remained true to their electoral program of 1885 and accepted the Republic, it is quite possible that they, and not the Radicals, would have become associated in government with the Opportunists. In that case, Boulanger would not have been brought into the cabinet. The General's later triumphs in various by-elections of 1888 were due largely to votes and generous subsidies from the Right, particularly the Orleanists. If the Orleanists had pursued their essential economic and political goals within the Republic, it is hardly likely that they would have given any aid to Boulanger. Indeed, Conservative participation in Republican politics would probably have lessened the ministerial instability upon which much of the Boulangist propaganda fed. The tragedy of the Boulanger affair lies in the fact that on several occasions the Right came within a hair's breadth of accepting the Republic.

The first of these occasions began late in August, 1886, as the leading newspapers of Paris carried announcements by

[44] Beau de Loménie, *op. cit.*, p. 142.

Raoul-Duval and Lepoutre that they were in the process of forming a Republican Right. In essence, they offered to accept France's present form of government in return for a conservative fiscal, economic, military, and religious policy. By so doing, Raoul-Duval explained, they hoped to strengthen the moderate wing of the Republicans, which they considered to be weakened by too close an association with the Radicals. Lepoutre expressed confidence that the new movement would win a large following. "I believe that two-thirds of the French citizens are completely indifferent to the form of government," he told reporters. "Above all, they want to be governed well and to carry on their business in peace." [45]

Even before these declarations, there had been some straws in the wind, indicating the possibility of such a combination, but they had led to bitter disputes within the Conservative party. That the moderate Republicans were chafing at their alliance with the Left was no secret. Steeg, their parliamentary leader, had accused Freycinet and his Opportunist ministers on July 11 of being vassals of the Radicals. Sensing the possibility of an entente, the Orleanist journalist, Kerohant, proposed that the Right support a purely Opportunist ministry in return for a conservative economic and social policy. Such a ministry, he explained,

would live as long as the Right let it live. Now, the Right cannot think of restoring the monarchy as long as it is a minority in parliament. Not being able to restore the monarchy, it would have no reason to oppose and to overthrow a Republican ministry which adopted as its program a policy of resistance to Radicalism, which rejected three-year military service and the progressive [income] tax, which kept to a system of order and economy in

[45] Maxime Lecomte, *Les ralliés: Histoire d'un parti, 1886–1898* (Paris: Flammarion, 1898), pp. 67–71.

financial questions, which eased the taxpayers' burdens, effectively protected agriculture and industry, and put an end to the war against Catholicism. There can be no alliance between the Right and the *Union des gauches* [moderates]. But there could be, under the conditions indicated, a truce of one year . . . renewable upon its termination.[46]

Even this timid attempt at seeking a *modus vivendi* with the moderates—it did not go so far as that of Raoul-Duval, who openly accepted the Republic—met with some strong Conservative opposition. Not unnaturally, the loudest objections came mainly from Bonapartists, who had a smaller stake in industry than the Orleanists and lacked their parliamentary traditions. Paul de Cassagnac rebuked Kerohant for his parliamentarism, saying: "There are not only legal means for founding a government. . . . For us to meet the men of the *Union des gauches* even half way—never, never!" [47]

The Comte de Paris was more realistic. From his enforced exile in London he issued instructions to Orleanist leaders in France on September 1, advising them against systematic opposition to the government. "It is not through daily polemics against the Republic that we shall arrive at inspiring France with the faith that she should have in us," he reminded them. Without mentioning Raoul-Duval's proposals, he warned: "The Right should not engage in anticonstitutional politics in the Chamber. It should fight only on conservative grounds and for conservative ideas." In this note, the Comte de Paris was simply reminding his followers of their stake in a regime which they themselves had founded. But because he did not want to stir up dissension among Conservatives, he waited before releasing his statement to the public until December 14, when a new cabinet had already been installed in office.[48]

[46] *Le Soleil,* Aug. 13, 1886.   [47] *L'Autorité,* Aug. 17, 1886.
[48] *Le Figaro,* Dec. 15, 1886.

Dissension was aroused when Raoul-Duval introduced his proposal for a republican Right to the Chamber on November 6. He chose his moment well: it was during debate on the budget, when the Left was pressing with increased vigor for a graduated income and inheritance tax. After reminding his fellow Conservatives of their common views with the Center on this question, Raoul-Duval called on them to make peace with the regime. Insults and catcalls greeted this suggestion. At the end of Raoul-Duval's speech, Paul de Cassagnac asked how many Conservatives were ready to support such a policy. Not one dared approve openly.[49]

The Conservatives showed their capacity for compromise less than a month later, however, after the fall of the Freycinet ministry. Putting aside their principles at least momentarily, they now sought a share of political power. On this occasion, Cassagnac no doubt expressed the feelings of most Conservatives when he criticized the Republicans for "the criminal stupidity which they have committed in excluding the Right—that is, more than a third of the nation—not only from the national administration, but even from the control of expenses, from the budget commission." [50] To make their support more appealing to the Republicans, the Conservative Deputies met on December 6 to approve a statement of policy, the principal clause of which was: "First of all, to engage in no systematic opposition." Such noble intentions were warmly seconded by Cassagnac, who now began to appear as a sort of rightist weathervane. "The Right," he solemnly proclaimed, "is a peaceful, legal opposition in good faith and not a party of insurrection." [51]

Not only the Conservatives, but the Radicals also sought a share of power in the next government and were therefore

[49] *J.O.C.* (1886), pp. 1743–1748.   [50] *L'Autorité,* Dec. 6, 1886.
[51] *Ibid.,* Dec. 8, 1886.

willing to modify their principles—at least for the time being. In the midst of the cabinet crisis, Henri Michelin, a leftist Deputy from Paris and later a leading Boulangist, rose in the Chamber on December 7 to ask that the question of constitutional revision be discussed. This proposal was immediately rejected by Barodet, president of the *Extrême gauche* and a known revisionist, who took a page out of Jules Ferry's book by saying that the moment was not opportune. What was needed now, he insisted, was Republican unity; revision of the constitution would come later. So it was postponed once more.[52] The Radicals appear to have experienced few pangs of conscience in putting aside one of their pet projects. After the 1885 elections only 57 per cent of the Radical Deputies actually wanted revision at all, as compared with 97 per cent in 1881.[53] A year of ministerial cohabitation with the Opportunists seems to have dampened Radical enthusiasm for the idea still further.

The spectacle of Conservatives and Radicals competing for the favors of the Opportunists illustrates a basic corollary to the principles of Center government: even as a minority, the Center holds the key to power. Right and Left could unite to overthrow a government, but that unity did not extend to forming a new one. For either side to be admitted into the ruling circle, approval by the Center was needed. The Center's discretionary power in cabinet crises necessitated certain concessions from the party that was to become its ally in government. If these concessions proved to be too much for the purists within that party to accept, it could withdraw from the coalition, thereby creating another cabinet crisis. Ministerial instability was thus built into a system of government by a Center minority.

[52] *La Justice,* Dec. 8, 1886.
[53] Jacques Kayser, *Les grandes batailles du radicalisme, 1820–1901* (Paris: Rivière, 1962), p. 141.

In the present instance, the overtures from the Right appear to have come too late, for the new government installed on December 8, 1886, was simply a repetition of the old. Only the Premier was different. He was a moderate Radical named René Goblet, who had been frequently at odds with Clemenceau. By his own admission, Goblet had no other plans than to continue the work of his predecessor.[54] Along with the other members of the Freycinet cabinet, Boulanger was back at his post. His presence allowed the new Premier to count on Radical support even while rejecting some of the most important Radical projects, such as separation of church and state.[55]

Although ostensibly secure, Boulanger's position had in fact suffered because he no longer had the support of the Opportunists. They had initially welcomed his accession to the War Ministry but became disenchanted six months later, after his attempt to remove General Saussier as military governor of Paris. Opportunists were immediately reminded of General Changarnier, who had been forced to resign from the same post by Louis Napoleon. When the cabinet refused to accept Saussier's resignation, Boulanger had to ask him to stay on, which he did.[56] Despite this satisfactory outcome, Jules Ferry remained suspicious of Boulanger. In a letter of July 2, 1886, to his brother Charles, he warned of the dictatorial tendencies of "this Bolivian-type general." [57]

An English rather than South American parallel to the French War Minister was discerned by Lord Lyons, who was then about to end his term as British ambassador to France. In a dispatch to London also dated July 2, Lord Lyons asked rhetorically "whether Boulanger is aiming at being a Crom-

---

[54] René Goblet, "Souvenirs de ma vie politique," *Revue Politique et Parlementaire,* CXLI (Oct. 10, 1929), 8.

[55] Antonin Débidour, *L'Eglise et l'Etat en France sous la Troisième République, 1870–1906* (3 vols.; Paris: Alcan, 1906), I, 383–384.

[56] *La République Française,* July 1 and 3, 1886.

[57] Jules Ferry, *Lettres* (Paris: Calmann-Lévy, 1914), pp. 407–408.

well or a Monk." To the British diplomat, the latter possibility—that of a royal restoration—seemed the more likely of the two. As if to prove his point, Lyons added rather cynically: "Then the Republic here has lasted sixteen years, and that is about the time which it takes to make the French tired of a form of government." [58] However tempting this analysis may be at first glance, it is well to remember that Lord Lyons personally had little use for the Republic and believed that an authoritarian regime was more suitable to the French temperament. In 1888 and 1889, when Boulanger did appear to threaten the regime, he no more resembled General Monk than he did a Bolivian. His success came from the ballot box, not the army.

Despite Boulanger's avowed loyalty to the Republic, however, his notorious ambition could at times make even loyal partisans uneasy. Already abandoned by the Opportunists, the General appears to have been reminded by the ministerial crisis of December, 1886, that his post as War Minister was not necessarily permanent. It was in this period that his contacts with some political adventurers of various leanings first became noticeable. Henri Rochefort even expressed alarm that Boulanger might be taken in by Rightists, a few of whom were making tentative overtures to him. Such warnings were decidedly premature—they were a subject of ridicule at the time [59]—but they did augur badly for the future.

[58] Thomas W. L. Newton, ed., *Lord Lyons: A Record of British Diplomacy* (2 vols.; London: Arnold, 1913), II, 367–368.
[59] Laur, *op. cit.*, pp. 211–213.

3

Tension with Germany
1887

"The Frenchman of today has no patriotism in the higher sense of the word, no sense of duty like the German." So wrote Count Münster, the German ambassador in Paris, to Bismarck late in 1886.[1] If only surface manifestations of patriotism are to be taken into consideration, Münster's judgment was generally correct. Certainly there was less drum beating, less respect for military authority in the Third Republic than in the German Empire. It was to making Frenchmen more patriotic, in the German sense of the word, that men like Paul Déroulède and Maurice Barrès devoted most of their energy. Déroulède in 1886 was president of an organization known as the *Ligue des patriotes,* which had been founded four years earlier to promote patriotism among French youth. In an obvious imitation of German methods, this French society laid great stress on gymnastics and rifle practice.[2] Barrès,

---

[1] Germany, Auswärtiges Amt, *Die Grosse Politik der Europäischen Kabinette,* ed. Johannes Lepsius, Albrecht Mendelssohn Bartholdy, and Friedrich Thimme, VI (Berlin: Deutsche Verlagsgesellschaft für Politik und Geschichte, 1924), 161; hereinafter cited as *Grosse Politik.*

[2] Raoul Girardet, "La Ligue des patriotes dans l'histoire du nationalisme français (1882–1888)," *Bulletin de la Société d'Histoire Moderne,* 12ème série no. 6 (1958), p. 4.

whose nationalistic activities were confined largely to the written word, freely admitted that the organization had been strongly influenced by German example. "The *Ligue des patriotes,*" he recalled, "was intended to be for France what the *Tugendbund* had been for Germany in 1813."[3]

Emulation of German methods was far from being confined to extreme nationalists. The defeat of 1870 appears to have convinced most French leaders that Germany was as a whole more advanced than France. Liberal French educators, for example, looked to Germany for ways to instill a sense of national purpose in their students, right up to the university level.[4] In the military sphere, Boulanger, like his immediate predecessors in the War Ministry, drew widely on German experience. His creation in 1886 of an officers' club in Paris called the *Cercle militaire* was an obvious imitation of a similar institution in Berlin.[5]

Boulanger's activities as War Minister did not, however, remain limited to internal reforms. He had taken office at a time when French nationalism was still inspired by Jacobinism and therefore largely the preserve of the Left. Indeed, in 1886, one can detect a growing militancy on the part of the Parisian masses toward Germany. Distrust of German intentions plus an increased confidence in France's strength appear to be the bases of such militancy. Several months before the Franco-German crisis of 1887, a leftist newspaper in the capital gave voice to popular nationalism in these terms: "Inas-

[3] Cited in Joachim Kühn *et al., Der Nationalismus im Leben der Dritten Republik* (Berlin: Paetel, 1920), p. 21n.

[4] Claude Digeon, *La crise allemande de la pensée française, 1870–1914* (Paris: Presses Universitaires de France, 1959), pp. 364–365.

[5] Alfred Ruhemann, *General Boulanger, "der Reformator des französischen Armee": Lebensbild des französischen Kriegsministers* (Berlin: Walther und Aplant, 1887), p. 47.

much as the next international conflagration must be betwee
Reaction and Revolution—with Bismarck on one side a
France on the other, so be it!" [6]

There seems to be no evidence that Boulanger sought
armed confrontation with Germany during his first year
War Minister. To enhance his own position, however, he
stantly emphasized the necessity of military readiness. On
point, as on many others, the French Right called h
danger to national well-being. Thus, as early as July,
the royalist commentator Philippe de Grandlieu uttere
cry, "Boulanger, *c'est la guerre!*" He viewed the War M
as a Jacobin candidate for dictatorship, whose milit
forms would inevitably lead the nation into war.[7]

Similar fears were expressed in Germany. At firs
came from unofficial quarters such as the press, which
to see a threat of war behind even the slightest refer
Boulanger to Alsace-Lorraine.[8] By the autumn of 1
German military attaché in Paris was reporting to
that the French War Minister's statements on mili
paredness were being picked up by a growing numbe
literate weeklies dedicated to *revanche*. Behind thei
titles, the message never varied: France must gird it
imminent aggression from Germany. Posters also
One, which was quickly torn down by the Fre
showed Boulanger marching at the head of a F
against Germany.[9]

[6] *Le Cri du Peuple,* April 1, 1886.
[7] *Le Figaro,* July 25, 1886.
[8] France, Ministère des Affaires Etrangères, *Docur
tiques français, 1871–1914,* 1ère série, VI (Par
Nationale, 1934), 264–265; hereinafter cited as *D.D.*
[9] *Grosse Politik,* VI, 146–154.

49

The Boulanger Affair

As these reports arrived in Berlin, the German capital was bracing itself for another test of strength between Bismarck and the Reichstag. The struggle took place over the Chancellor's new seven-year military appropriation bill, and in it the name of Boulanger was to figure prominently. Bismarck had already singled out Boulanger to the Reichstag in March, 1886, as a possible danger to the peace of Europe. Recalling the effects of the first French Revolution on France's neighbors, he asked rhetorically if Boulanger might not lead the army of a Socialist French revolution against monarchical Europe. What else could one expect of a war minister who had announced so blithely that today's workers were tomorrow's soldiers? [10] Jules Ferry easily saw through Bismarck's purpose. In a letter of September 8, 1886, to the Opportunist journalist Joseph Reinach, he wrote that the German government was calling Boulanger "General *revanche*" in order to frighten its own people into submission.[11]

Such were the tactics employed by Bismarck when the new septenate was presented to the Reichstag on November 25, 1886. Fearing that it might not pass over strong Socialist and Centrist opposition, the Chancellor pointed to what he called the growing threat of militarism in France. Although he did not at first mention Boulanger by name, the German press was quick to take over from there and condemned the French War Minister in no uncertain terms. Just how genuine Bismarck's expressed fear of Boulanger was still remains a mystery. Surely it cannot be denied that the Chancellor's designs were admirably served by the notoriety of that ambitious French

[10] Germany, *Stenographische Berichte über die Verhandlungen des Reichstags,* III; VI. Legislaturperiode, II. Session 1885/1886, 1659; hereinafter cited as *Verhandlungen.*

[11] Jules Ferry, *Lettres* (Paris: Calmann-Lévy, 1914), pp. 426–427.

general. As Bismarck was to admit later: "I could not invent Boulanger, but he happened very conveniently for me." [12]

In Paris, meanwhile, Münster became alarmed at the new talk of war in the German press—the result, he believed, of a serious misunderstanding of French intentions. He therefore hastened to reassure Bismarck in a dispatch of December 21, 1886, that the Goblet ministry wanted peace above all. It was Germany and not France, he implied, that was creating the current tension. The new military bill and the debates over it in the Reichstag frightened Frenchmen into believing that a German attack on their homeland was imminent. It was therefore "natural," said Münster, that Boulanger and Aube should base their re-entry into the government on the condition that an extraordinary appropriation of 360 million francs be granted to the War Ministry and 150 million to the navy. "The increase [in strength] of the German army must necessarily have reminded the French of the imperfections of their own army, and it will be easier for Boulanger than for anyone else to obtain the necessary credits from the parliament." Under the present circumstances, he concluded, Boulanger's position as War Minister was considerably enhanced. [13]

Münster's message elicited no reply from Bismarck. Once it became apparent that the war fever in Germany had not abated, the German diplomat took the extraordinary step of writing to Kaiser Wilhelm I directly. In a letter of December 30 he noted that in France "a wind of peace is blowing across the country." Déroulède and other chauvinists might rattle sabres if they liked, said Münster, but they had only a small following among Frenchmen generally. Even Boulanger was speaking only of peace. [14] As soon as Bismarck learned of

[12] Cited in A. J. P. Taylor, *The Struggle for Mastery in Europe, 1848–1918* (Oxford: Clarendon Press, 1954), p. 308.
[13] *Grosse Politik*, VI, 157–159.   [14] *Ibid.*, pp. 160–162.

Münster's report, he castigated the old ambassador roundly (1) for addressing the Kaiser directly and (2) for minimizing what he called the Boulangist menace. "If His Majesty and the confederated governments shared the views exposed by Your Excellency," remarked the Chancellor bitterly, "the Imperial government would hardly be in a position to support and defend the military bill convincingly before the Reichstag." [15]

When the military bill came up for a vote on January 11, 1887, Bismarck's defense of it was as convincing as possible. Unlike some of his previous speeches, this one did not cover France with invectives. Bismarck freely admitted that Jacques Bonhomme, the typical French peasant, was an essentially peaceful soul. But without mentioning the name of Boulanger, he warned that Premier Goblet might well be replaced in the near future by someone of warlike intent.[16] The Reichstag, however, refused to be moved and passed a military law for a period of only three years. Bismarck replied by dissolving parliament on January 14 and calling for new elections in order to obtain a favorable majority.

The Chancellor's action appears to have been inspired by two motives. In the first place, he wished to insure future policy against the possibility of his being replaced by a liberal. Kaiser Wilhelm I was already close to ninety and in poor health: his likely successor, Friedrich III, was known for his relatively progressive views.[17] Another reason was no doubt Bismarck's wish to maintain control over a legislature which, since 1871, had become increasingly bold. Although the Chancellor claimed that Europe was at the brink of war, he was openly contradicted in the Reichstag by the Deputy Bam-

[15] *Ibid.*, pp. 163–166.

[16] *Verhandlungen*, Vol. IV, Session 1886/87, p. 339.

[17] Erich Eyck, *Bismarck and the German Empire* (2nd ed.; London: Allen & Unwin, 1958), pp. 284–285.

berger, who insisted that peace was more secure than at any time since the Franco-Prussian conflict. It was this sense of security which had allowed the Reichstag to assert itself. An assembly elected amid popular fears of war was likely to be more docile.[18]

To drive home his point on the danger of war, Bismarck summoned 72,000 reservists only one month before the elections for military exercises in Alsace-Lorraine. He also privately warned Herbette, the French ambassador in Berlin, of this supposed danger, saying: "If Boulanger becomes Premier or President of the Republic, it means war!" Herbette recognized that the whole "Boulanger question" was pivotal to Bismarck's stand before the Reichstag and before the German people.[19]

Yet if Bismarck had wished to make Boulanger still more popular with the French masses, he hardly could have succeeded better. The crisis over the German septenate immediately split French opinion into two clearly defined camps. Moderate and conservative elements, fearing that France would certainly be defeated in a new war with Germany, sought to appease their eastern neighbor wherever possible. Thus, the influential Opportunist organ, *La République Française,* suggested that Boulanger be refused the arms credits he had requested. To grant them, the paper warned, would lend substance to Bismarck's contention that there was a danger of war from France.[20] The conservative *Figaro* went even further and claimed that war could be averted only if Boulanger were compelled to resign as War Minister.[21]

---

[18] G. Valbert, "La dissolution du Reichstag et la politique électorale en Allemagne," *Revue des Deux Mondes,* LXXIX (Feb. 1, 1887), 669–676.

[19] *D.D.F.,* 1ère série, VI, 425–428.   [20] Jan. 22, 1887.

[21] Jan. 23, 1887.

Fear of war also gripped the French Left, whose normal reaction, however, was to give even more support to Boulanger instead of abandoning him. The people looked at the present War Minister for their protection, said Henri Rochefort, who predicted that if Boulanger were expelled from the government, some twenty thousand Parisians would immediately fill the boulevards, shouting protests.[22] Münster reported a recent conversation with Freycinet, who revealed that many French politicians wished to be rid of Boulanger; but the importance attached to the War Minister in Germany had made his position virtually unassailable in France.[23] As tension mounted between France and Germany, the bookstalls of Paris were flooded with a wave of penny biographies of Boulanger, describing his past military triumphs and heralding his future ones.[24]

Encouraged by this new popularity, Boulanger decided to fill the role assigned to him as the savior of national honor. He moved to accept Bismarck's challenge: without the knowledge of the cabinet, he ordered building materials for the construction of military installations in French Lorraine. Word of this move soon reached the German press, which demanded an immediate explanation from the uninformed French government. When Bismarck let it be known privately that Boulanger's actions could lead to war, Windthorst, the leader of the Catholic Center party, relayed this information to the newly elected deputies in the Reichstag from Alsace-Lorraine. These deputies were all *protestataires;* that is, they protested the annexation of their homeland to Germany and maintained chief loyalty to France. They sped to Paris and warned their

[22] *L'Intransigeant,* Jan. 21, 1887.

[23] *Grosse Politik,* VI, 169–170.

[24] Gabriel Monod, "Contemporary Life and Thought in France," *Contemporary Review,* LII (Sept., 1887), 430–431.

counterparts from France's eastern departments in the Chamber of the gravity of the situation. Foreign Minister Flourens then exacted a promise from Boulanger not to undertake any similar actions without prior consent of the government.[25]

Still anxious to prove himself, however, the War Minister conceived a new plan. He drafted an order summoning several French divisions for maneuvers in the East, only a few kilometers from where the Germans were training, and showed it to the President of the Republic. Grévy was stunned. "Don't you realize that this would mean war?" he asked. "I am ready," replied the brash General, who threatened to resign if the order were not approved. Grévy, who later recounted the incident to Münster, called Boulanger's bluff; no French troops were sent anywhere near the German border.[26]

By trying to beat Bismarck at the latter's own game, Boulanger had—in modern parlance—helped "escalate" the tension to the point where war was a distinct possibility. French diplomats, however, recognized their country's handicaps and did everything possible to preserve the precarious peace. In a telegram of January 25, Flourens instructed Herbette in part:

As for General Boulanger himself, you must not let him be discussed directly, just as we could not allow ourselves to discuss a German minister; but you may say that in our country it is not the War Minister who makes the final decision as to peace or war, and that the firm desire of the entire government—including the Chambers, which represent public opinion—is to maintain peace.[27]

Bismarck claimed to be unconvinced. Diplomatic protocol prevented him from demanding Boulanger's ouster from the

[25] *D.D.F.*, 1ère série, VI, 416–417; cf. Auguste Lalance, *Mes souvenirs, 1830–1914* (Paris: Berger-Levrault, 1914), pp. 54–55.

[26] *Grosse Politik*, VI, 203–205.

[27] *D.D.F.*, 1ère série, VI, 426n.

French government. Instead, he used an indirect method of achieving the same end by warning Herbette: "That man is planning a *coup d'état!*" Now it was the Frenchman's turn to be unconvinced. He predicted that calm would return after the Reichstag elections.[28] A few weeks previously, in fact, he had expressed to Bismarck the French government's sincere desire to see the septenate passed by the Reichstag. Only then, he reasoned, could normal relations between the two countries be resumed.[29]

Relatively normal relations were indeed resumed, but not until German public opinion had been roused to a fever pitch on January 31 by an article in the semiofficial Berlin *Post,* entitled "On the Knife's Edge." This journal, which had warned of war between France and Germany in 1875, now exclaimed that Boulanger had complete control of the situation in France and was ready to launch an offensive against Germany at any moment. The following day, the German military attaché in Vienna wrote to Herbert von Bismarck, the German foreign minister, that the latter's Austrian colleague, Count Kálnoky, was unfavorably impressed by this outburst. "The Count considers it inopportune that the German press is exaggerating the importance of Boulanger and thereby makes his ouster more improbable." [30] In Paris the shock created by the article in the *Post* was so great as to precipitate a fall in the *rente* by 2 francs 50.[31] As British and Russian diplomats asked Bismarck to ease the pressure, the latter obliged by recalling German troops from the field on February 18. Calm was restored in time for the Reichstag

---

[28] *Ibid.,* pp. 427–430. [29] *Ibid.,* pp. 401–402.
[30] *Grosse Politik,* VI, 171–172.
[31] Edmond and Jules de Goncourt, *Journal: Mémoires de la vie littéraire* (22 vols.; Monaco: Imprimerie Nationale, 1956–1958), XIV, 192.

elections of February 21, which gave the Chancellor his favorable majority. The septenate was accordingly voted into law on March 11, 1887.[32]

THE SCHNAEBELÉ AFFAIR

France and Germany were again at swords' points after April 21, 1887, when a French frontier official named Schnaebelé was enticed across the border into Germany and arrested for espionage. In this instance, it appears that neither government desired the incident, yet both must share responsibility for the crisis which followed. The initial blame falls on Gautsch, the German police commissioner at Ars-sur-Moselle, who on April 13 and 19 sent letters of safe-conduct to Schnaebelé, inviting him to discuss official business on the German side of the border. When the Frenchman was arrested, the German government's first reaction was to claim that he had actually been engaged in espionage at the time. French Foreign Minister Flourens, however, set the record straight by sending Herbette copies of Gautsch's two letters. When confronted with this evidence on April 25, Herbert von Bismarck admitted that a trap had, in effect, been set. Apparently Gautsch's action had not been approved in advance by the German foreign ministry.[33]

Partly because of this evidence, Bismarck announced in a letter of April 28 to Herbette that Schnaebelé was being sent back to France. The Chancellor explained that inasmuch as the latter had been on official business at the time of his arrest, he would be released in order not to discourage other frontier officials from carrying out their normal duties. He emphasized, however, that Schnaebelé did confess to espionage—a

[32] André Daniel, *L'année politique, XIV* (Paris: Charpentier, 1887), 19–26.
[33] *D.D.F.,* 1ère série, VI, 512, 519.

crime all the more serious because he had taken advantage of his border post to commit it. Such abuses of privilege, he explained, could hinder the normal functioning of international relations, which by their very nature depend on mutual trust between officials of different countries.[34] The French government was thus put on notice to avoid a repetition of such an incident.

From this message, as well as from the correspondence which preceded it, it is evident that Bismarck sincerely wished to avoid a crisis at this juncture. Yet for the vast majority of Frenchmen, who had no access to the diplomatic courier, the Schnaebelé affair seemed to be merely another example of German bullying. Henri Michelin expressed the belief, widely held among Parisians, that the German chancellor was seeking to provoke France into a war. "Monsieur Bismarck has always cherished only one dream: *to wipe out France.*"[35] Even after Schnaebelé's release, Alexandre Millerand warned: "After such a hot alert, the government would be criminal not to take every precaution so as to be ready—I say completely ready—for any eventuality."[36] Fear of war was equally strong on the French Right. If the Conservatives repeatedly advised caution during the affair, it was because they seriously doubted the Republic's ability to achieve victory.[37]

Fear of war was probably a major factor in prompting Bismarck to free Schnaebelé. The day before the Chancellor wrote to Herbette, he had received a message from a German military attaché in Paris, reporting the state of French public opinion. "The exasperation of the masses," he observed, "is currently very great." Germany might be legally justified in arresting Schnaebelé, but such incidents could only increase

[34] *Grosse Politik,* VI, 187–189.   [35] *L'Action,* April 24, 1887.
[36] *La Justice,* April 30, 1887.
[37] *Le Gaulois,* April 26–27, 1887.

Boulanger's popularity and might even bring on war. With apparent surprise, the diplomat reported that German agents had discovered no unusual activity at the Paris railroad stations. Even the War Minister manifested himself far less than during the previous crisis. Boulanger's only public act was to cancel leaves in a number of regiments, but even this measure was not general.[38]

If Boulanger was not conspicuous during the Schnaebelé affair, it was not for want of trying. While the affair was still in progress, Boulanger asked the cabinet that the French ambassador to Germany be recalled and that 50,000 French troops be mobilized along the German border. Premier Goblet, who appears to have lost his grip on reality at this point, approved the measure. It was blocked only by the determined opposition of Flourens, Rouvier, and President Grévy.[39] Even after the crisis was resolved, Goblet refused to admit that he and Boulanger were wrong. In a conversation with Herbette, who was visiting Paris on May 1, the Premier remarked: "The incident is ended, good! But perhaps it would have been preferable to end by war all these German quarrels." [40] Nor would Boulanger admit his error. On May 10, he presented to the Chamber a bill to permit mobilization exercises for the army. Since this measure necessitated the appropriation of additional funds, it was sent, with the Chamber's approval, to the budget committee.[41]

The bill never left committee, for exactly a week later, on May 17, the Goblet ministry was overthrown—Boulanger and all. On the basis of available evidence, it cannot be proved definitely that any but the budgetary question then discussed

---

[38] *Grosse Politik*, VI, 186–187.   [39] *Ibid.*, pp. 191–192, 206.

[40] Emile Bourgeois and Georges Pagès, *Les origines et les responsabilités de la Grand Guerre* (Paris: Hachette, 1921), p. 229.

[41] *J.O.C.* (1887), p. 972.

was responsible for the government's fall. There are indications, however, of a concerted effort by moderates to remove Boulanger by defeating the ministry. Flourens told Münster confidentially on May 10 that he and several of his colleagues were hoping to get rid of the War Minister shortly.[42] Their desire was no doubt given added impetus by the verdict of the Leipzig trials, which showed that Boulanger had instituted the practice of using frontier officials, such as Schnaebelé, as spies.[43] Rumors, which came into the open a year later, indicated that leading French generals were most dissatisfied with Boulanger's organization. They discreetly made known their belief that France's military establishment was in such a poor state as to make the country totally unprepared for war.[44]

It was hardly a secret that the major powers of Europe were anxious to see Boulanger removed as War Minister. When a new government was formed without him under Maurice Rouvier, the Germans were the first to rejoice. Herbert von Bismarck wrote to Münster on June 3, saying: "We view it as a peaceful sign that M. Rouvier and his colleagues have succeeded in doing away with this troublemaker, dangerous for the peace." The German ambassador was asked to convey this view to Rouvier and let him know that the German government would do everything possible to facilitate the new ministry's conduct of foreign affairs.[45] Yet if Boulanger's dismissal was of prime importance to Berlin, the French domestic situation required that the fall of the Goblet cabinet appear to be the result of a purely internal problem. Otherwise, it might be

[42] *Grosse Politik*, VI, 189.

[43] Emile Bourgeois, *Manuel historique de politique étrangère* (4 vols.; Paris: Belin, 1926) IV, 35–36.

[44] Charles de Mazade, "Chronique de la quinzaine," *Revue des Deux Mondes*, XC (Nov. 15, 1888), 468.

[45] *Grosse Politik*, VI, 192–193.

suspected that France's record in the recent crisis was less than blameless.[46]

BOULANGER STEPS DOWN

Whether or not Boulanger was the cause of the ministry's demise, he quickly became the main consideration in the formation of a new government. Although the anti-Goblet majority of May 17 was composed chiefly of Conservatives and Opportunists, some Radicals had voted against the cabinet in the belief that only the budget was at issue. Within two days after the vote, however, they began to suspect that the War Minister alone was the real target.[47] At the possibility that Boulanger might not be included in the next cabinet, his supporters now organized a movement in his favor. Henri Rochefort even warned that the dismissal of Boulanger could have the same effect as that of Necker, whose abrupt removal by Louis XVI had led to the storming of the Bastille. Rochefort, in his typically extravagant language, now warned of equally revolutionary action on behalf of Boulanger, whose retention in the government had become the chief demand of the Left.[48] By the same token, the Conservatives insisted, out of opposition to both his foreign and domestic policy, that he be ousted.[49]

By this time, Boulanger had clearly become, in the eyes of both Right and Left, the very incarnation of Radicalism. As such, his participation in a new government was a prerequisite for Radical support. That this support was still desired by the Center is shown by President Grévy's invitation to Charles

[46] Léon Goulette, *Avant, pendant et après l'affaire Schnaebelé* (Paris: Bayle, n.d. [1887]), pp. v–vii.

[47] *La Lanterne*, May 20, 1887.

[48] *L'Intransigeant*, May 20, 1887.

[49] *L'Autorité*, May 19, 1887; *Le Figaro*, May 25, 1887.

Floquet on May 24 to discuss the formation of a new "government of republican concentration." Floquet, a Radical who stood somewhat further to the left than Goblet, was apparently acceptable to the Opportunists as long as Boulanger was excluded from the cabinet. Under these conditions, however, the Radicals refused to support Floquet, who regretfully announced the next day that he could not accept the task.[50]

Meanwhile, the General's supporters busily petitioned the Chamber and the President of the Republic to keep Boulanger at his post as War Minister. On May 20, the *Cercle républicain d'Indre-et-Loire* sent a letter to this effect to Grévy. A similar petition was sent by the city council of Lyons, which had met in special session to discuss the matter. Perhaps the most unusual (and certainly unprecedented) petition was the one signed by 324 civilian employees of the War Ministry.[51] Boulanger's failure to dissociate himself from this last petition only served to harden the Opportunists' opposition to him.[52] The General likewise failed to discourage a spectacular gesture by Rochefort, who called on all admirers of Boulanger to register their protest by voting for him in the Paris by-election of May 22. Although the previously unopposed Radical candidate won handily with 219,929 votes, Rochefort's suggestion, which was made only a day before the election, produced 38,457 ballots for Boulanger.[53]

Now that the Center was thoroughly disenchanted with the conduct of Boulanger's followers, the Right made discreet but persistent overtures for collaboration with the Opportunists. First, the Conservatives repeated their pledge made during the

---

[50] *La Lanterne,* May 27, 1887.   [51] *L'Action,* May 23, 1887.
[52] *La République Française,* May 25, 1887.
[53] *L'Intransigeant,* May 24, 1887.

last ministerial crisis not to engage in any systematic opposition.[54] Then Baron de Mackau, their leader in the Chamber, made two unsolicited visits to Grévy, during which he promised that his party would maintain a position of benevolent neutrality toward an all-Opportunist cabinet, sympathetic to the wishes of the Right. The result of these overtures was the Rouvier ministry, which was voted into office on May 30 by a combination of Conservatives and Opportunists. To Albert Deberly, Conservative Deputy from the Somme, it seemed as if Raoul-Duval's cherished wish had come true— except that there was no formal alliance here, just an unwritten understanding.[55]

Formal alliance or not, the mere fact that the Right was willing to support a Republican ministry even while not participating in it was without precedent since 1871. The new Conservative stand had been prepared to some extent by the declaration of the Comte de Paris in September, 1886, and by that of Baron de Mackau four months later. On being elected president of the Conservative Union, the latter had made a speech in favor of a constructive policy by the Right to help heal the country's internal wounds.[56] The apparent fruition of such a policy was greeted favorably by most segments of the Right, now eager to move closer to the seat of power. Speaking for the Orleanists, the journalist de Pène predicted that the new ministry "could open new horizons" in cooperation between Right and Center.[57]

Just as the Right greeted the new government with satisfac-

[54] *Le Gaulois,* May 19, 1887.

[55] Maxime Lecomte, *Les ralliés: Histoire d'un parti, 1886–1898* (Paris: Flammarion, 1898), pp. 92–94.

[56] Charles de Mazade, "Chronique de la quinzaine," *Revue des Deux Mondes,* LXXIX (Feb. 1, 1887), 714–715.

[57] *Le Gaulois,* May 30, 1887.

tion, the parliamentary Left took the latest developments in a spirit of utter dismay. Having prevented the formation of a government of Republican concentration by their insistence that Boulanger be retained in his post, the Radicals now accused the Opportunists of open betrayal. For them, the ex-War Minister was no longer the main issue—save as a symbol of their own exclusion from the government. Rochefort led the attack on the new cabinet, calling it "the German ministry" [58] and referring to Rouvier as "the protégé of the Right." [59] Pelletan saw the Conservative-Opportunist entente as a return to clericalism, imperialism, and perhaps even the monarchy itself.[60] Irrespective of Boulanger's fall from office, the entire French Left was smarting at its defeat.

Boulanger apparently wished to take advantage of this feeling in order to win sympathy for himself. On leaving his post, he revived a privilege which had fallen into disuse since 1875, and addressed the following order of the day to the army:

Officers, noncommissioned officers, and enlisted men:

Inasmuch as the cabinet of which I was a part has resigned, the President of the Republic has entrusted to other hands the War portfolio.

On leaving the army command I wish to thank all those who have seconded me in the patriotic task of making our means of defense equal to any test.

You will be, under the orders of my successor, what you have been under mine: devoted to your professional duties and faithful to the constitutional laws, respect for which must, in our heart, dominate all other feelings.

I shall be the first to set for you the example of this twofold military and Republican discipline.[61]

[58] *L'Intransigeant,* June 1, 1887.   [59] *Ibid.,* June 2, 1887.
[60] *La Justice,* May 31, 1887.
[61] *Année politique,* XIV (1887), 123.

The General's critics were quick to note that such a declaration of purpose was at best completely unnecessary. "What outgoing War Minister ever thought of not returning quietly to the ranks?" asked *Le Temps* irritably.[62] To Gabriel Monod it seemed that Boulanger "pointed to his retirement as an example of respect for the law in a way which implied that he might have been tempted to violate it." [63]

Nonetheless, the General's manifesto did help to keep his name in the public eye; the leftist press did the rest. When the government named Boulanger division commander at Clermont-Ferrand, the Parisian dailies loyal to him published the time of his scheduled departure from the Gare de Lyon, plus a detailed description of his route to the station.[64] Boulanger was supposed to leave on July 8 at eight o'clock in the evening. At about six o'clock, some five to six hundred youths assembled near the General's residence at the Hôtel du Louvre to whip up enthusiasm. They sang *En r'venant de la Revue* and sold color portraits of their hero. Within half an hour, as a result of their activity, a crowd of about three thousand enthusiasts and curiosity-seekers was gathered in front of the hotel, eagerly awaiting the arrival of Boulanger, who appeared with his retinue at 7:30. Clusters of people now hung on to his carriage, trying to prevent it from leaving; but Boulanger was able to reach the railroad station by 7:45.[65]

At the Gare de Lyon itself, an awesome demonstration took place, which retarded Boulanger's departure by two hours. The Paris chief of police, Lépine, recalls that before Boulanger reached the station, a crowd estimated at some twenty thousand persons had already filled the Place Diderot and its environs. Using a secret passage, Lépine gained access to the train platforms, which were then empty. Suddenly, with the

[62] June 1, 1887.   [63] *Loc. cit.,* 430.
[64] *L'Intransigeant,* July 9, 1887.   [65] *Le Temps,* July 11, 1887.

apparent complicity of the station employees, all gates opened, and the mob invaded the entire station.[66] So many people walked onto the tracks that the railroad crew was not able to bring Boulanger's train into the station until nine o'clock. Then by blocking the tracks, the people prevented that train from leaving. By evading his admirers and climbing aboard another locomotive, the General was able to reach Charenton, where another train took him to his destination.[67] Frustrated in their attempt to keep Boulanger in Paris, his more hot-headed supporters then left the Gare de Lyon, shouting: "To the Elysée!" and "Down with Grévy!" They were easily dispersed, however, at the Place de la Bastille by a force of 200 policemen.[68]

Just what the demonstration of July 8, 1887, signified in political terms has been obscured by a vast amount of tendentious writing. Perhaps the most widely held view remains that of Nazi party historian Walter Frank. To Frank, the events at the Gare de Lyon indicated that the French masses longed for a dictator capable of waging a war of *revanche* against Germany.[69] In those days before public opinion polls, however, concrete proof of popular revanchist feeling is difficult to find. One German historian, eager to show that French nationalism was largely responsible for the First World War, has seen evidence of such feeling in the chauvinistic lyrics of a few café songs sung in the winter and spring of 1887.[70] Yet it is well to remember that the French public was at the time genuinely

[66] Louis Lépine, *Mes souvenirs* (Paris: Payot, 1929), p. 68.

[67] Auguste Boucher, "Chronique politique," *Le Correspondant*, CXLVIII (July 25, 1887), 387–388.

[68] Lépine, *op. cit.*, pp. 26–27.

[69] Walter Frank, *Nationalismus und Demokratie im Frankreich der Dritten Republik, 1871 bis 1918* (2nd ed.; Hamburg: Hanseatische Verlagsanstalt, 1941), pp. 160–167, 182.

[70] Kühn, *op. cit.*, pp. 26–27.

frightened of a possible invasion by Germany.[71] Any consideration of café songs as proof of a widespread desire in France for *revanche* should be taken against the background of this fear.

As for the theory that the demonstration at the Gare de Lyon revealed a deep-seated desire on the part of the French people for a dictator, this is at best an extrapolation from a charge later made against the General—not the French people —by the French government. In 1889, when the government was looking about for any available weapon to use against Boulanger, it accused him of having attempted a *coup d'état* that night. This accusation rests on very slim evidence. It is true that at a meeting of anarchists and revolutionaries held on July 5, 1887, that famous alumna of the Commune, Louise Michel, reported that Boulanger had discussed such a possibility with some Deputies of the far Left and the far Right. Their plans failed to materialize, however, because they depended on Boulanger's reinstatement as War Minister and the support of the Army high command, neither of which had been forthcoming.[72]

The motives of those who participated in the Gare de Lyon demonstration are perhaps best explained by the leftist journalists who encouraged it. "Yesterday's manifestation," commented Henri Michelin, "was . . . not in favor of one man, but in favor of the principles he personifies: *national defense and dignity of the Republic.*"[73] Indeed, for the French Left of that time, the two principles seemed to be virtually inseparable. Since the revolutionary wars of 1793, the Republic had been enshrined in the leftist mystique as the staunchest de-

[71] Cf. *supra*, pp. 54–58.

[72] Archives Nationales Françaises, F[7] 12445, July 6, 1887; hereinafter cited as A.N.F.

[73] *L'Action*, July 11, 1887.

fender of national honor. To those who thought of the Republic in terms of 1793, it must have appeared little short of treasonous for the government to accept parliamentary support from the Right. From his perch on the Jacobin fringe, Eugène Mayer wrote: "In the ovations given to the General there was nothing personal. It was at once a patriotic manifestation and a protest against the cabinet, nothing more." [74]

A similar view was expressed in the Chamber by Clemenceau three days after the demonstration. This was the speech in which the Radical leader is said to have broken formally with Boulanger, thereby cutting him off from his base of political support.[75] In fact, it meant nothing of the sort. Clemenceau's speech was but one of several made that day in opposition to the Rouvier ministry by Radicals. Although he criticized the Gare de Lyon demonstration and Boulanger's apparent encouragement of it, he tried to bring out its true significance.

I say that this popularity [of Boulanger] has come too quickly to someone who liked noise too much, or who, to speak more equitably, did not avoid it enough. . . . But we must see what this War Minister's situation was, what he had done, and why good people, excellent patriots, were involved in the scenes at the Gare de Lyon.

These people, explained Clemenceau, were paying homage to the General's Republican initiatives as War Minister and protesting the end of Republican concentration in government. It was to the latter that Clemenceau referred when he said: "The Boulanger question is a misfortune; it is a misfortune for all of us—for you [Rouvier] as well as for me." [76] The misfortune

[74] *La Lanterne,* July 11, 1887.
[75] Cf. Adrien Dansette, *Le boulangisme* (Paris: Fayard, 1946), pp. 100–102.
[76] *J.O.C.* (1887), pp. 1161–1162.

was that Boulanger had been allowed to divide the Republicans.

No declaration by Clemenceau at this point could have destroyed Boulanger's political base, since that had already been lost in the formation of the Rouvier government. Although the Radicals still supported the General, they were now excluded from power. A few politicians of the extreme Jacobin faction, however, wished to see Boulanger back in government regardless of his support, or lack of it, in the Chamber. They called themselves Boulangists—a new term, but one destined to be repeated often during the next two years.

4

The Right Changes Course 1887

Condemned to relative obscurity at Clermont-Ferrand, a severe demotion, Boulanger began to fade from the French political scene. The last important public demonstration in his favor during the year 1887 took place on July 14, the anniversary of his first public triumph. It was led by Paul Déroulède, who organized a band of urchins to attend the Longchamp military review and shout: "Long live Boulanger!" "Resign!" and "Down with Ferry!" Some of the spectators took up the cries of Déroulède and his claque, but these were largely drowned out in the general noise and excitement.[1] When Henri Rochefort tried to speak on Boulanger's behalf in another part of Paris, he was hooted off the platform.

The continuing success of the Conservative-Opportunist entente demonstrated that the Center was fully capable of governing without Boulanger in the War Ministry. Although the Boulangist press claimed that the new cabinet ministers would not dare to show their faces in the provinces that summer, they visted Rouen, Le Havre, Saint-Quentin, and Senlis, and were invariably well received.[2] Inasmuch as Boulanger's fol-

[1] *La Justice,* July 15, 1887.
[2] Gabriel Monod, "Contemporary Life and Thought in France," *Contemporary Review,* LII (Sept., 1887), 435.

lowing was centered mainly in Paris, the warm reception given to the government outside the capital is not surprising.

THE BOULANGISTS

Of those whose hostility to the new ministry went beyond the confines of the Chamber, the most conspicuous was Déroulède. A veteran of the Franco-Prussian War, he had helped organize the *Ligue des patriotes* in 1882, following encouragement by Gambetta and other leading Republicans. In keeping with article 32 of its charter, this organization took no stand on internal politics during its early years and was generally favorable to the government. With the advent of the second Ferry cabinet, however, Déroulède and his *ligueurs* drifted into the opposition on both foreign and domestic questions.[3] As early as the fall of 1884, Déroulède publicly accused Ferry of being the ally of Bismarck.[4] A year later, he entered politics as an independent candidate for the Chamber from Paris and won some 100,000 votes.[5] Although his appeal for support was officially nonpartisan, it did mark a falling-out between Déroulède and France's Republican "establishment."

As chief financial contributor,[6] Déroulède was often able to set policy for the *Ligue* by 1887, but not without antagonizing some of its members. Divided among 500 branches throughout the country, the organization reached its peak membership figure of about 82,000 in 1886 and declined numerically thereafter.[7] A principal factor in its decline was

[3] A.P.P., B a/976, March 13, 1889.

[4] Georges Buisson and A. Henri Canu, *M. Paul Déroulède et sa Ligue des patriotes: la vérité* (Paris: Savine, 1889), p. 30.

[5] *Le Drapeau*, Oct. 3 and Dec. 16, 1885.

[6] *Ibid.*, April 29, 1888.

[7] Johannes Ziekursch, *Politische Geschichte des neuen deutschen Kaiserreiches* (3 vols.; Frankfurt: Societäts Drükerei, 1927), II, 183.

the Boulanger question. Following the Leipzig trials, in which several Alsatians and one Frenchman were accused by Germany of high treason for having belonged to the *Ligue,* Déroulède organized a rally on their behalf at the Cirque d'Hiver. Once he began to speak, however, it became apparent that he was scarcely interested in the Alsatians, but had started the meeting in order to protest the removal of Boulanger. In this attempt he failed miserably. All the local committees of the *Ligue* in the provinces promptly disavowed Déroulède's speech, and many individual members resigned, throwing the organization into great disorder.[8]

Although no effectively organized movement for Boulanger existed in 1887, none was really needed. At this point in his career, the General seems to have had only one ambition: to win back his post of War Minister.[9] To help him in this endeavor was clearly the aim of Charles-Ange Laisant, a positivist mathematician and left-wing Deputy from Paris. Immediately after Boulanger's transfer, Laisant addressed a pamphlet to his constituents, explaining why he was a Boulangist —surely one of the earliest public uses of the word. His reasons were perfectly straightforward: "Because I am a patriot; because I desire peace; and because I am a Republican." [10] According to Laisant, it was Boulanger's enemies, Bismarck and Rouvier, who created the Boulangist phenomenon. "By declaring myself a Boulangist," he reasoned, "I find the means, in a single word, to protest against the Right, against the Rouvier cabinet, against Prussian policies—and for our homeland." [11]

[8] Monod, *loc. cit.;* cf.; Raoul Girardet, "La Ligue des patriotes dans l'histoire du nationalisme français (1882–1888)," *Bulletin de la Société d'Histoire Moderne,* 12ème série, no. 6 (1958), p. 5.

[9] Maurice Barrès, *L'appel au soldat* (Paris: Juven, 1911), p. 90.

[10] Charles-Ange Laisant, *A mes électeurs: Pourquoi et comment je suis boulangiste* (Paris: Mayer, 1887), p. 5.

[11] *Ibid.,* pp. 22–23.

Laisant deeply wished to see Boulanger return to the War Ministry, but clearly ruled out any illegal actions, since it would be opposed by the Republican masses which supported the General. He warned, however, that there were others, on the Right, who lacked these scruples.

In certain monarchist circles, the cult and the love of force are pushed to a degree of aberration beyond normal imagination. I have heard some, with my own ears, express regret that General Boulanger, during the demonstration at the Gare de Lyon, did not decide to march on the Elysée and take it over, relying on popular consent. As if, in addition to the sentiments of honesty and Republican rectitude which guide him, General Boulanger did not understand that the same friends who hailed him so warmly on his departure would have blown his brains out along the way between the Gare de Lyon and the Elysée.[12]

Within a year after having written this passage, Laisant was to participate in the formation of a Boulangist party, whose plans for the General, while never clearly defined to the public, went beyond the War Ministry. During its brief existence, this party consistently adhered to the letter, if not the spirit, of the law. By warning that force might be used, however, Laisant helped give the Boulangist movement an air of illegality, which it never completely lost.

Once he arrived in Clermont, Boulanger used every means that was not explicitly illegal in order to regain his former post. His chief confidant, now as in the future, was Alfred Naquet, the Jewish Senator from the Vaucluse, who was already well known for his positivist views. As a Deputy, Naquet had been a champion since 1871 of the graduated income tax and since 1875 of the referendum. His sole parliamentary success, however, was the passage of a law legalizing

[12] *Ibid.*, p. 27.

divorce in 1883. The lethargy shown by the Chamber toward his first two projects convinced Naquet that France's political system would have to be drastically reformed if the popular will (i.e., that of Naquet) were to make itself felt. Impressed by Boulanger's Republicanism, Naquet eventually chose the General to be the instrument of such reform.[13]

Naquet's earliest political writings indicate an almost mystical faith in universal suffrage as an expression of the national will. "Universal suffrage and the Republic are one and the same thing," he asserted.[14] A republican regime is therefore to be judged by a single criterion: the extent to which the people's wishes, as expressed by universal suffrage, are translated into political acts. In a true republic, there are no obstacles to such expression, and even the most complicated problems can be resolved by "free discussion." For this reason, Naquet had little use for socialism and its conception of class. The social problem would quickly disappear, he predicted, just as soon as the voice of the people could be heard in government.[15]

From this position, which was published in 1873, Naquet identified himself as an "advanced Republican"—far to the Left on constitutional questions, but rather less so on economic ones. Whereas the Socialists took an economic view of politics, the "advanced Republicans" took a political view of economics. In 1873, Naquet stood entirely within the tradition of the Jacobin Left by proposing, as the most representative form of government, a weak executive dominated by a unicameral legislature.[16]

By 1883, Naquet was still deeply involved in constitutional

[13] Sybil [Charles Benoist], *Croquis parlementaires* (Paris: Perrin, 1891), pp. 92–93.

[14] *La République radicale* (Paris: Germer-Baillière, 1873), p. 16.

[15] *Ibid.*, pp. 45–46.   [16] *Ibid.*, pp. 105.

questions, but had broken with leftist tradition on a crucial point. Instead of favoring a weak executive as did the Radicals and the extreme Left, he now advocated complete separation of powers. The success of the American system, he maintained, recommended such a change for France.[17] Unlike almost everyone else on the Left, Naquet seems to have grasped the importance of a strong executive for the pursuance of reform. To shield himself against charges of wanting a dictatorship, he added that the executive could be composed of one man or several. Personally, he favored a directory, but considered the composition of the executive to be a question of minor importance.[18]

Although these proposals were academic at the time they were published, they received concrete expression in the Boulangist campaign of 1888 and 1889. In all his public pronouncements on the constitution, Boulanger was to draw exclusively on Naquet's ideas. Insofar as the movement had a formal political credo, Naquet was its author. When the Senator from the Vaucluse made his proposals for constitutional reform in 1883, Ferry had already begun his notorious delaying tactics. Naquet therefore despaired of obtaining revision through the process outlined in the 1875 constitution and decided to take the issue to the people. Once the voters were made fully aware of the evils in the present constitution, he predicted, "universal suffrage will . . . have the last word. It will simply impose integral revision as a mandate on all the Senators and Deputies elected by the nation." [19] Such having been his plan, it is easy to understand why Naquet later supported Boulanger with such intensity. The General was to be the vehicle by which a parliament dedicated to revision could be elected.

[17] *Questions constitutionnelles* (Paris: Dentu, 1883), p. 90.
[18] *Ibid.,* pp. 73–74.   [19] *Ibid.,* p. 63.

It was not until Boulanger's ouster from the government that the two men actually became collaborators, even though they appear to have known each other since at least 1886. In a newspaper article of August of that year, Naquet mentioned his personal acquaintance with the General and praised the latter's devotion to the Republic.[20] A few months later, the Senator resumed his attacks on the constitution, calling it a vestige of Orleanism.[21] His proposals for a new regime were essentially similar to those announced in 1883.[22] The gains registered by the Left in 1885 and the ensuing Radical participation in government did not lessen Naquet's desire for constitutional change. On the contrary, the virtual abandonment of revision by the Radicals apparently intensified his quest.

In mid-1887, therefore, both men found themselves outside the "mainstream" of French public affairs. Each, in his own way and for his own reasons, was seeking to divert that stream in his direction. Boulanger's first surviving letters to Naquet date from this period. They do not mention revision of the constitution, but discuss, in rather vague terms, the General's chances of entering the government. From his new post at Clermont-Ferrand, Boulanger expressed complete confidence in a letter to Naquet dated July 18. "I have only one answer to give you," he wrote. "*Let us wait.*" [23]

Boulanger did not wait long, however. Three days later, an unsigned article appeared in the left-wing daily, *La France,* relating what purported to be two attempts to corrupt the

[20] Cf. Georges Grison, *Le général Boulanger jugé par ses partisans et ses adversaires* (Paris: Librairie Illustrée, 1889), p. 239.

[21] Alfred Naquet, "Le parlementarisme," *Revue Bleue,* XXIII (Dec. 25, 1886), 801.

[22] Alfred Naquet, "Le régime représentatif," *Revue Bleue,* XXIV (Jan. 22, 1887), 102–103.

[23] France, Bibliothèque nationale, N.A.F. 23783, no. 5.

former War Minister. The first was said to have taken place during the Schnaebelé affair, when ninety-four French generals promised to follow Boulanger if he took matters into his own hands and made war on Germany. In the second, which supposedly occurred just after the overthrow of the Goblet ministry, some rightists called on Boulanger to stage a *coup d'état*.[24] In neither story were the participants identified, but the article's purpose was clear. It constituted a warning that unless Boulanger were brought back into a Republican cabinet, he might be bought out by those hostile to the Republic. Such a possibility was quickly laughed off by the Opportunists, who applauded Jules Ferry's contemptuous description of Boulanger as "a music-hall Saint-Arnaud." [25]

Propaganda in the General's favor continued to circulate in Paris for several months after he left the government. If pro-Boulanger café songs were now sung less frequently than during the crises with Germany, there was still a considerable stock of Boulanger portraits, medals, pipes, scarf pins—and even soap—that had to be sold. The manufacturers of most, if not all, of these products had used the General's name in order to benefit from his popularity, and only secondarily to further it.[26] Of a quite different nature was an imitation five-franc piece bearing Boulanger's image with the inscription: "Boulanger, ex-Minister of France, July 14, 1887." The police stopped circulation of these coins on July 7, at which time some 40,000 had already been sold at a wholesale price of six

[24] *La France*, July 21, 1887.

[25] Charles de Mazade, "Chronique de la quinzaine," *Revue des Deux Mondes*, LXXXII (Aug. 15, 1887), 947–948. General Saint-Arnaud, as War Minister, organized Louis Napoleon's *coup d'état* of December 2, 1851.

[26] Frederick Turner, *General Boulanger* (London: Swan, Sonnenschein, 1888), pp. 114–115.

francs per hundred. No indication of the buyers' names or motives is revealed in the police report.[27]

Although it is uncertain who initiated such propaganda in 1887, the most likely choice is a certain Count Dillon, who was in charge of Boulanger's publicity a year later. Dillon, whose noble lineage is at best obscure, had been a classmate of Boulanger's at Saint-Cyr. Having made a fortune overnight as president of a Franco-American cable company in 1878, Dillon, who greatly admired American advertising techniques, was ideally suited to organize propaganda for the General.[28] Unlike the other members of Boulanger's inner circle, Dillon was not a leftist. If he had any deep political convictions, he kept them well hidden. Whether or not he actually was a royalist, as he later claimed to Arthur Meyer of *Le Gaulois,*[29] he certainly was no democrat. It is reasonable to suppose, therefore, that his hopes for Boulanger were different from those of the far Left. When the Rouvier ministry fell in November, 1887, the Boulangist Deputy, Le Hérissé, announced to the press that the General would accept the post of War Minister in the new cabinet.[30] But was this enough for Dillon?

Legitimate suspicions about Boulanger's real intentions were naturally aroused by the appearance, late in 1887, of a placard entitled: "Boulanger, the Savior of France." It was signed by a public relations man named André Magué, who later identified himself as a leftist republican seeking "national renewal" for France.[31] Unlike previous appeals for the Gen-

[27] A.N.F., F⁷ 12445, July 20, 1887.

[28] A.P.P., B a/906, Feb. 18, 1889.

[29] Mermeix [Gabriel Terrail], *Les coulisses du boulangisme* (Paris: Cerf, 1890), p. 84.

[30] *Le Gaulois,* Nov. 21, 1887.

[31] Magué, *Le proscrit de Jersey: Etat actuel de la France* (Neuilly: Marceau, 1890), pp. 22–23.

eral, this one paid little attention to his ability in foreign affairs and emphasized internal politics. Boulanger had almost no experience in the latter field; but since the war scare was now past, his partisans obviously needed a new approach. Most unusual was the goal set forth for the former War Minister.

The tradesman who asks only that his business prosper, the farmer who asks only for an increase in the yield of agriculture, and the worker whose only desire is the development of industry and the [fair] distribution of its profits have already understood the role of Boulanger and impatiently await his arrival at the nation's highest office.

As President of the Republic, Boulanger would rid France of an evil called parliamentarism, which was said to be ruining the Republic. In this context, the term referred less to parliamentary government itself than to its abuse by the procrastinating politicians of the Center.[32]

Sentiments of this nature could possibly have originated with Dillon, but they were far more akin to those of the General's most recent associate, a Bonapartist journalist named Georges Thiébaud. As a member of the "Appeal to the People" wing of the party, led by Prince Jérôme, Thiébaud failed to win a seat in the Chamber during the general elections of 1885. This defeat appears to have increased his desire to find a new Napoleon for France, the existing Bonapartist pretenders being unequal to the task. He first cast about in Conservative circles, but found no one popular or ambitious enough to fill such a role. In any event, it was not so much the Republic that Thiébaud opposed as the men in high office. He

[32] André Magué, "Boulanger, le sauveur de la France" (Paris: Magué, 1887).

would be quite content with a Republic led by a really strong personality. Under these conditions, General Boulanger seemed to be the logical choice.[33]

Thiébaud approached Boulanger toward the end of 1887 with the proposal that the latter win a popular following by running in parliamentary by-elections in various parts of the country. The General, whose military status prevented him from entering politics, refused to commit himself at that time.[34] To do so, he would have needed a broader political base than the few malcontents then intriguing for him could provide. Yet even at that very moment, this broader base of support was being prepared—albeit inadvertently—by none other than the Comte de Paris.

THE PRETENDER'S MANIFESTO

Spread across the front pages of France's royalist newspapers on September 15, 1887, was a set of instructions from the Comte de Paris to his followers, which constitute the most unusual document in the history of French royalism. Against the traditions of his house and the interests of his party, the Orleanist pretender recommended that the monarchy be restored by a plebiscite. The new regime, he promised, "will be strong enough to reconcile the practice of universal suffrage with the guarantees of order requested by the country, disgusted with Republican parliamentarism." All kinds of liberties were promised: local, municipal, provincial —even parliamentary, plus freedom of the press and of association. The only liberties which the Comte failed to guarantee were those which mattered most: ministerial responsibility and the annual voting of the budget by parliament.[35]

[33] Charles Joly, "Un nouveau Diogène: M. Georges Thiébaud," *La Nouvelle Revue,* LVII (March 15, 1889), 341–347.

[34] Mermeix, *op. cit.,* pp. 38–39.

[35] *Le Gaulois,* Sept. 15, 1887.

In effect, this strange proclamation announced that royal opposition to the Republic would henceforth be extended to include its parliamentary regime. The paradox was that this regime was Orleanist in its conception: it had been founded to serve as the vehicle for a restoration of the Orleanist monarch. By urging restoration by a plebiscite, the pretender was turning his back on the very constitutional laws that his own lieutenants had drafted. Since the July Monarchy, the house of Orleans had stood for parliamentary government. By using the expression "Republican parliamentarism," the Comte de Paris was tacitly admitting that, somewhere along the way, the monarchy had lost its option on the Third Republic.

The pretender's manifesto shows how impressed he was with the methods and resulting success of the Bonapartists. Within the Conservative party, it was the Bonapartists who had the most *éclat*: they were both rightist and modern. Such qualities enabled them to retain much of their support in the countryside, despite the ignominious defeat of Napoleon III and the absence of a valid successor. As early as 1884, a royalist journalist named Louis Teste had recognized that a return to the old monarchy, or even to the July Monarchy, was impossible, given the current lack of public sympathy. If there was to be any restoration, he explained, it would have to be of the Second Empire with a royal claimant at its head.[36] This was essentially the proposal made by the Comte de Paris.

As might be expected, the warmest praise of this proposal came from Paul de Cassagnac, who wanted a restoration of the Second Empire but disliked both Bonapartist claimants. By discarding parliamentarism, noted Cassagnac, the Comte de Paris had come up with the constitution of 1852. "The monarchy is now blended with the Empire. The fundamental idea [of each] becomes identical."[37] Critics of the manifesto agreed that it reflected a certain Bonapartist mystique. To the

[36] Cited in *ibid.*, July 31, 1888.   [37] *L'Autorité*, Sept. 16, 1887.

moderate and semiofficial *Temps,* it symbolized "the conversion of the representative of traditional monarchy to the Caesarian doctrine of empire." [38] Eugène Veuillot, brother of the late Louis and, like him, a staunch Legitimist, bitterly accused the Orleanist pretender of abandoning whatever shred of true royalism he once had. In effect, said Veuillot, the Comte de Paris was admitting that "there is no more king." [39]

More cogent criticism came from within the pretender's own party. The Marquis de Castellane recognized that most of his fellow Conservatives had no intention of overthrowing the present regime. He advised them not to attack the Republic, to which a majority of Frenchmen were firmly attached because it provided material, if not moral, order. Royalist campaigns were therefore useless. What was asked for was a change of men, not a change of parties, still less a change of institutions. Besides, of the two hundred-odd Conservatives in the Chamber, half would do anything to prevent the other half from attaining power. "The distance is as great from a Bonapartist to a royalist as from a royalist to a [moderate] Republican." [40] It was therefore in the Orleanists' own interest to cooperate with the Opportunists, with whom they shared many common economic concerns, rather than to try to change the regime.

Immediately after the Comte de Paris published his manifesto, the Radical enemies of the Rouvier ministry predicted that no further dealings between the Opportunists and the Right would be possible. They had been making such predictions ever since the cabinet had been formed, however, and this one was no more accurate than the others. A rupture between the Center and its rightist allies did not take place

[38] Sept. 16, 1887.   [39] *L'Univers,* Sept. 15, 1887.
[40] Marquis de Castellane, "Le parti conservateur," *La Nouvelle Revue,* XLIX (Dec. 1, 1887), 534–551.

until two months later; it was severely aggravated, but not caused, by the manifesto. The Comte de Paris had wisely chosen to make his surprise declaration at a time when the Chamber was not in session, and the most important political figures were absent from Paris.

It was apparent, moreover, that few royalists were then prepared to exert themselves for a monarchical restoration. Even that pillar of Orleanism, the Duc d'Aumale, did not choose to give his millions to the royalist campaign fund. Instead, he invested them in a company run by anticlerical Republicans.[41] In the purely political sphere, the Right continued to show general satisfaction with its working relationship to the government. Only a day after the manifesto was issued, Cassagnac gave the somewhat illogical but correct assurance that the Conservatives would not abandon the ministry so long as it continued its present policy.[42]

That the Conservatives had not abandoned the government was amply demonstrated by their attitude toward the by-election held in the Orne on October 16, 1887. In the general elections of 1885, that department had elected five Conservatives out of its allotment of six Deputies. One of these was Baron de Mackau, Orleanist leader in the Chamber and president of the Conservative Union. When a vacancy was created by the death of one of the Orne's Conservative Deputies, Mackau and the three others issued a joint declaration on October 1, announcing that their party would present no candidate in the by-election. Reflecting obvious embarrassment at the Orleanist pretender's manifesto, this statement explained that for the moment calm was needed; one more Conservative in the Chamber was not worth the hatred and anger that would re-

[41] J.-J. Weiss, "Le manifeste et le ministère," *Revue Bleue*, 3ème série, XIV (Oct. 1, 1887), 417–418.
[42] *L'Autorité*, Sept. 17, 1887.

sult from another electoral contest. A more likely reason for the Conservatives' abstention was the position of the Republican candidate, Christophle. As a member of the Left-Center (actually the most conservative element among the Republicans), he took a stand on economic questions that was virtually identical to that of the Orleanists.[43]

Economic interests, however, were not the only ones that mattered. At this point in the Third Republic's history, ideological and, more specifically, constitutional issues still played a large role in French politics. By abandoning the regime founded by his own party, the Comte de Paris disparaged the Orleanist constitution of 1875. Now, this misbegotten document had few defenders left. All Republicans, even the moderates, had to pay lip service to the idea of revising the constitution because of its Orleanist origin. On the far Left were a small group of Deputies who insisted on changing the constitution altogether. It so happens that these were the same Deputies who supported Boulanger—not because he had yet made any pronouncements on the constitution, but because they saw in him a symbol of "advanced Republicanism." After the pretender's manifesto, the position of the Boulangist Deputies and that of the Right began to move closer together.

A SCANDAL BREAKS: WILSON

Before the entente between Conservatives and Opportunists was broken, French politics was to pass through a major scandal, which ended in the forced resignation of the President of the Republic. Ironically, it was Grévy himself who set the entire train of events in motion. Acting on the suggestion of the War Minister, General Ferron, he removed Brigadier

[43] *Le Gaulois,* Oct. 1, 1887

General Caffarel from active duty on October 7, 1887.[44] As bits and pieces of the affair became public, it was revealed that Caffarel, as Deputy Chief of Staff, was accused of having used improper influence in questions of arms procurement. The accusation against him rested on captured letters from a *demimondaine* named Madame Limouzin, who had boasted to her civilian admirers that her influence in the War Ministry enabled her to get a certain brand of cartridge accepted for use with the Lebel repeating rifle. In this connection, she asserted that she had obtained several interviews with Boulanger while the latter was still War Minister.

General Ferron, who had never concealed his distaste for his publicity-seeking predecessor, seized on this occasion to disparage Boulanger's record as War Minister by implying that he had been negligent, or worse. In a speech of October 9 at Chartres, Ferron discussed the Lebel rifle in these terms: "I cannot reveal the extent to which its manufacture has progressed, but I can tell you that when I arrived at the [War] Ministry, the weapon's production left something to be desired." [45] Quite understandably, Boulanger sought to defend his reputation. He immediately convoked reporters to Clermont-Ferrand, where he told them that as War Minister, he had granted Mme. Limouzin exactly one appointment. Within five minutes, he recalled, he recognized her purpose and asked her to leave. Now he was indignant that his name should be besmirched. "I cannot avoid the conclusion that the Caffarel affair is directed against me." Ferron was jealous of his popularity, he charged.[46]

After reading this interview, the War Minister asked Boulanger to state whether or not the words ascribed to him actu-

[44] André Daniel, *L'année politique,* XIV (Paris: Charpentier, 1887), 256.

[45] *La Justice,* Oct. 11, 1887.   [46] *La Nation,* Oct. 12, 1887.

ally were his. A day later, Boulanger admitted that the interview, as published in the newspapers, was textually correct. For this breach of discipline, Ferron had him confined to quarters for thirty days.[47] By showing a capacity for making forceful decisions, the government won praise from its Conservative allies, who predicted—correctly, in this instance—that the General's popularity would suffer as a result.[48]

The scandal did not stop there, however. It was soon discovered that Mme. Limouzin's influence extended beyond the field of weapons procurement to that of military and state medals. The trail of decorations led to the Elysée Palace, where Daniel Wilson, the son-in-law of President Grévy, had been doing a brisk business in the sale of Legion of Honor ribbons! When the police tried to protect Wilson's reputation by removing certain incriminating letters from the Limouzin file, the Chamber voted on November 5 to create a twenty-two-member commission to investigate the entire affair. The motion which proposed its creation was introduced by the Radicals, opposed by the Center, and finally approved by the Conservatives, who did not wish to appear as protectors of Wilson. Yet the Conservatives obviously did not want to see the Rouvier ministry fall. They saved it in the vote of confidence which followed.[49]

This was the last time that the Conservatives voted for Rouvier. His cabinet fell on November 19 as the first step in a concerted effort by the Right and the Left to force the resignation of Grévy. Unlike his enterprising son-in-law, the chief of state was not accused of immoral conduct. Since the law did not require his resignation under the present circumstances, he

[47] *Le Temps,* Oct. 15, 1887.
[48] *Le Gaulois,* Oct. 14, 1887; *L'Autorité,* Oct. 16, 1887.
[49] *J.O.C.* (1887), pp. 1942–1943.

thought it his patriotic duty to remain at his post. Public opinion, however, would not be satisfied until he left. To compel the President to resign, the Right and Left consistently withheld their support from each of the Center politicians whom he asked to form a new cabinet.[50] On realizing that his continued presence at the Elysée was only prolonging the ministerial crisis, Grévy finally resigned on December 2, 1887.

With the fall of the Rouvier ministry, more was lost than simply the Presidency of Jules Grévy; the unofficial alliance between the Opportunists and the Conservatives also came to an end. Ever since Rouvier had taken office, the Radical politicians felt cheated out of what they considered their rightful place in power. The Wilson affair provided the Left with an ideal opportunity to regain its former position of influence by splitting the Right from the Center. Its cries of indignation at Wilson's scandalous conduct should not be taken at their face value; everyone in the Chamber had known privately about the sale of decorations for some time.[51] Yet once Grévy's resignation came to depend on a new cabinet crisis, the Conservatives could no longer support the government lest they be tarnished themselves by the scandal. By mid-November, royalist committees all over France were urging their Deputies to overthrow the cabinet.[52] So when Clemenceau, citing lack of public confidence in the ministry, interpellated it on the *rente*, the Conservatives joined forces with the Radicals against the Center.[53]

[50] Adrien Dansette, *L'affaire Wilson et la chute du président Grévy* (Paris: Perrin, 1936), pp. 122–129.

[51] Denis W. Brogan, *The Development of Modern France, 1870–1939* (London: Hamish Hamilton, 1959), p. 199n.

[52] A.N.F., F⁷ 12549, Nov. 17–19, 1887.

[53] *J.O.C.* (1887), pp. 2066–2068.

After the government's fall, both Right and Left tacitly agreed that it meant the end of the experiment in Opportunist-Conservative cooperation. On the following day, Cassagnac took stock of the situation and asked: "Did we do right? Unfortunately, I have some doubts." [54] Cassagnac seems to have grasped intuitively that the Right, which had played a truly conservative role while collaborating with the government, had now become a party of disorder.[55] From the Left, Pelletan called for a meeting of all Republican Deputies in order to elaborate a common policy.[56] With Rouvier out of office, the Radicals were eagerly looking forward to another government of Republican concentration.

They were to be bitterly disappointed. As members of the Senate and the Chamber met in joint session at Versailles on December 3 to elect a new President of the Republic, the most probable choice seemed to be Jules Ferry, who was favored by most Opportunists as a means of conciliating the Right.[57] So intense was leftist opposition to Ferry that riots broke out in Paris protesting his possible election. The favorite of the Radicals was one of their own number, Charles Floquet. As a compromise, however, they accepted a pale Opportunist named Sadi Carnot, grandson of "the organizer of victory" in the French Revolution. On learning of Carnot's election, Parisians cried with relief: "At least it's not Ferry! Long live the Republic!" [58] Such relief was premature at best. To end the unusually long ministerial crisis, Carnot chose as Premier one of his closest friends, Pierre Tirard, who assembled a

[54] *L'Autorité,* Nov. 21, 1887.

[55] Cf. Eugen Weber, "The Right in France: A Working Hypothesis," *American Historical Review,* LXV (April, 1960), 558.

[56] *La Justice,* Nov. 20, 1887.

[57] *La République Française,* Nov. 29, 1887.

[58] *La Lanterne,* Dec. 5, 1887.

cabinet of fellow Opportunists. The Radicals, who had precip-
itated the crisis, conspicuously failed to profit by it.[59]

In fact, no one really drew any immediate profit from the
affair. The government, which now had only vacillating support from the Radicals, was less stable than ever. No direct
benefit accrued to Boulanger, who failed once more to regain
his old post of War Minister. Late in November, 1887, while
Grévy was trying desperately to stay on as President, he had
reportedly offered Clemenceau an opportunity to form a cabinet with Boulanger as War Minister, in order to win the Radical leader's support. Without the approval of the Opportunists,
however, these negotiations came to nought.[60] Several days
later, on November 29 and 30, the royalist leaders, Mackau
and Martimprey, are said to have approached Boulanger with
a promise of Conservative support for a ministry in which he
would return to his old post. Inasmuch as such support depended on Boulanger's public approval of a monarchical restoration, however, the General refused the offer.[61] Boulanger
was never to make a public declaration in favor of the monarchy; his later alliance with the royalists was based on complementary, not identical, interests.

An indication of what these interests would be arose only
two days after the fall of the Rouvier government. On November 21, 1887, two different motions in favor of revising the
constitution were introduced in the Chamber. The first came
from Jolibois, a Bonapartist Deputy, who proposed that the
trend of executive subordination to the legislature be reversed.
He was followed by the extreme Jacobin, Michelin, who also

[59] Jacques Kayser, *Les grandes batailles du radicalisme, 1820–1901*
(Paris: Rivière, 1962), p. 163.

[60] Alexandre Zévaès, *Au temps du boulangisme* (Paris: Gallimard,
1930), p. 75.

[61] Mermeix, *op. cit.,* pp. 62–66.

proposed revision, but of an entirely contrary nature. The only way to cure the Republic's ills, he claimed, was to rid it of its present Orleanist constitution.[62]

In the final vote, both motions were defeated. The one presented by Jolibois was approved by a vast majority of Conservative Deputies, plus Michelin, but was opposed by everyone else. Michelin's proposal won the votes of the entire Left, but was opposed by the Right and the Center.[63] Both motions fared extremely well, nonetheless. When Michelin had asked for revision in December, 1886, it was Barodet who persuaded the Left to oppose it. This time, Barodet seconded the motion. Frustration at having been excluded from the Rouvier government apparently made the Radicals revisionist by late 1887. The new position of the Conservatives reflects the influence of the Orleanist pretender's manifesto. Ignoring the advice of the Marquis de Castellane, the Conservatives now carried the instructions of the Comte de Paris to their logical conclusion by demanding revision of the very constitution which most of them had originally favored. Now that the royalists were freed by Rouvier's fall from any governmental responsibility, they began to engage in a policy of negativism, which served only the interests of General Boulanger.

The attack on the regime had begun.

[62] *J.O.C.* (1887), pp. 2071–2072.   [63] *Ibid.,* pp. 2076–2077.

5

Boulanger the Politician
1888

~~~~~~

After the disorder of the previous months, the year 1888 began calmly and gave no indication of the upheavals to follow. Surveying the preceding twelve months, Charles de Mazade saw as a "heroicomic diversion the rise and fall of General Boulanger, the so-called necessary Minister, once loudly popular and today unheard-of." [1] Mazade spoke too soon; on January 2, 1888, Boulanger secretly crossed the border into Switzerland to see Prince Jérôme Napoleon, who was spending his exile at Prangins. The General made the trip at the suggestion of Thiébaud and without the knowledge of his friends on the far Left. On telling Jérôme of his intention to enter politics, the former War Minister received vague promises of aid.[2] The elder Bonaparte's love of intrigue made him an obvious patron for a general-turned-politician. But as Boulanger later admitted privately, Jérôme was certainly the most isolated, if not the most completely forgotten, political figure of France.[3]

[1] "Chronique de la quinzaine," *Revue des Deux Mondes*, LVIII (Jan. 1, 1888), 236.
[2] Mermeix [Gabriel Terrail], *Les coulisses du boulangisme* (Paris: Cerf, 1890), pp. 46–50.
[3] Henri Rochefort, *Les aventures de ma vie* (5 vols.; Paris: Dupont, 1897), V. 179.

Thus began the strangest and most indecisive political adventure in the history of the Third Republic. Having been excluded on two successive occasions from the War Ministry, Boulanger now took his case to the French people in a kind of serialized plebiscite based on the discriminate use of by-elections. A precedent for such action already existed in the protest vote for Boulanger in the Paris by-election of May 22, 1887.[4] On that occasion, the vote had a specific object: the retention of Boulanger as War Minister. The object of the General's campaign of 1888 and 1889 was far less precise. At first, he won votes as a protest against appeasement and political corruption; later he campaigned for revision of the constitution and against the Opportunists. Because the General's program was deliberately vague, anyone with a grievance was naturally attracted to the movement which bore his name. By the same token, however, no one knew what Boulanger's own intentions were—perhaps not even the General himself. So his political demise after the elections of 1889 left only a small void.

THE FIRST BY-ELECTIONS

Following Boulanger's visit to Prangins, he was again approached by Georges Thiébaud, who repeated his earlier plan to present the General in the seven by-elections to be held on February 26, 1888. Thiébaud explained that he had no intention of making Boulanger a Deputy, since, as an army officer, the General was ineligible to run. He did wish to organize what he called a "national concentration" around the General's name, adding that a good showing would disprove the contention that Boulanger had lost his popularity. Ballots would be printed with Boulanger's name and distributed to the voters, who would be asked to vote for him on the first ballot

[4] Cf. *supra*, p. 62.

and for anyone else on the second. As Thiébaud put it: "The important thing is not to be elected, but to have votes everywhere." [5]

Accordingly, campaign posters began to appear in the departments concerned early in February. Voters were asked to support Boulanger on the first ballot—not to elect him, but to demonstrate French patriotism. By so doing, they would stand up to Bismarck, who, it was claimed, was still exultant over having forced Boulanger out of the War Ministry. Since the passing of Thiers and Gambetta, continued this message, France had lacked a truly national policy. Boulanger alone was able to awaken national feeling in the Chamber. The appeal for votes ended with the ringing cry: "Patriots of all parties, vote for General Boulanger!" It was signed by Thiébaud, who bore the title "President of the Committee of Initiative in Paris." [6]

After the elections, Thiébaud claimed that there was no committee as such, save himself. But the decision to run Boulanger had been taken in consultation with a few of the General's closest friends, who contributed 45,000 francs to help pay for campaign expenses.[7] The actual work, however, was done mainly by Thiébaud, who began his tour of the seven departments on January 25, made speeches, and distributed campaign literature and predesignated ballots as widely as possible. The Bonapartist journalist admitted that he saw in Boulanger a new Napoleon.[8]

When the results of the first ballot arrived, they showed that although Boulanger ran last in every contest but one, he

[5] Maurice Barrès, *L'appel au soldat* (Paris: Juven, 1911), pp. 110–111.

[6] André Daniel, *L'année politique*, XV (Paris: Charpentier, 1888), 51–52.

[7] A.P.P., B a/1496, April 4, 1889.   [8] *Le Figaro*, Feb. 28, 1888.

amassed a total of close to 55,000 votes in the seven departments. They were distributed, most unevenly, as follows: [9]

Hautes-Alpes

Flourens (Opportunist)	12,617
Euzière (Radical)	11,094
Boulanger	126

Côte-d'Or

Cernesson (Radical)	33,691
Philipot (Opportunist)	26,251
Boulanger	9,487

Loire

De la Berge (Opportunist)	42,752
Chollet (Opportunist)	42,421
Boulanger	14,083

Loiret

Augère (Opportunist)	41,625
Babier (Radical)	40,773
Brierre (Conservative)	33,985
Dumas (Conservative)	32,778
Boulanger	4,663

Maine-et-Loire

De Lacretelle (Conservative)	61,782
D'Angers (Opportunist)	29,542
Boulanger	12,015

Haute-Marne

Roret (Radical)	23,344
Darbot (Opportunist)	16,231

[9] A.N.F., C 5300 A 70 to A 5306 A 76.

Dubreuil St.-Germain (Conservative)	6,581
De Rouvre (Conservative)	4,910
De Beurges (Conservative)	3,234
Boulanger	945
Leroy-Beaulieu	543

Marne

Bourgeois (Opportunist)	48,018
Boulanger	16,240

In the Loire, where Boulanger was openly favored by the So-cialists, he appears to have owed much of his large vote to them. Elsewhere, patriotism seems to have been the deciding factor in his successes, especially from Radical and Bona-partist voters.[10] Where one or more of the three main polit-ical groups of France was absent, Boulanger generally fared better than where all were fully represented.

That Boulanger received many votes from the Left is not surprising, since it was from that quarter that he originally entered the government. The Left had no monopoly on patri-otism, however. Frenchmen of all political persuasions were sincerely disturbed at their country's decline in territory and prestige since 1870. Parlor historians could, if they liked, point to France's diminished realm since 1814 and infer that decadence had set in. To such people, Boulanger appeared as the great redeemer, the great restorer of the nation's original glory. So great was the General's prestige that in some of the seven departments his name was on the lips even of young children. A contemporary report mentions a Catechism class where children were being instructed on "the general resur-rection of the flesh." One little girl, unable to understand what it all meant, first stared blankly at her examiner for a few

[10] *Le Temps,* Feb. 28, 1888.

seconds and then blurted out: "General resurrection . . .
Boulanger!" [11]

Admiration for Boulanger in Catholic circles indicates that
love of country could outweigh purely domestic considerations in motivating voters to choose a candidate. Because of
their anticlerical policies, the Opportunists and Radicals had
little chance of winning Catholic votes; but the Bonapartists
were in a better position. Although Bonapartism was not a
clerical movement in its inception, it grew increasingly pro-
Catholic in the early years of the Third Republic as its more
anticlerical elements dropped off to become Republican. A
sign of this evolution can be seen in the creation, in January,
1886, of the newspaper *L'Autorité,* with its proud motto:
"For God, for France!" In a speech at Armentières on July 12
of that year, the paper's editor, Paul de Cassagnac, referred to
the recently formed Conservative Union as France's "national
party." He also linked patriotism and religion, saying that
"a country without faith, without belief, is a country which
quickly loses loyalty to the family and to the homeland." [12]
The fact that Boulanger's electoral propaganda was signed by
a known Bonapartist probably enabled many Catholics to vote
for the General with a clear conscience, especially since it was
just a protest vote.

The vote for Boulanger also represented a protest against
the current state of national politics, which had been considerably soiled by the Wilson scandal. As a result of having abandoned the Opportunists in November, 1887, the Conservatives
were in a position to benefit from their former associates'
embarrassment. In the Senate elections of January 5, 1888,
the Conservatives gained only three seats, a modest success at

[11] X, "Fragments de plébiscite," *Revue Bleue,* 3ème série, XXV
(March 10, 1888), 291–293.
[12] *L'Autorité,* July 16, 1886.

best. On closer examination, however, it was revealed that where Republicans did win, it was by smaller margins than previously. As in 1885, many of the Opportunist victors had disavowed their party's record in order to blend in with the Right. The Center's poor showing was widely considered to be the result of public dismay at signs of political corruption.[13]

By the time the by-elections took place, Wilson had already been arraigned before the lower court, so that the scandal received continued public notice. While regretting Boulanger's large vote, Camille Pelletan ascribed it to the disrepute into which the politicians in power had fallen as a result of the Wilson affair. "The evil," Pelletan observed, "does not come from General Boulanger; its origin is in the misdeeds committed [by politicians]." Impatience at the government's apparent acceptance of the international *status quo* also prompted some Frenchmen to vote for a general on horseback. "One can say that, until now, there has been nothing in his conduct of the sort which prepares the way for dictators." Pelletan expressed the hope that Boulanger would dissociate himself from those who had presented his candidacy.[14]

Boulanger seemed only too happy to oblige. In a letter to the War Minister of March 9, which was widely published in the press, the General formally withdrew from politics. He had just been the object of propositions (from an unnamed source) to run in future by-elections, he reported. Because of his military duties, Boulanger expressed the desire to put an end to demonstrations in his favor. He asked his friends "not to waste on me votes which I cannot accept." [15]

The War Minister was not fooled, however. His office was already in possession of the telegraphic correspondence be-

---

[13] Charles de Mazade, "Chronique de la quinzaine," *Revue des Deux Mondes,* LVIII (Jan. 15, 1888), 465–466.
[14] *La Justice,* March 8, 1888.   [15] Rochefort, *op. cit.,* p. 118.

tween Boulanger and Dillon from February 22 to 28. The intercepted messages left no doubt that the General was an active participant in his own election campaign. On the day of the elections, he wrote to Dillon: "I approve everything." Immediately afterward, Boulanger gave further instructions: "Have learned of the results; very good. Now we must work on the press and public opinion." [16]

Acting with rare discretion, the War Minister formed a council of inquiry, which investigated Boulanger's activities and, on March 15, announced that he was being released from active duty. Although mention was made of the General's recent foray into politics, the ostensible reason for his release was that he had made three unauthorized trips to Paris on February 24, March 2, and March 10. A commander of an army corps was not allowed to leave the territory of his command without the prior consent of the War Minister. So on the surface, only a breach of discipline was at issue. Yet the public sensed its political content, and scattered pro-Boulanger demonstrations broke out in Paris.[17] The General sought to increase his popular favor by declaring to the press that he had gone to Paris simply to visit his ailing wife.[18]

THE PROTEST COMMITTEE

On learning of his release, Boulanger made another trip to Paris, where, in the words of a newspaper favorable to him, "important decisions were made this morning in a meeting held by the General and some of his friends at the home of a Deputy." [19] Immediately after the meeting, those friends

[16] Cited by Joseph Reinach, *Les petites catilinaires,* Vol. I: *La foire boulangiste* (Paris: Victor-Havard, 1889), pp. 160–161.

[17] Raoul Frary, "Chronique politique," *La Nouvelle Revue,* LI (April 1, 1888), 748–749.

[18] *Le Figaro,* March 18, 1888.   [19] *La France,* March 17, 1888.

present announced on March 16 that they had formed a so-
called "Republican Committee of National Protest." With
Naquet as president, the Committee included the leftist
Deputies Borie, Brugeilles, Chévillon, Susini, Duguyot, La-
guerre, Laisant, Laur, Le Hérissé, Michelin, and Vergoin.
Also participating were Déroulède, Lalou of *La France,*
Mayer of *La Lanterne,* and Rochefort of *L'Intransigeant.*
Monetary contributions were accepted at the offices of these
newspapers.[20] They were to be used for the purposes stated in
the Committee's first public declaration:

General Boulanger has just been made the victim of an infamous
measure, which is now condemned by all patriots.

But his friends and other men who are resolved not to abandon
the cause of the homeland have the right and the duty to assert
national feeling through his name.

A Committee is being constituted for this purpose under the
name of: Republican Committee of National Protest. It will
sponsor the candidacy of General Boulanger in by-elections, not
to have him enter the Chamber, but as a means of protesting
against a government which is not inspired by a sense of patriotism.

Once this protest is made in each department, the voters will
choose their definitive, Republican representative. At present, we
propose the candidacy of General Boulanger to the voters of the
Bouches-du-Rhône and the Aisne.[21]

By this declaration, Boulanger's leftist partisans openly
adopted the tactics originally suggested by Thiébaud. In a few
weeks, their protest over the General's release from active
duty was to become a plebiscite for a different sort of Republic. Although there was considerable disagreement both within

[20] A.P.P., B a/976, May 2, 1888.
[21] Cited in Maxime Lecomte, *Les ralliés: Histoire d'un parti, 1886–
1898* (Paris: Flammarion, 1898), pp. 116–117.

and without the Protest Committee as to the exact nature of such a regime, the Boulangist movement never ceased to be oriented toward the Left. Since the Dreyfus affair, historians have usually considered nationalism and the plebiscite to be wholly within the preserve of the French Right. Yet, as André Siegfried pointed out in 1913, these phenomena belong equally to the Left.

There are in fact sincere democrats, particularly Radicals of a certain type, who, more interested in universal suffrage than in parliament, tend openly or obliquely to set [governmental] authority on a national base by withdrawing it from the fluctuations of parties. They are at heart proponents of the plebiscite, who, without always admitting it, prefer governmental force to liberty.[22]

These dissident Radicals formed the hard core of Boulanger's following. Convinced that most politicians in the Chamber were thwarting France's national will, they sought to use the General as a means of arriving at a direct consultation of the French people.

For Alfred Naquet, the Committee's president, the Boulangist venture was the culmination of a long political career as a dissident Radical. Even during the Second Empire Naquet had been known as a militant republican. In 1867, while professor at the Faculty of Medicine in Paris, he had helped organize a peace conference at Geneva, which ended in a vote condemning the policies of Napoleon III. For this act of disloyalty, Naquet was imprisoned for fifteen months and stripped of his title of *agrégé*. He later participated in the Government of National Defense and was elected to the National Assembly in 1871 as a Radical from his native depart-

[22] André Siegfried, *Tableau politique de la France de l'ouest sous la Troisième République* (Paris: Colin, 1913), p. 485.

ment of the Vaucluse. As a Deputy he opposed creation of the Senate and favored the income tax, the right of workers to organize without restrictions, and complete amnesty for the Communards. When Gambetta threw his support behind the 1875 constitution, Naquet severed all ties with him and was re-elected to the Chamber in 1876 and 1881 as an intransigent. He resigned in 1883 to run for the Senate, where he pressed for passage of his law on divorce. Even after the divorce law was finally accepted in 1884, Naquet remained an anomaly in the conservative upper house; in 1888 and 1889 he was its only Boulangist.[23]

Next in political seniority on the Protest Committee was Laisant, a graduate of the *Ecole Polytechnique* who had served as a captain of engineers in the Franco-Prussian War. During the siege of Paris, Laisant directed work on the fort of Issy and was decorated with the Cross of the Legion of Honor. Elected to the Chamber from Nantes in 1875, he was the first to ask, in 1876, that military service be reduced to three years —a proposition that won him considerable popularity even though it was initially rejected by the Chamber. Laisant also favored complete amnesty for the Communards and church-state separation. In the elections of 1881, he was opposed by both a royalist and a moderate Republican; only after his two rivals withdrew did he win on the second ballot. While serving as a Deputy, he founded a journal called *La République Radicale,* in which he regularly attacked what he referred to as "the infamous Chamber" of 1881. Laisant was once more re-elected to the Chamber in 1885, this time on a Radical and intransigent slate from Paris.[24]

[23] Adolphe Robert, Edgar Bourloton, and Gaston Cougny, *Dictionnaire des parlementaires français* (5 vols.; Paris: Bourloton, 1890), IV, 480–481.

[24] *Ibid.,* III, 540–541.

The Committee's youngest member was Georges Laguerre, who in 1888 was only thirty. Laguerre, who was related to Thiers through his mother, had been originally destined for Saint-Cyr but studied law instead. On being admitted to the bar in 1879, he soon expressed radical views in sharp contrast with those of his family and became associated with Clemenceau. As legal expert for Clemenceau's journal, *La Justice*, Laguerre won celebrity in 1882 for having espoused the cause of striking miners in Lyon, Saint-Etienne, and Montceau-les-Mines. A year later, he defended Louise Michel, who had been arrested for demonstrating on behalf of the unemployed. Laguerre entered the Chamber for the first time in 1833, as a result of a by-election in the district vacated by Naquet. Still an associate of Clemenceau, Laguerre tried to obtain constitutional revision so as to eliminate the Senate in 1884. He was re-elected as a Radical in 1885 but thereafter sat with the intransigent Left. From this position he continued to argue in favor of a graduated income tax.[25]

The other Deputies on the Protest Committee had all been elected to the Chamber on or after 1885; their entry into national politics coincided with that of Boulanger. In the case of Henri Michelin and Francis Laur, the General's remarks on the Decazeville strike were encouraging. It was Michelin who had interpellated the government on its attitude toward the strikers. Prior to his election as an intransigent Deputy from the Seine in 1885, he had been mayor of the seventh *arrondissement* of Paris and had risen to become president of the city council.[26] Laur had been a mining engineer before seeking political office. On entering the Chamber as Deputy from the Loire, he proposed a series of labor reforms in the mines, which were all rejected. The most important of these measures stipulated that miners were to be paid weekly and that their

[25] *Ibid.*, III, 585.   [26] *Ibid.*, IV, 368.

salaries could not be attached. During the strike at Decazeville, Laur offered his services as mediator; they were accepted by the miners but rejected by the company. At this
point he began his association with Boulanger.[27]

Of the remaining Deputies who joined the Committee at its
inception, none had made a lasting mark in the Chamber.
Within the year, Brugeilles and Duguyot were to leave the
Boulangist movement and return to the Radicals. They shared
with their fellow Committee members, however, an essentially
Jacobin position and a lack of experience in national politics.
Common to all the Boulangist Deputies was their perch on the
leftist fringe, which kept them far removed from real political
power. Most of them had entered the Chamber as part of a
vast outpouring of opposition to the ruling Opportunists in the
general elections of 1885. Even as a minority, however, the
Opportunists continued to hold fast to the reins of government. Their virtual monopoly of power was made even more
apparent after Boulanger's dismissal from the War Ministry.
By 1888, the extreme Jacobin Deputies were convinced that
they could not influence the course of politics within parliament. They therefore sought to ride to power on General Boulanger's coattails.

Just as Boulanger was moving into his new home on the rue
Dumont-d'Urville, the Protest Committee set up business at 4,
rue de Sèze. Its claim that the General was not seeking public
office, for which he was still technically ineligible, was greeted
by widespread disbelief. On the Right it was rumored that,
within the Protest Committee, a kind of shadow cabinet had
already been created.[28]

Rumor or not, it was evident that Boulanger had taken one
further step in the direction of full commitment to politics. By
removing him from active duty, the government greatly facil-

[27] *Ibid.*, III, 626–627.   [28] *Le Figaro*, March 18, 1888.

itated this step; but in view of his correspondence with Dillon, it really had no other choice. Another disturbing sign was the appearance, on March 13, of *La Cocarde,* the first newspaper to call itself specifically "Boulangist." Its early issues, however, were devoted far less to praise of the General than to a plan for revision of the constitution. France's present regime, the paper claimed, "is only a grotesque and hypocritical imitation of the monarchy." Democratic reforms were being postponed or blocked altogether by the Senate and by the fact that a government, in order to have support in the Chamber, had to take in at least some Ministers who wished to maintain the *status quo.* By eliminating both the Senate and the cabinet system of government, the French people could finally make their needs felt. "We propose to remake a constitution by which the nation will govern itself, with a single agent [*commis*] to whom it will give its orders, who must account to it for his acts, and who will be revocable at will." [29]

Public reaction to the new journal was initially ecstatic. Circulation on its first day of publication was 150,000 copies and rose to 400,000 for the next four days before falling to a steady but comfortable 50,000–55,000, just above that of *L'Intransigeant.*[30] The paper's claim to represent Boulanger, however, was repeatedly contested by the General himself. In a letter to Laguerre, which the latter read to the Chamber on March 20, Boulanger affirmed: "I have not participated either in the creation of the newspaper *La Cocarde* or in its composition. Never have I inspired a single article; none of my friends has contributed to its foundation, even by financial aid." [31] Lest it be thought that this was merely another pious denial, we should note that Boulanger wrote to his confidant, Naquet,

[29] *La Cocarde,* March 13, 1888.
[30] A.N.F., F⁷ 12445, April 10, 1888.
[31] *J.O.C.* (1888), pp. 1097–1098.

in June, saying: "As for *La Cocarde,* I have no power over its editorial content." [32]

Despite its impressive circulation, *La Cocarde* apparently embarrassed Boulanger more than it helped him. The paper's first editor-in-chief was Georges de Labruyère, former editor of the anarchist *Cri du Peuple* and lover of its new editor, Séverine. Their names were conspicuously absent from the list of guests at the General's official functions throughout 1888.[33] At the time of *La Cocarde*'s first appearance, neither Boulanger nor the Protest Committee had made any public statement concerning revision of the constitution. Although the leading Boulangists all favored revision, they did so as individuals and had, in fact, some extremely varied ideas as to the exact nature of their new Republic. When Boulanger finally did propose revision openly, his statement reflected Naquet's ideas, rather than those of *La Cocarde.* Inasmuch as Labruyère was never formally associated with the Committee, it is quite probable that he used the label "Boulangist" simply to win support for his own revisionist plans.

At this juncture in Boulanger's campaign, his main point was not constitutional revision, about which he had still said nothing, but protest against the government for having relieved him of his military duties. The extent of this protest, as registered in the by-elections of February 26, impressed the Right because it caused the government so much embarrassment. Paul de Cassagnac, who was still no admirer of the General, obviously relished interpellating the government on March 20 concerning its reasons for removing him from the active list. Cassagnac asserted that the movement which used Boulanger's name, though illegal, simply represented widespread discontent with Opportunism. If Boulanger was in any

[32] Bibliothèque nationale, N.A.F. 23783, no. 23.
[33] A.P.P., B a/1496, Jan. 7, 1889.

way undisciplined, he said, it was because the Republicans had earlier encouraged his political ambitions in an attempt to use the army for their own ends.[34]

Most impressed of all were the Orleanists. While their leading newspaper could publish a poem mocking Boulanger as late as March 14,[35] its journalists were already beginning to show him a grudging respect. A day earlier, Louis Teste had begun to see a relationship between the new course outlined by the Comte de Paris and Boulanger's campaign. "For the monarchist party," he observed, "two aspects of Boulangism are not displeasing: the reawakening of the principle of authority and the rejuvenation of the idea of the plebiscite, which the Comte de Paris intends to make the basis of his monarchy." Teste advised his fellow royalists to keep out of the Boulangist movement, which seemed to him to have no future. Instead, they should learn to imitate the General's methods.[36] Cornély went one step further and ventured the prediction that Boulanger would be useful in bringing down the Republic. "I do not like Boulanger, but I cultivate him." Yet the very fact that Cornély's editorial was an answer to objections from royalist readers who still abhorred any contact with Boulanger indicates that open collaboration could not take place overnight.[37]

In view of the Conservatives' current political behavior, collaboration with Boulanger must have seemed the most logical outcome. By February, 1888, the Right in the Chamber was determined to vote against the cabinet as a matter of principle. In this, it was joined by the Boulangist Deputies, leaving only the Opportunists and the more moderate Radicals to support the ministry. The Conservatives thereby contributed greatly to

---

[34] *J.O.C.* (1888), pp. 1087–1096.
[35] *Le Gaulois,* March 14, 1888.   [36] *Ibid.,* March 13, 1888.
[37] *Ibid.,* March 21, 1888.

the very parliamentary instability which they so piously condemned. Yet if a new ministerial crisis took place, it was a
foregone conclusion that the new Premier would be Floquet,
who in principle should have been even less acceptable to the
Right than Tirard. Such considerations did not affect the Conservatives, however, as they continued to practice *la politique
du pire* (to make matters worse before they get better).[38]

For the Republicans trying to maintain the government, the
creation of the Protest Committee marked the point of no
return in the career of General Boulanger. "One can no
longer deny it," cried Pelletan. "They are really asking for a
plebiscite; they really want a dictator." On March 18, more
than fifty Radical Deputies signed a declaration condemning
"the intrusion of military leaders into politics" as harmful to
the Republic.[39] For the Opportunists, Boulangism "is not a
new word designating a new thing: it is merely a mask for the
old Caesarism, that evil which has settled in the very marrow
of the Latin race." [40]

Latent Caesarism, therefore, was the Opportunists' explanation for Boulanger's popularity—even before his really
important political successes. This explanation has found as
much favor with later historians [41] as it did with its authors.
An innate French predilection for the man on horseback is
used to explain Boulanger's success, which in turn is used to
prove the theory. Aside from this circular argument, however,
such an explanation overlooks two chief aspects of the problem. One is that the Republican politicians who accused their

[38] Raoul Frary, "Chronique politique," *La Nouvelle Revue,* LI
(March 1, 1888), 219–220.

[39] *La Justice,* March 20, 1888.

[40] *La République Française,* March 17, 1888.

[41] Cf. Adrien Dansette, *Le boulangisme* (Paris: Fayard, 1946), pp.
369–371; J. E. C. Bodley, *France* (2 vols.; New York: Macmillan,
1898), II, 388.

compatriots of Caesar-worship were motivated at least in part by a refusal to recognize their own failings. By chiding the voters for so-called political immaturity, these critics neatly avoided asking themselves whether the protest vote was at all justified. Another point overlooked is that, throughout his political career, Boulanger repeatedly emphasized his devotion to the Republic. None of the leftists in his inner circle seems to have wanted a dictator.

SUCCESS IN THE AISNE

When Boulanger entered the lists in the Aisne and the Bouches-du-Rhône, his campaign had taken on a truly professional appearance. For one thing, the General was no longer dependent solely on his close friends for financial support; the Duchesse d'Uzès, a wealthy royalist disillusioned with the Comte de Paris, made a contribution of 25,000 francs. Later, after the royalists officially allied themselves with Boulanger, her donations were to grow to three million francs.[42] Another advantage now enjoyed by the General was the open and active campaigning by his Committee. Its propaganda stressed military readiness and more effective government:

VOTERS,

In domestic affairs the government has shown its total impotence; in foreign affairs, it has shown its completely cringing attitude.

The Parliament, led by Ministers without any patriotic energy, has not accomplished a single Republican reform.

Equality before military service is still an empty word.

The violent and antinational measure which strikes General Boulanger gives you the opportunity to protest this pernicious policy.

France *rejects all dictatorships*. The question is not one of

[42] Mermeix, *op. cit.*, 87–88.

bringing a man to power, but rather of affirming, in the name of a Republican and patriotic soldier, the very existence of the nation.

The name of Boulanger means: *Public liberties, Democratic reforms internally, Dignity in foreign affairs. . . .*[43]

In this declaration, the questions of patriotism and internal reforms were found to be complementary. As the campaign progressed, the General's propaganda was to lay increasing emphasis on domestic issues; but an undertone of nationalism was always present. For the "advanced Republicans" of this period, the two factors could hardly be separated.

In the Aisne, Boulanger's lieutenants gave speeches everywhere, saying that their candidate was not running against the Republican contenders and would be withdrawn after the first ballot. The *Ligue des patriotes,* still active in that department, helped by distributing propaganda flysheets and predesignated ballots for the General. Parisian newspapers favorable to Boulanger were also widely distributed.[44] On March 21, the Protest Committee suddenly withdrew the former War Minister's candidacy in both contests on the grounds that it did not want to give the government any excuse for punishing him further.[45] Despite this pledge, however, the campaign did not cease in either department. The General's friends redoubled their efforts to see him elected, and his newspapers urged patriots to vote for him as a protest even though he had officially withdrawn.[46]

Of the two departments concerned, the Aisne was the more important. Bordering on Belgium, it had been the scene of two sieges during the Franco-Prussian War: at Laon and Saint-Quentin. In the general elections of 1885, the Aisne had returned an entire slate of Republicans—mainly Radicals—to the Chamber. At the same time, it had a strong Conservative

[43] *L'Intransigeant,* March 20, 1888.
[44] *Le Figaro,* March 28, 1888.
[45] *La Lanterne,* March 23, 1888. [46] *Ibid.,* March 24, 1888.

organization, thus leaving the Opportunists with a relatively small share of the vote. In the cities there was a small but growing Socialist party. A victory for Boulanger in the Aisne would therefore be interpreted as a sign of great personal popularity among various types of voters. In this variety, however, the leading parties in the Aisne had one common trait: they were all anti-Opportunist.

The General's most serious contender in the Aisne was the Radical candidate, Paul Doumer, who was then assistant to the mayor of Laon. He campaigned actively on a program of protection of French workers from immigrant competition, three-year military service for all, tax reduction, separation of church and state, public assistance for the countryside, and state-financed insurance.[47] The Conservative candidate was an eighty-year-old royalist named Jacquemart, who did not campaign personally, but issued an electoral manifesto favoring peace and order. Boulanger, he said, was "the war candidate." [48] Whether this accusation helped the Conservative cause is open to question. Similar warnings made by the Right during the two crises with Germany seem only to have increased the General's already large following.

Boulanger's success in the Aisne by-election was tremendous: he received about 45 per cent of the total votes cast and almost twice as many as Doumer, his nearest rival. An indication of where the General's votes came from may be had from a comparison of the first and second ballot results.[49]

March 25		*April 8*	
Boulanger	45,125	Doumer	42,244

[47] *La Tribune du Département de l'Aisne,* March 9, 1888.
[48] *Journal de Saint-Quentin,* March 21, 1888.
[49] A.N.F., C 5300 A 70.

110

Doumer	26,933	Jacquemart	33,444
Jacquemart	24,753	Boulanger	11,614
Carré	4,576	Langrand	3,121
Langrand	2,411		

Before the second ballot, the Opportunist candidate, Carré, had withdrawn in favor of Doumer. Yet even if Doumer did succeed in winning all of Carré's votes, he seems to have owed more than twice as many to Boulanger. Conversely, it is apparent that at least two-thirds of the General's votes on the first ballot came from Radicals and Socialists. This conclusion is borne out by the fact that Boulanger's greatest margins of victory were in the cities of Saint-Quentin and Vervins, and that the Bonapartists in the countryside were reported to have deserted Jacquemart.[50] Even with the Bonapartist vote, the General appears to have owed most of his success at the polls to the Radicals and Socialists in the cities.

Along with Boulanger's victory in the Aisne came a most shameful performance in the Bouches-du-Rhône. From the start, the General's campaign there had been egregiously mismanaged; in fact, there should never have been a campaign at all. The idea of entering Boulanger in the Bouches-du-Rhône came from Georges Laguerre, who at thirty was the youngest member of the Protest Committee. In acting as he did, Laguerre apparently overlooked two important differences between the election in the Aisne and that in the Bouches-du-Rhône. Whereas the former was a first ballot between relatively unknown candidates, the latter was a second ballot, dominated by the well-known former Communard, Félix Pyat. On the first ballot of March 11, Pyat had been strongly challenged by two Radicals, but they withdrew in his favor

[50] *Le Glaneur de St-Quentin,* March 27, 1888.

111

once Boulanger's candidacy was announced.[51] Despite the General's official withdrawal a few days later, Francis Laur arrived in Marseilles on March 23 to continue the campaign. He toured the department, speaking for Boulanger and denouncing Pyat as an anarchist revolutionary.[52] Such tactics availed little, for Pyat won handsomely with 40,273 votes, as against 23,719 for a monarchist named Hervé and 12,496 for the Opportunist, Fouquier. Boulanger's tally was a mere 1,071, of which 868 votes came from the city of Marseilles.[53]

Not even so humiliating a defeat could detract, however, from the General's dazzling success in the Aisne. Most dazzled seem to have been the Radicals, who were groping for some way to explain Doumer's poor showing on the first ballot. While admitting that many of Boulanger's votes came from the Left, Pelletan claimed that Conservative support had given the General his margin of victory. The acquittal of Wilson on March 25 and "a do-nothing government" were also held responsible. To remedy the situation, Pelletan proposed that an energetic, Republican government enact truly progressive reforms.[54] Yet this solution contained an element of internal contradiction. If Boulanger's electoral success was really due to rightist favor, then no amount of Republican reforms could be expected to head him off. The Radicals kept to this approach, however, and for a time even succeeded in imposing it on the Opportunists.

As a direct result of the General's continued political activity, he was dishonorably discharged from the army on March 26, 1888. He immediately entered his candidacy for the by-election to be held in the Nord on April 15, having just withdrawn from that in the Aisne, and addressed a manifesto to

[51] *Année politique,* XV (1888), pp. 67–69.
[52] *La Lanterne,* March 25, 1888.   [53] A.N.F., C 5301 A 71.
[54] *La Justice,* March 27, 1888.

the normally Republican Nord electorate. It began on a patriotic note: "When I was Minister, I said: *'If I wanted war, I would be a fool; if I did not prepare for it, I would be a wretch.'* My feelings have not changed." To be strong, France needed a government which could act, but the present regime prevented effective action (he did not explain how). "For the impotence of the Assembly there is only one remedy: dissolution of the Chamber, revision of the Constitution. It is to this end that all my efforts will be directed. *Long live France! Long live the Republic!*" [55]

Boulanger's profession of faith in the cause of constitutional revision marked the beginning of an entirely new phase of his career. No longer was he merely protesting some personal injury; he now became the titular head of a revisionist party with an avowed, if ill-defined, political goal. At the same time, the General helped broaden his field of electoral activity. Now that he was legally free to seek public office, he used the prospect of a new regime to win the votes of all the politically discontented.

The General's declaration also prompted the Radicals to make revision their key demand in a frantic attempt to outbid him for public favor. On March 31, the day after the declaration was published, Pelletan introduced a motion in the Chamber for the consideration of constitutional revision. It was categorically opposed by Tirard, who argued: "The government considers that it would be dangerous today to add another element of agitation to those already manifest in the country." Pelletan's motion was seconded by Clemenceau, who claimed that the time had come to give France a truly Republican constitution. It passed by a vote of 268 to 237, thanks to the support of such royalists as Mackau, Lareinty, and Martimprey. Their ideas on revision were naturally far

[55] *La Cocarde,* March 31, 1888.

removed from those of the Radicals, but they gladly took advantage of this opportunity to discredit the regime further. For having opposed the motion, Tirard was obliged to resign.[56]

The ensuing ministerial crisis was one of the shortest on record, since a successor to Tirard had virtually been agreed upon in advance. Charles Floquet, the white hope of the Radicals, took office as Premier on April 3. Amid loud applause from the Left, he announced in his ministerial declaration that his government "does not fear any seriously elaborated reform." Yet this statement was merely a prelude to his main point: "The question of revision of the Constitution, which has just been laid before the Chamber is one of those which command the greatest calm and reflection.[57] No doubt about it: Floquet understood perfectly that he had been called to office in order to preside over a change in the regime.

Although Floquet did not commit himself specifically to a particular form of constitutional revision, it was apparent that he had dissociated himself from the regime as it then was. Now there was virtually no important political figure to defend it.[58] By tacitly espousing the cause of revision, the Premier seemed to confer a sort of political legitimacy on the programs of the Comte de Paris and Boulanger. In modern parlance, such a policy would be called "me-tooism." Then, as now, it proved to be an utter failure.

[56] *J.O.C.* (1888), pp. 1245–1246. [57] *Ibid.*, p. 1253.
[58] *L'Autorité,* April 1, 1888.

6

The Revisionist Campaign

1888

When Boulanger declared himself openly in favor of revision of the constitution, he did more than please his friends on the Protest Committee. He prepared the way for full support by the Orleanists. Although the Boulangists had a vastly different conception of revision from that of the Orleanists, the very fact that both favored a change brought them closer together. Accounts vary as to which of the two parties initially proposed real collaboration. Arthur Meyer of *Le Gaulois* related that he was approached just before the by-elections of February 26 by Dillon, who claimed that Boulanger was being sought by all parties (!) to enter politics. Meyer realized, he says, that if the royalists did not take advantage of the General's popularity, the Bonapartists would. So he immediately proposed to leading Orleanists that they try to restore the monarchy with Boulanger's help. Although the Comte de Paris was hesitant at this stage, the Duchesse d'Uzès immediately contributed 25,000 francs to the General's cause.[1]

This version of the case raises a few serious questions. First of all, it contradicts the account of Mermeix, who dates the

---

[1] Meyer, *Ce que mes yeux ont vu* (Paris: Plon, 1911), pp. 71–72.

first contribution by the Duchesse d'Uzès from the Aisne by-election campaign and not that preceding the by-elections of February 26.[2] One may also ask why Meyer was so afraid of competition from the impoverished Bonapartists, who could not offer Boulanger more than a small fraction of the funds soon to be dispensed by the Orleanists. If indeed a threat of Bonapartist competition did exist, it is difficult to explain why Meyer rushed to subsidize the General's campaign at a time when that campaign was being run solely by a Bonapartist, Georges Thiébaud.

More probable is the version given by Pierre Denis, one of Boulanger's followers. According to this account, it was Meyer who made the initial offer of collaboration. Sometime in March—not February—1888, he is said to have proposed to Dillon what he called a "parallel march" of the two factions. He explained it in this way: "We have the same adversaries; let us first combat them together; afterward, we shall see." By its extremely vague character, this proposition typifies the Boulangist-Orleanist alliance. Each party to the agreement wished to use the other as its tool.[3] As soon as the Orleanists realized that Boulanger could no longer serve this purpose, they left him.

For about a year and a half, the alliance worked to the apparent satisfaction of both parties. What the Orleanists and many other Conservatives sought from Boulanger was his leftist following. Although they never admitted it publicly, the Conservatives seem to have realized that they were bound to remain a minority in France for the foreseeable future. With the votes of dissident Republicans brought in by Boulanger, however, they might become a majority. Inasmuch as the

[2] Cf. *supra,* p. 108.

[3] Pierre Denis, *Le mémorial de Saint-Brelade* (Paris: Ollendorf, 1894), pp. 106–109.

General had to make pro-Republican pronouncements in order to win such votes, the royalists appear to have made no attempt to censure or even to influence his avowed program.

In any case, Boulanger carefully avoided any detailed description of his program during his political tours of the departments. For he received much more than financial aid from the Right. In the provinces especially, he owed many thousands of votes to Conservative support. Like the Conservatives, the Boulangists appear to have recognized their minority status. They hoped that the votes of the Right, added to those of the Left, would give them the necessary majority to effect their form (or forms) of constitutional change. By making an ill-defined revision of the constitution the main issue in his campaign, Boulanger arrived at the broadest common denominator to encompass various kinds of political discontent.

THE DORDOGNE ELECTION

An example of the importance to Boulanger of Conservative favor can be had in the by-election which took place in the Dordogne on April 8. Neither the General nor most of his lieutenants wished to see him a candidate in this contest; their real interest was the by-election in the Nord, which was to cement their alliance with the Orleanists. Thiébaud, on the other hand, had not abandoned his strategy of having Boulanger win votes everywhere. With the help of *La Cocarde,* he entered the General as a candidate in the Dordogne as well as the Aude, where a by-election was to be held the same day. Even after Boulanger withdrew from both contests on March 30, Thiébaud continued the campaign.[4]

In the general elections of 1885, the Dordogne and the

[4] Mermeix [Gabriel Terrail], *Les coulisses du boulangisme* (Paris: Cerf, 1890), p. 80.

Aude had both returned an entire slate of Republican Deputies. But whereas the Republicans (mainly Radicals) were supported by an absolute majority of the electorate in the Aude, they seem to have won by default in the Dordogne. The latter department, which bordered on the Bonapartist stronghold of the Charente, had a very strong Jeromist following. Implacably hostile to the monarchy, Jeromist voters had either abstained or else favored the Opportunist candidates in the Dordogne, rather than support a Conservative list composed exclusively of royalists.[5]

For these Jeromists, the by-election of April 8 became an opportunity to avenge the slight of 1885. They took control of the Conservative Committee in the Dordogne and successfully resisted a royalist attempt to present a candidate who had been defeated in the 1885 general elections. On the eve of the by-election, the department's leading Bonapartist organ expressed current Jeromist sentiment by entitling its lead editorial: "Anything rather than royalty." [6] Anything, in this instance, turned out to be Boulanger, since the local Bonapartist politicians decided not to present a candidate and instead collaborated with Thiébaud. As a protest against the present government, Bonapartist voters were urged to support Boulanger. "The General demands DISSOLUTION AND REVISION OF THE CONSTITUTION: this is also our twofold aim." [7] On April 4, market day in Périgueux, Bonapartist political workers distributed two ballots marked for Boulanger and campaign literature signed by Thiébaud to nearly every passer-by.[8]

The General's opponent in the Dordogne was a Radical lawyer named Clerjounie, who in a pre-election rally on April 4 publicly favored Floquet and revision of the constitution.

[5] *L'Indépendant de la Dordogne,* April 6, 1888.
[6] *L'Echo de la Dordogne,* April 9, 1888.
[7] *Ibid.,* April 1, 1888.
[8] *L'Avenir de la Dordogne,* April 6, 1888.

With Floquet as Premier, he argued, the revisionist movement led by Boulanger had lost its *raison d'être*. Clerjounie praised the General for his patriotism and for his accomplishments as War Minister, but criticized him for having violated military discipline.[9] By taking up the cause of revision, Clerjounie and his fellow Radicals thought that they were attacking the very roots of Boulangism, but they were sadly mistaken. Their error was in taking the revisionist movement at its face value. The current dissatisfaction for which Boulanger had become the principal outlet was directed less at the regime itself than at governmental policy. The General himself virtually admitted as much. Even while calling for a new constitution, he added that "the Chamber has become completely alien to the aspirations of the country." [10] Coming from a Chamber already discredited in the eyes of many, Floquet's plan to consider revision was rejected in advance by those at whom it was primarily aimed: the partisans of General Boulanger.

From the results of the April 8 by-elections it became possible to determine the importance of Boulanger to the Conservative cause. The General won in the Dordogne by the impressive majority of 59,555 votes to 35,759; but he immediately declined the office in order to be still eligible for election in the Nord.[11] In the consistently Republican department of the Aude, however, the Radical candidate took a commanding lead on the first ballot, with 24,363 votes to 18,767 for the Opportunist runner-up. Boulanger placed a poor third with only 8,440.[12] Taken together, the two elections show that he had great appeal to voters of the Right. Thiébaud had acted on his own and had presented the General's candidacy in order to demonstrate this appeal.

The lesson was not lost on leaders of the Bonapartist party.

[9] *Ibid.*, April 6, 1888. [10] *La Cocarde*, March 31, 1888.
[11] A.N.F., C 5303 A 73; *L'Intransigeant*, April 11, 1888.
[12] A.N.F., C 5301 A 71; *La Justice*, April 13, 1888.

Before April 8, Paul de Cassagnac claimed that Boulanger had no following among Conservative voters and therefore threatened only the Republicans. He concluded that it availed the Bonapartists nothing to abstain from presenting a candidate in a by-election where the General was entered.[13] A few days after the Dordogne election, Cassagnac saw the situation in an entirely different light. "I confess that the election in the Dordogne has me completely baffled," he began. Being accustomed to seeing Boulanger as a creature of the Left, he could not immediately understand how the General had received so many votes from the Right. So he changed his opinion of the former War Minister. "The Boulangist movement—as the election in the Dordogne . . . clearly shows—is anti-Republican and antiparliamentary, an awakening of the country in the direction of authority. Out of one hundred Boulangists there are *ninety* Conservatives."[14] From Clément de Royer, president of the Paris committee for Prince Victor, came a similar conclusion. "The rest of us [Bonapartists] can only rejoice at what is now going on. It is an awakening of the French people in favor of our ideas. . . . General Boulanger's program in the Nord may be accepted by everyone; it contains nothing contrary to our doctrines."[15]

The Dordogne election showed Bonapartists of all shades that Boulanger could rally the rank and file of their voters, who were too disillusioned with the party's two lackluster pretenders to go to the polls. That is what had happened in that department during the general elections of 1885. Unless some drastic remedy was applied, an even greater danger existed:

[13] *L'Autorité,* April 12, 1888.   [14] *Ibid.,* April 13, 1888.

[15] Cited in *La Justice,* April 9, 1888, to show Radical voters what the paper claimed were Boulanger's true colors. This may be considered an early, and not too successful, attempt at proving guilt by association.

namely, that many individual Bonapartists, increasingly annoyed at their party's internal squabbles, would leave the party altogether. It is not necessary to accept Cassagnac's figures concerning the Dordogne election to understand his hope that Boulanger would lift the Bonapartists out of these squabbles. This had been Thiébaud's strategy from the start.[16] Now it seemed to be working as planned.[17]

Therein lay the great danger for the Radicals. Having been the first to sponsor Boulanger, they understood his political assets perhaps better than any other progovernment party. Pelletan therefore berated the General's leftist partisans, saying: "Is a single one of these Radicals unaware that what he [Boulanger] says: revision, dissolution, *improvement in the conditions of working men* (O! the brochures from Ham!) is calculated to make him the Bonapartists' man?" [18] The Radical leaders feared that Boulanger would be able to carry along not only elements of the Left but many Conservatives as well. This explains why the Radicals called for liberal reforms while at the same time accusing Boulanger of being a creature of the Right. Their demands were addressed to the Opportunists; their accusations, to the far Left.

VICTORY IN THE NORD

As a result of his election in the Dordogne, Boulanger now enjoyed the open and unabashed support of the Bonapartists. His victory in the Nord would give him similar support from the royalists. Unlike the generally agricultural Aisne and the impoverished Dordogne, the department of the Nord was one

[16] Mermeix, *op. cit.,* p. 45; Maurice Barrès, *L'appel au soldat* (Paris: Juven, 1911), p. 111.

[17] It did work. Oswald Taillefer, the Bonapartist candidate who placed third on April 8, won the follow-up election on July 22 (A.N.F., C 5303 A 73).

[18] *La Justice,* April 10, 1888.

of the wealthiest and most highly industrialized in all of France. In the early years of the Third Republic, it was divided into two roughly equal political blocs: the Conservatives usually dominated the Flanders countryside, while the Republicans led in most cities and towns. Industrial suburbs went one way or the other according to local interests: textiles were generally Conservative, but mines and metallurgy mainly Republican. Because of the public desire for a balanced budget and higher tariffs, the department elected an entire list of Conservatives in 1885. In the by-elections of 1887, however, the Nord sent two Republicans to the Chamber. Republican gains were greatest in the countryside, which by then had recovered from the agricultural crisis of 1884. The Republican cause was also furthered, in a partisan sense, by a new, militantly Republican prefect, who granted favors only to the party faithful. As in other departments, many Conservative voters left their party in 1886, following irresponsible talk by its leaders of a monarchical restoration.[19]

In view of Republican difficulties in 1888, the Orleanist chiefs who ran the Conservative party in the Nord might reasonably have hoped for a victory in the by-election to be held on April 15. With Boulanger a candidate, however, they decided to abstain from the contest. This decision was made chiefly by Meyer and Martimprey, the latter a Deputy from the Nord. The Comte de Paris, who was in Spain at the time, was not informed of their plans. If Boulanger won in the Nord, the pretender was expected to approve this kind of "parallel march" in other by-elections as a matter of policy.[20]

[19] Jacques Néré, "Les élections Boulanger dans le département du Nord" (unpub. complementary thesis, Doctorat ès lettres, University of Paris, 1959), pp. 95–96.

[20] Mermeix, *op. cit.*, p. 96.

In many ways, therefore, the election in the Nord constituted a test case.

To insure that the test would be successful, Meyer and Dillon approached wealthy Orleanists for contributions, which soon reached 200,000 francs.[21] This sum was used to pay for the most intense propaganda employed to date in a French by-election. As a rule, Frenchmen seeking election to the Chamber during this period were most frugal about their campaign expenses. A Republican candidate normally spent about 8,000 francs, or about one-sixth the amount allowed his English counterpart; and a royalist could be expected to spend even less.[22] Perhaps the closest parallel to the well-financed electoral machine which worked for Boulanger in the Nord could be found in the United States. In Floquet's words, Dillon "Americanized" the Boulangist campaign.[23]

Thanks to Dillon's management and Orleanist money, the campaign had the effect of a steamroller. Boulanger's chief lieutenants—Laguerre, Le Hérissé, Laur, and Vergoin—carried their message to the entire department in person, followed by newsboys selling *La Lanterne* and *L'Intransigeant*. Billboards were soon covered with publicity for the General, while ballots marked with his name and campaign leaflets reached even the most isolated farms in Flanders. "People in this part of the country," wrote one observer, "were not accustomed to this kind of electoral activity, conducted . . . with such powerful publicity." [24] Boulanger's campaign literature carried a simple message: greater honesty in government and

[21] *Ibid.*, pp. 89–90.
[22] J. E. C. Bodley, *France* (2 vols.; New York, Macmillan, 1898), II, 139–140.
[23] Meyer, *op. cit.*, p. 71.
[24] *La République Française*, April 9, 1888.

a militant policy toward Germany. Pictures of the General were also distributed in enormous quantities. By April 15, it was estimated that one of these was on the wall of almost every peasant house in the department.[25]

Another factor which undoubtedly helped Boulanger's cause in the Nord was the position taken by the department's influential Conservative newspapers. Although they had received official orders from party headquarters in Paris to remain neutral, their attitude in fact changed from one of coolness toward Boulanger to hesitant but open approval.[26] Typical of this change was the position of the leading Catholic organ in the Nord, *La Vraie France,* which began simply by opposing the General's Opportunist adversary, Foucart. As late as April 6, the paper expressed satisfaction that a Radical journal, *Le Nord,* had just abandoned Boulanger because of his plebiscitary intent. Two days before the election, however, the Catholic journal moved a step closer to approval of Boulanger by noting, "The Boulangist campaign has literally driven the Opportunists crazy." Finally, with the election only a day off, this paper arrived at open support in these terms: "Boulangism . . . is not a goal in itself; it is an instrument." [27] The theme that the Opportunists must be beaten by every available means was stated even more explicitly by another Conservative newspaper of the region:

Above all, we are enemies of the Opportunists, and we believe that Boulanger's success will be a mortal blow to this party, which has terrorized the Nord for seventeen years, which persecutes religion, and which, on the pretext of doing favors for friends, deprives us of the equality and the justice to which all Frenchmen are

[25] "Chronique politique," *Le Correspondant,* CLI (April 25, 1888), 404–405.

[26] Néré, *op. cit.,* pp. 120–121.

[27] *La Vraie France,* April 2–14, 1888.

entitled. We realize that all remedies do not take effect, and that certain ones are dangerous; but when the situation is desperate, we must try anything.[28]

Whatever the influence of the Conservative press in the Nord on its readers' voting, it is apparent that these papers were already under some pressure from readers to favor Boulanger. Support for the General from the rank and file of Conservative voters manifested itself at least a week before approval from the rightist press. It did not seem to embarrass the Boulangist press in Paris, except *La Cocarde,* which felt obliged to explain why Boulanger, a man of the Left, was winning favor on the Right.

The Conservatives in the Nord are not enemies of Republican institutions, but they are the declared enemies of parliamentarism and of the pernicious political system which has been practiced these last years. . . . No one can say that the General will have the votes of reactionaries, for in the Nord, the word Conservative . . . means protest.[29]

This attempt to distinguish between Conservatives in the Nord and those elsewhere was awkward at best.

Still more awkward was the position of the Republicans. First to decide how to face Boulanger were the Radicals, whose party congress for the Nord met at Lille on April 2. Since their candidates had been pushed aside in previous Republican nominating conventions in the department, they were too embittered to join forces with the Opportunists.[30]

[28] Cited in "Chronique politique," *Le Correspondant,* CLI (April 25, 1888), 403–404.

[29] *La Cocarde,* April 7, 1888.

[30] Maxime Lecomte, *Le boulangisme dans le Nord: Histoire de l'élection du 15 avril* (Paris: Librairie Illustrée, 1888), pp. 46–47.

After considerable discussion, they resolved not to present any candidate and instead issued the following explanation:

The Radical congress of the department of the Nord, considering that the Radical party should not assume responsibility for the discredit heaped on parliamentarism by the actions of the Opportunists, has decided that there is no reason to present a candidate at the [Republican] congress on April 4.

The Radicals then called on Boulanger to expose his views on constitutional revision in detail and without equivocation. He was further asked to explain what reforms he intended to initiate. Once he did so, they said, "the Radicals of the Nord will know their duty and vote according to their principles." Wisely, Boulanger remained silent; his henchmen continued to make speeches on his behalf, but avoided any precise commitments as to his program.[31]

When the general Republican congress for the Nord met two days later, it quite naturally chose an Opportunist, one Paul Foucart, an august member of the department's *haute bourgeoisie*. The new candidate had little to recommend him to the mass of the electorate; in 1884, he had strongly condemned a coal miners' strike at Anzin.[32] On accepting his party's call, Foucart declared himself opposed to constitutional revision on the grounds that a constitution is only as good as the men charged with implementing it. Other than a nod in the direction of old-age pensions paid by the state, Foucart gave no indication of wanting to change the political *status quo* in any way. On the contrary, his only electoral manifesto was devoted almost entirely to attacks on Boulan-

[31] Louis Maury, *M. Boulanger devant l'opinion publique* (Poitiers: Millet, Descoust & Pain, 1888), pp. 29–30.
[32] Lecomte, *Le boulangisme,* pp. 70–71.

ger, whom he accused of dictatorial ambitions and, of all things, of having no program! [33]

The leading opportunist organ in the Nord also spent more time in criticizing Boulanger (and thereby drawing still more attention to him) than in praising the Republican candidate. On election day, the paper's front-page editorial spoke only of Boulanger, the warmonger. It warned its readers:

You will not forget that as Minister of War, General Boulanger, by his bellicose attitude, nearly involved us, without allies, in a war with Germany, when we were not yet ready, and nearly exposed us to a new invasion, a new dismemberment of the homeland.[34]

Such a warning may have had precisely the opposite effect of the one intended, since many voters still admired Boulanger's firmness toward Germany. Although subsequently available evidence shows him to have been extremely reckless, his stand in 1887 did give his compatriots a sense of pride which they had not experienced since 1870.[35]

Foucart's conservatism only antagonized the Radicals, who waited in vain for Boulanger to present his program. Exasperated at the inaction on both sides, they joined some of the less revolutionary Socialists of the department and presented their own candidate, a civil engineer with a long Radical past named Emile Moreau. The new candidate's program was certain to please those who nominated him: it included (1) a new constitution with a unicameral legislature, (2) separation of church and state, (3) three-year universal military service, and (4) economic and social reforms, notably a reduction in working hours for labor. What hampered Moreau most of all was the lateness of his candidacy: he was nominated a bare

[33] *Le Progrès du Nord,* April 6–7, 1888.
[34] *Ibid.,* April 16, 1888.   [35] Cf. *supra,* pp. 53–54, 95–96.

three days before the election, and his program was released only two days before.[36]

By the time Moreau entered the fray, Boulanger had already built up a commanding lead in popularity among voters in the Nord. A Conservative journalist named Heulhard judged a week before the election that the support of the Radicals and most industrial workers for Boulanger was as good as won.[37] An indication of the General's popularity among the proletariat can be seen in a plea addressed by a group of miners in the Pas-de-Calais to their brethren in the Nord. It warned that Boulanger, if elected, would revive the Second Empire. Not that the present regime was perfect:

We have not yet obtained from the Republic what we had a right to expect from it; but at the very moment that a reforming ministry has taken office, this is not the time to give ourselves up to a soldier. Brothers of the Nord! We beg you: do not be fooled. Between Boulanger, the ally and protégé of the Bonapartists, and Foucart, the anticlerical Republican, do not hesitate.[38]

Many miners in the Nord did not hesitate an instant; they went right ahead and voted for Boulanger. Foucart's anticlericalism alone was not likely to improve their salaries or working conditions.

To counter the charge of Caesarism, Boulanger's chief lieutenants issued a proclamation late in the campaign, in which they took great pains to impress upon voters in the Nord that his previous candidacies did not count. He was running in that department on a clean slate, they insisted. "Whatever lies have been posted or published, bear this in mind about our campaign: General Boulanger is a Republican. He is a candidate

---

[36] *La Justice,* April 14, 1888. [37] *Le Figaro,* April 9, 1888.
[38] *La Justice,* April 14, 1888.

in the Nord and nowhere else." Once elected to the Chamber, they promised, Boulanger would introduce "sincere and democratic reforms." [39] By this pledge, Laguerre, Laur, and company seemed to refute Rochefort's claim of the previous week. "All we ask for," he then maintained, "is the return of General Boulanger to the War Ministry." [40] But that would simply be a return to the past, which few Frenchmen now appeared to want. To those who voted for the General, he represented the hope of future change; and everyone was free to interpret this hope in his own way.

As expected, Boulanger's victory in the by-election of the Nord was overwhelming. He won 172,853 votes to 75,901 for Foucart and 9,647 for Moreau. That his success was not due entirely to Conservative support may be seen from a comparison with the results of 1885, when the Right was at its highwater mark. In the general elections of that year, the Conservative list in the Nord won 165,309 votes for its first candidate and 161,099 for its last. Figures for the unified Republican list were 122,987 and 113,711, respectively. In the by-election of April 15, 1888, the final returns for some of the department's leading cities were as follows: [41]

Lille		Tourcoing	
Boulanger	14,524	Boulanger	5,407
Foucart	9,686	Foucart	4,784
Moreau	2,975	Moreau	647

Roubaix		Dunkirk	
Boulanger	7,948	Boulanger	7,263
Foucart	2,131	Foucart	1,004
Moreau	1,567	Moreau	519

[39] *Ibid.*, April 13, 1888.   [40] *L'Intransigeant,* April 8, 1888.
[41] A.N.F., C 5306 A 76.

As this sampling shows, Boulanger's most impressive margins of victory were in normally Conservative Roubaix and Dunkirk. In divided Lille, he won by a smaller margin, while in traditionally Republican Tourcoing, Foucart made his best showing.

If Boulanger owed most of his votes to the Right, his gain over the Conservatives' totals of 1885 were made at the expense of the Republicans. In normally Conservative Flanders, Boulanger polled somewhat fewer votes than the Conservatives in the by-elections of 1887 and far less than they had in 1885. In the non-Flemish countryside, his totals were slightly less than what the Conservatives had received in 1885. His real advance over the Conservatives' vote in the last general elections was in the industrial centers where Republican strength had been greatest.[42] Immediately after the election, Alexandre Millerand estimated that Boulanger had received approximately 112,000 votes from the Right and some 60,000 from Republicans. The Radicals took little comfort, however, in the assurance that the General would not have won without Conservative support. Since it was generally agreed that the vast majority of Boulanger's Republican votes came from the Left, the Radicals argued that, to win the Left away from him, more reforms, of the type proposed by Moreau, were needed.[43] A recent study, based on intensive research, indicates that even more Republicans voted for Boulanger in the Nord than Millerand thought: about 70,000 instead of 60,000.[44]

More than anything else, the by-election of April 15 in the Nord showed that the needs of Boulanger and those of the Right were complementary. Supported by only a handful of

[42] Néré, *op. cit.*, pp. 170–174.   [43] *La Justice*, April 16, 1888.
[44] Jacques Néré, "Le vrai visage du boulangisme" (unpub. ms., Paris, 1961), p. 137.

extreme Radicals, the General could not hope to win more than a very few departments in the whole country. The Conservatives were somewhat better off; but although they might win as much as a third of the seats in the next Chamber, a majority was highly improbable. When the Comte de Paris proposed that the monarchy be restored by a plebiscite, he was making a tacit admission that it could not be restored by conventional parliamentary means. At the same time, however, he gave no indication as to how such a plebiscite was to be organized within the framework of France's present regime. Nor did he explain why the French electorate, which failed to elect a Conservative majority to the Chamber, was expected suddenly to produce an Orleanist majority in a plebiscite. To the makers of Orleanist policy, Boulanger seemed to provide an answer to both questions.

Boulanger's victory in the Dordogne had sealed his alliance with the Bonapartists; his success in the Nord sealed one with the Orleanists. A foretaste of the latter pact was provided by Cornély immediately after the General's election in the Nord.

Well now, the General is victorious. Therefore the Republic has been defeated. . . . It matters little to us which fractions or subfractions of the diverse opinions formed the General's majority. That majority exists, and it signifies: no more parliamentarism!
. . . And if the term "national party" is applied to the group of people who utter this cry, then we fall into this group; we are of this party.[45]

On April 24, the Comte de Paris put the finishing touches on the alliance in the form of a new declaration to his party. He recalled his instructions of September 15, 1887, in favor of abandoning the regime and boasted that "the [latest] events

[45] *Le Gaulois*, April 16, 1888.

131

have proved me right." Without mentioning Boulanger by name, he added: "The recent, striking manifestations of universal suffrage are the cry of a France tired of this kind of regime and seeking deliverance from it." What the country wanted most, he claimed, was revision of the constitution. "The monarchists did not wait for the present crisis before demanding revision. I included it myself in their program, and I remind them of it today." The revisionist movement would lead straight to restoration of the monarchy, he predicted. Therefore, all loyal monarchists should support it.[46]

Before issuing this statement, the Orleanist pretender had made an agreement with Dillon according to which no Conservative candidate would henceforth run in any by-election where Boulanger was being presented. Conversely, Boulanger was not to run or sponsor another candidate in a department where a Conservative was already entered.[47] Before the General's "electoral steeplechase" ended, he was to win four more by-elections: three in the provinces and one in Paris. Except for the last, these took place in departments which had Conservative majorities in 1885. Although Dillon's agreement cannot provide the sole explanation for Boulanger's subsequent successes, it did influence his course of action.

The function of constitutional revision in the alliance between Conservatives and Boulangists was that of a means, rather than an end. It acted as a catalyst which enabled the two parties, so different in their political philosophies, to join forces until the general elections of 1889. During that period, neither side took up the question in detail. In a speech before his closest supporters on April 27, 1888, Boulanger attacked what he called parliamentarism because it "leaves ministers at the mercy of the parliament," but he did not explain how he would change the system. Again disclaiming any dictatorial

[46] *Le Gaulois,* April 25, 1888.   [47] Mermeix, *op. cit.,* p. 109.

ambitions, he asserted that he wanted revision in order to consolidate the Republic and to make "the other [unnamed] reforms" possible.[48] The General's lack of a specific program was applauded by Cassagnac, who commented: "Programs never served any useful purpose." Since both Boulanger and the Conservatives favored revision, "we may go part of the way together." [49] A specific revisionist program on either side might well destroy the fragile entente just concluded.

VARIETIES OF REVISIONISM

Not only did Conservatives and Boulangists fundamentally disagree about the nature of the new regime which they were working together to achieve, but within Boulanger's circle itself there was a wide range of opinions concerning France's future constitution. When the Comte de Paris proposed a sort of Bonapartist monarchy in his first manifesto, the immediate reaction of his followers was to praise the scheme publicly and to return to politics as usual. Save for a few recalcitrant Legitimists, who naturally opposed the Orleanist pretender's idea, it was not analyzed or even openly discussed by the royalists. For most of the leading Boulangists, however, revision of the constitution was not merely a means, but an end in itself. Yet because they differed among themselves as to its eventual content, they postponed serious discussion of revision until a new parliament could be installed.

The convening of a new parliament could await the next general elections, or it could follow an early dissolution of the present one. By proposing dissolution as well as revision in his address to voters of the Nord, Boulanger appeared to want to hasten the process of replacing the present constitution by a new one. The broad term "revision" really obscured the fact that the General's most ardent supporters did not seek revision

[48] *L'Autorité,* April 29, 1888.   [49] *Ibid.,* April 30, 1888.

in the sense used when the constitution was revised by Ferry in 1884. They wanted, not mere amendments, but a completely new draft. Having already asserted that the present Chamber was alien to France's aspirations, Boulanger implied that it could not be expected to adopt a new constitution. He nonetheless kept the promise made by his chief aides to voters in the Nord [50] and took his seat in the Chamber for the sole purpose of proposing revision.

As Deputy from the Nord, Boulanger entered the Chamber for the first time since resigning from the War Ministry and on June 4, 1888, immediately introduced a bill for consideration of revision of the constitution. First, he offered his own analysis of France's current political difficulties. They were caused, he argued, by "a completely false conception of the Republic," which was being treated by the Opportunists as their personal property. As a result, many loyal Republicans voted Conservative in 1885. "The three million votes from the [Conservative] opposition were not, as claimed the next day, a manifestation in favor of the monarchy; they expressed a scathing protest against the present state of affairs." The same protest, Boulanger continued, was behind his own electoral successes. After this reasoned statement, however, the new Deputy from the Nord seemed to contradict himself by shifting all the blame to the constitution. "The constitution of 1875 is neither Republican nor democratic. It is oligarchic and parliamentary," making the Chamber supreme.[51]

The proposed solution which followed was only a bare and somewhat vague outline of a constitution, as if its sponsor wished to avoid detailed involvement in the question. "I believe," he began, "that France would easily become accustomed to doing without a President of the Republic." But since the country already had one, Boulanger was willing to

---

[50] Cf. *supra*, pp. 128–129.   [51] *J.O.C.* (1888), pp. 1627–1628.

keep that institution if the people so desired. The entire question as to whether the country was to be governed by an individual or a directory would be left to a constituent assembly. What really mattered, he said, was that the executive possess real power and not be responsible to parliament. On the other hand, the executive could be deposed by the people if it failed to carry out its popular mandate. Boulanger was ready to eliminate the Senate; but if the nation really wanted it, he said that it should be elected by universal suffrage. To make sure that the government would always be responsible to popular will, he suggested referendums on all important issues, on the Swiss model.

Uncertain as they were, Boulanger's proposals drew fire from Clemenceau, who had been one of the original proponents of revision and still favored it, but not at the expense of the Chamber. In the ensuing debate, the Deputy from the Nord was supported by his own little band, plus most of the Conservatives, who revealed their motives with absolute candor. The royalist de la Rochefoucault announced that he would vote for revision as a step toward restoration of the monarchy, while the Bonapartist Jolibois predicted that it signified a return to Empire. Floquet then mocked Boulanger, exclaiming: "At your age, Sir, Bonaparte was dead, and you are but the Sieyès of a stillborn constitution." On this note, the Premier asked for a vote, by which Boulanger's bill was rejected, 377 to 186.[52]

Although few of his listeners seem to have realized it, none of Boulanger's proposals to the Chamber on constitutional revision was truly original. Each can be found in the writings of Naquet published in 1883.[53] On the very day that Boulanger introduced a bill for revision to the Chamber, a new Paris daily named *La Presse* was being readied for publication.

[52] *Ibid.*, pp. 1636–1638.   [53] Cf. *supra*, pp. 74–75.

With Georges Laguerre as its editor and publisher and other members of the General's committee as frequent contributors, this may rightly be considered the official Boulangist organ. Its first issue carried an article by Naquet praising Boulanger's motion as proof that the General did have a program.[54] Two days later, Naquet admitted that Boulanger had been inspired by some(!) of his ideas. If applied, he claimed, they would be a perfect safeguard against dictatorship.[55]

Not all the leading Boulangists, however, agreed with Naquet that the answer to France's problems was increased independence for the executive. In orthodox Jacobin tradition, many of them favored just the opposite: making the executive completely subordinate to a unicameral legislature. Foremost among these was Henri Michelin, a Jacobin with socialist leanings, whose newspaper, *L'Action,* had begun continuous publication in November, 1886, without any noticeable ties to the General. When the Freycinet ministry had been overthrown, Michelin, who was also a Deputy from Paris, took advantage of the ministerial crisis to propose revision before the Chamber.[56] In the pages of *L'Action,* he argued against a *replâtrage*—literally a replastering—of the Freycinet cabinet under a new Premier.[57] When such a replastering did in fact take place, he ridiculed the ministry, especially Boulanger, whom he called an overly ambitious "ham actor." [58]

To all appearances, then, Michelin became a partisan of General Boulanger in the hope of using him as a means to effect revision of the constitution in a traditionally Jacobin sense. The kind of revision Michelin sought was implied by his colleague, Planteau, who claimed that there should be no

[54] *La Presse,* June 6, 1888.   [55] *Ibid.,* June 8, 1888.
[56] Cf. *supra,* p. 44.   [57] *L'Action,* Dec. 4, 1886.
[58] *Ibid.,* Dec. 11, 1886.

executive at all. An executive belonged to the monarchy or the Empire, but not to the Republic, which had greatly suffered, he maintained, from abuses of power by its ministers. Instead of ministers, Planteau proposed an agent, revocable at will by the Assembly, who would do its bidding and—since unicameral legislatures were considered by the Jacobin Left to be the perfect expression of the popular will—that of the people.[59] Speaking before Michelin and twenty-four other partisans at the Café Riche, Boulanger promised: "If someone in the constituent assembly proposed the abolition of the Presidency of the Republic, I would do more than approve the motion; I would be the first to vote for it." [60] Generous though this pledge may have seemed, it was a far cry from the elimination of all ministerial posts.

At all events, Boulanger's speech before the Chamber on June 4, 1888, plainly did not satisfy Michelin. Three weeks later, the latter announced to reporters that a progressive program, elaborated by himself and some (unnamed) associates, would soon be presented to Boulanger. If the General did not accept it publicly, warned Michelin, he stood to lose his supporters on the Left.[61] The program was indeed presented to the Boulangist central committee in mid-July. Its main points were the use of popular referendums for all important issues and a unicameral legislature elected by thirds every two years. The Assembly was to control its "agent" and name judges to the higher courts. All basic freedoms were guaranteed, but not, as in France's post–World War II constitutions, the right to work. Other reforms not pertaining to the constitution included revision of the civil and commercial codes, as well as an end to direct taxation. State revenues were to be derived exclusively from a graduated income tax and a capital gains

[59] *Ibid.*, Dec. 6, 1886.   [60] *La Cocarde*, April 29, 1888.
[61] *Le Matin*, June 26, 1888.

tax. Appended to these economic reforms were the usual Radical demands for free public education, universal military service, and separation of church and state. Boulanger did not express his views on this program, since he was then on tour in Brittany.[62] So far as is known, the General never did commit himself to such a program, until Michelin, in exasperation, left the movement late in 1889.[63]

When *La Cocarde* began publication, Boulanger had not yet made even a vague pronouncement in favor of revision. The paper's original plan for revision was virtually a carbon copy of Michelin's.[64] But after the General's manifesto to the electorate of the Nord, this so-called "Boulangist organ" embarked on a wildly erratic course. An unsigned editorial of April 3, 1888, mocked all proposals to eliminate the Senate, on the grounds that it was the Chamber and not the upper house which had enacted the measures against Boulanger. Following this tacit admission that men, not institutions, were responsible for the country's ills, there came the highly original observation that all talk of revision was irrelevant since there was really nothing to revise.[65] In strictly legal terms, France had no constitution, only a set of basic laws.

Lest readers become confused over such hairsplitting, Mermeix stepped in several weeks later and announced: "There are revision and revision." The type sponsored by Boulanger was what he favored, he explained, because it would make the President of the Republic directly responsible to the Chamber.[66] Boulanger may have promised such an arrangement to Mermeix privately, since he did talk out of both sides of his mouth. But he does not seem to have made any public proposal to this effect—certainly not in his speech to the Cham-

[62] *Le XIXe Siècle*, July 16, 1888.   [63] Cf. *infra*, pp. 223–224.
[64] Cf. *supra*, p. 104.   [65] *La Cocarde*, April 3, 1888.
[66] *Ibid.*, April 27, 1888.

ber on June 4. The General's words on that occasion were reproduced by *La Cocarde* without comment, save the most perfunctory kind of approval.[67] Indeed, it appears that most of the revisionists, such as Mermeix, had little understanding of what an executive really was. By 1888, the President of the Republic was largely a figurehead without any real executive power. Yet his office was under fire from the Left because of its original role as a springboard for monarchical restoration.

In its opposition to such institutions as the Senate and the Presidency of the Republic simply as institutions, the French Left often lost sight of economic problems. From the Boulangists came few concrete solutions to ease the distress of the urban proletariat. Their more advanced economic thinkers, such as Michelin, mixed economic reforms with those of a purely ideological nature. Michelin's most far-reaching proposal, the graduated income tax, was hotly opposed by some other Boulangists. *La Cocarde* was most petulant: "Once the income tax is made law, two categories of citizens will be created—the rich and the poor—who will no longer be equal." (As if they were equal then!) Since the rich would naturally demand new privileges for paying higher taxes, went the argument, the principle of universal suffrage would be undermined.[68] Wisely, Boulanger did not let himself become involved in discussions of this rarefied nature. In the urban economic sphere, he simply promised an end to unemployment and to restrictions on strikes and changing jobs.[69]

When discussing both constitutional and economic questions, Boulanger avoided detail as much as possible. For one thing, he does not appear to have possessed sufficient intellect to deal with these matters in detail. Besides, he did not wish to

[67] *Ibid.,* June 6, 1888.   [68] *Ibid.,* Dec. 12, 1888.
[69] *Programme du général Boulanger* (Paris: Bonne-Nouvelle, 1888).

antagonize any of his followers by seeming to favor one particular solution over another. Finally, as Professor Néré points out, the French masses would not have welcomed a lengthy discussion of the constitution.

The popular masses to which Boulangism appealed were not especially interested in the different constitutional modalities, which they could hardly understand anyway. In their eyes, revision of the Constitution was essentially a means of eliminating parliamentary impotence and therefore of accomplishing the long-promised social reforms, which were to put an end to their misery.[70]

Revision was therefore a political catch-all. Aside from its intrinsic appeal to the hard-core Boulangists, it offered all the discontented some hope for change. Thus, the posture adopted by Boulanger in the Nord by-election of April 15, 1888, was maintained throughout his political career.

[70] *Néré,* "Le vrai visage du boulangisme," p. 139.

7

Reversals and More Success

1888

Boulanger's impressive victory in the Nord by-election of April 15, 1888, raised him to the height of his popularity. Before taking his seat in the Chamber, he made a speaking tour of France's northern departments in May in order to consolidate his popular support. This tour showed how varied his following was. At Dunkirk, Bonapartists came in the greatest numbers to acclaim him; at Lille, his audience was composed mainly of Radicals; at Anzin, it was primarily Socialist. Everywhere, there were Catholics, irritated at the government's religious policy, who cheered him on. The General did his best to accommodate his different audiences. To the Right he would cry "Long live France!" while to the Left it was "Long live the Republic!" Invectives against parliamentarism were in order for the Bonapartists at Dunkirk. At Lille, he pleased both monarchists and Radicals by attacking the Opportunists. At Anzin, he drew cheers from industrial workers by promising to end what he called "wage slavery." Wherever he went, Boulanger upheld the principle of "religious liberty." Designed to appeal to Catholics, this slogan was nonetheless sufficiently general so as not to offend anyone.[1]

[1] Auguste Boucher, "Chronique politique," *Le Correspondant* CLI (May 25, 1888), 790–792.

Shortly after the General's victory in the Nord, his committee discarded the word "protest" and renamed itself simply the "National Republican Committee." Its president was Boulanger; but Naquet, as vice-president, appears to have been entrusted with the important decisions. Vergoin assumed the post of secretary, while Dillon became treasurer. It was by a committee decision that Laguerre was made director of *La Presse*. That paper was one of several means used by the committee to guide the Boulangist movement. Others included the organizing of meetings, rallies, and demonstrations, as well as the publication and distribution of flysheets, brochures, and songs. In order to give the movement an illusion of spontaneity, the committee in Paris did not establish department and *arrondissement* branches from above. Instead, it sent delegates into the provinces to help local Boulangists organize such branches autonomously. Only a few such local committees styled themselves openly Boulangist. Others were called "revisionist" or "dissolutionist-revisionist," so as not to discourage voters who might be suspicious of Boulanger as a person. Front organizations in Paris, such as the *Ligue d'action républicaine* and the *Fédération républicaine révisionniste,* had the same purpose.[2]

All this preparation was made in view of the general elections to be held in the fall of 1889. The first Boulangist committee outside of Paris was the one for the Loire, founded on April 19, 1888. Five more departmental committees were created that year, but most came into existence later.[3] In a newspaper interview of August, 1888, Boulanger revealed that he planned to organize revisionist committees "in every commune of France where possible." Since revision of the constitution had to be voted by the Chamber, a lower house

[2] A.P.P., B a/976, Nov. 2, 1889.
[3] A.N.F., F⁷ 12446, Jan. 13, 1892.

favorable to revision would have to be elected. "In order to attain this goal in 1889, I shall enter my candidacy in every department! In the departments where I have to withdraw, I shall try to have revisionist Deputies elected in my place." [4]

The extent to which Boulanger's strategy concorded with that of the royalists is illustrated by Arthur Meyer's explanation of the Conservative position three weeks earlier:

The Conservatives will present a revisionist list in each department. . . . General Boulanger, for his own part, will run on the same program.

In all departments where the representation is completely Conservative . . . and where it is not threatened by the Republicans, General Boulanger's support will be unnecessary. In the other departments where General Boulanger can bring us the votes of disenchanted Republicans or of "floaters," who are more numerous than many like to think, we shall vote for him.

General Boulanger will be elected in a certain number of departments; since he cannot be the Deputy from more than one, he will resign in the others, where Conservatives will be elected in his place, as in the Dordogne. [5]

Except for differences in terminology, the strategies of the two parties are so similar that there can be little doubt that they were elaborated in common. Both reveal a dismally low opinion of the average voter, who was expected to cast his ballot like a mere robot for whatever candidate Boulanger happened to designate. As the different elections of 1888 and 1889 were to show, however, the behavior of the French electorate was not as mechanical as Boulanger and Meyer seemed to think.

SOME BY-ELECTION DEFEATS

At the time that the first revisionist committee outside Paris was being created, Boulanger was Deputy from the Nord and

[4] *Le Figaro*, Aug. 21, 1888.   [5] *Le Gaulois*, July 31, 1888.

honor bound to serve only his constituents. He could not, therefore, run in any other by-elections without seeming to betray his great majority in the Nord. So when *La Cocarde* announced on April 23 that the General was being presented in by-elections to take place in the Isère and the Haute-Savoie on April 29, two official Boulangist papers, *La Lanterne* and *L'Intransigeant,* vigorously denied that he was a candidate.[6] In rebuttal, *La Cocarde* insisted that such a denial must come from Boulanger himself.[7]

Not until May 10 did the General publicly announce his withdrawal from the contests in both normally Republican departments. In the meantime, he had amassed only 833 votes on the first ballot in the Haute-Savoie; and although his tally in the Isère was sufficient to deprive the Opportunist or the Radical candidate of a clear majority, he still finished only a poor third. Despite a rash of campaign posters, which appeared in the Isère just after the first ballot, Boulanger received just 14,374 votes, as against 40,488 for the Radical winner and 37,923 for the Opportunist in second place. No Conservative had entered the contest,[8] indicating that perhaps the General's candidacy had been planned by his committee and not merely by *La Cocarde.*

In light of his failure in the Haute-Savoie and the Isère, Boulanger no longer waited until the eleventh hour before withdrawing. When a parliamentary vacancy occurred in the Charente, he lost no time in declining to run and instead recommended Paul Déroulède to the voters of that department as a fellow Charentais. Noting that they shared the same program, Boulanger asserted: "A vote for Paul Déroulède is a

[6] *L'Intransigeant,* April 24, 1888.

[7] *La Cocarde,* April 24, 1888.

[8] A.N.F., C 5304 A 74; Boucher, "Chronique politique," *Le Correspondant,* CLI (May 25, 1888), 795.

vote for me." [9] Just before the election took place on June 17, Mermeix revealed that he had asked the General to run. A majority of the Boulangist directorate, however, decided to enter Déroulède in order to prove that they constituted a real party and not just the train of a popular military figure. Even if voters in the Charente preferred Boulanger to Déroulède, most members of the committee had not forgotten the General's pledge to represent only the Nord. If it were not kept, they argued, he might lose his base of support. [10]

Other than being a native of the Charente, Déroulède had little to recommend himself to that department's largely Bonapartist electorate. In the Charente there was far less apprehension over the German question than in the Nord or the Aisne. As in most of France, voters in the Charente viewed Déroulède simply as a warmonger [11]— an opinion which hardly changed after the death of Kaiser Friedrich III on July 15. In an open letter to the electorate, Déroulède tried to make political capital out of the German Emperor's passing by representing it to be a gain for the war party in Germany. [12] Whatever the truth of this claim, its only noticeable effect on the people of the Charente was to make them even more prudent, for fear of exciting more war fever. [13]

Déroulède was further handicapped by the fact that he had to face Conservative opposition in this by-election. Since the agreement concluded by Dillon and the Right provided for Conservative abstention only where Boulanger himself was a candidate, Déroulède had to expect opposition. Boulanger actually broke his part of the agreement by entering his lieutenant in a department which had consistently favored the Bonapartists since 1871. So intense was Boulangist propa-

[9] *L'Action,* June 1, 1888.   [10] *La Cocarde,* June 18, 1888.
[11] *Ibid.,* June 18, 1888.   [12] *L'Intransigeant,* June 18, 1888.
[13] *Le Temps,* June 18, 1888.

ganda directed at Bonapartist voters in the Charente that *La Cocarde* felt obliged to explain to its leftist readers why the party was seeking support on the Right. It tried to reassure them by saying that "in the Imperialist [i.e., Bonapartist] army, the voting troops are democratic." A living political party had to recruit members at the expense of others; the "democratic" Bonapartists would vote for Déroulède.[14]

As the results of the first ballot showed, the majority of Bonapartist voters in the Charente remained faithful to their party and gave its candidate, Gellibert de Seguins, 31,439 votes. An Opportunist named Weiller took second place with 23,993 votes, followed by Déroulède with 20,674. Although the Boulangist candidate did not fulfill the hopes of his sponsors, he did lead his rivals in the department's two largest cities, Angoulême and Cognac. About half of Déroulède's votes were estimated to have come from Conservatives and the other half from Radical voters.[15] His inroads on the Right prompted Cassagnac to issue a backhanded compliment: "M. Déroulède's failure is relatively honorable." [16]

It was still a failure, however. Even Boulanger's promise to visit the Charente if Déroulède were elected had been of small help to the latter.[17] Naquet blamed his candidate's defeat on "a department which until now has been a fief of Imperialist [i.e., Bonapartist] reaction" and immediately announced Déroulède's withdrawal. Since the votes for Déroulède and Weiller combined were greater than those given to Gellibert de Seguins, Naquet called on the Opportunist to leave the field as well, in favor of a new candidate, who was to be a "Repub-

[14] *La Cocarde,* June 16, 1888.

[15] A.N.F., C 5301 A 71; *Le Temps,* June 19, 1888.

[16] *L'Autorité,* June 20, 1888.

[17] André Daniel, *L'année politique,* XV (Paris: Charpentier, 1888), 163.

lican revisionist." [18] As Weiller proved uncooperative, the Boulangist central committee issued a directive for those who had supported Déroulède on the first ballot to vote for the Opportunist on the second. At least Weiller was a Republican, it noted, while Gellibert de Seguins represented what it mistakenly termed "the monarchy." [19]

Even after Déroulède officially withdrew, predesignated ballots for him continued to arrive in the Charente. The Boulangist press virtually admitted that he was still in the race by noting that his partisans could not be stopped from voting for him if they really wanted to.[20] Yet the "National Republican Committee" had found it necessary to give open support to an Opportunist rather than to a Bonapartist, with whose party it was actually allied. No example illustrates better than this the importance attached by the Boulangists to their Republican loyalties. Even as their connections with the Right became increasingly apparent, they always insisted on their devotion to the Republic—a devotion which, within the context of their aims to revise the constitution, was perfectly sincere. Their Republicanism was of no immediate benefit to Déroulède, however, whose total vote was cut by almost half on the second ballot. The Bonapartist entry won easily.[21]

Following this setback, Boulanger resolved to fulfill the second part of his promise to his constituents and appeared before the Chamber for a second time, on July 12. On this occasion, he asked the lower house to do nothing less than vote its own dissolution. He argued that it had been the scene of such disgraceful conduct that the French people were fast growing disgusted with all those responsible for the disorder. Meanwhile, he warned, the monarchists were anxiously wait-

---

[18] *La Presse,* June 22, 1888. [19] *Ibid.,* June 24, 1888.
[20] *Le Temps,* June 30, 1888.
[21] *Année politique,* XV (1888), 164.

ing in the wings until the parliamentarians finally succeeded in killing the Republic. To avoid such a disaster, the Deputies had only to ask the President of the Republic to dissolve the Chamber and then allow a new "National Republic" to be established—presumably with Boulanger at its head. This the Deputies refused to do, for they were not easily deceived by the ambitious General's unashamed attempt at blackmail. Seeing that his cause was lost in the Chamber, Boulanger resigned on the spot, but not until he and Floquet had exchanged a heavy volley of insults.[22]

In nineteenth-century France, insults often led to duels, and this case was no exception. On the morning of July 14, the two protagonists faced each other at swords' points in the garden of Count Dillon. Eager for a quick victory, Boulanger rushed at his adversary and impaled himself on the near-sighted Premier's sword, which ran through his neck. An error of less than half an inch kept the wound from being fatal. Once the foolhardy General was taken to the hospital, Floquet left to dedicate a monument to Gambetta on the Place du Carrousel, where he was enthusiastically received. The spectacle of a reputedly dashing warrior losing a duel to a civilian led to a sharp fall in Boulanger's popularity. Even café singers like Paulus were changing their repertoires from Boulangist to anti-Boulangist songs.[23]

Regardless of this public humiliation, Boulanger had set his course before the duel. On resigning as Deputy from the Nord, he had issued two public declarations. The first was addressed to his constituents in the Nord, explaining why he was giving up his seat in the Chamber after having promised to represent them faithfully. He claimed that he had fulfilled his campaign

[22] *J.O.C.* (1888), pp. 2092–2096.

[23] Gabriel Monod, "Contemporary Life and Thought in France," *Contemporary Review*, LIV (Dec., 1888), 903–904.

pledge to demand revision and dissolution, but that these were blocked by an obstructionist majority in the Chamber. This majority, he implied, would be swept out in 1889. By opposing his motions, Boulanger argued, the politicians insulted both him and the Republic. "My dignity and yours," the voters of the Nord were told, "oblige me to accept the challenge and to ask France to decide between my insulters and me." Here was the first open admission by Boulanger that he was seeking a plebiscite.

In his second declaration, the General repeated this challenge and asked the voters of the Ardèche, where a by-election was to take place on July 22, to be the first to judge.[24] On that same date, there was to be a by-election in the department of the Rhône as well; but Boulanger chose not to run there, indicating the selective nature of his plebiscite. In the 1885 elections, the Rhône had returned a full slate of Republicans to the Chamber, while the Ardèche had gone Conservative by a narrow margin.[25] Even with Conservative support, however, the General's campaign in the Ardèche suffered heavily from the fact that it was conducted from a hospital bed at a time when his condition was still critical. Having declared himself a candidate little more than a week before the election, Boulanger was unable to mount a full-scale campaign, such as he had enjoyed in the Nord.

Although the Conservatives presented no candidate in the Ardèche, Boulanger was by no means assured of many votes from the Right. While the local Conservative Committee remained neutral throughout the short campaign, the department's leading rightist newspaper advised the General not to run. His duel with Floquet had badly injured his reputation, it

[24] *L'Intransigeant,* July 15, 1888.
[25] "Chronique de la Semaine," *Revue Bleue,* 3ème série, XLIII (July 28, 1888), 174.

observed.[26] There were, moreover, many monarchists in the Ardèche who apparently refused to vote for any Republican —even if that Republican was named Boulanger. Only in its last two days did the General's campaign take on any of the animation of former contests. Thanks to the efforts of Thiébaud, Boulanger received a public declaration of support from Léon Chevrau, a former Bonapartist Deputy from the Ardèche.[27] Such aid availed little, however, as the election results showed Boulanger with only 27,454 votes, while Beaussier, his Opportunist adversary, won handsomely with 43,295.[28] On all sides of the political arena, it was agreed that the General's defeat in the Ardèche was a heavy blow to his chances.[29]

THE TRIPLE BY-ELECTION VICTORY

While Boulanger's political position was thus being progressively eroded, four new parliamentary vacancies were created: two in the Nord and one each in the Somme and the Charente-Inférieure. With the General's popularity at its apparent nadir, the government saw no danger in scheduling the by-elections for all three departments on the same day, August 19. It was not expected that Boulanger would run in all three, let alone win.[30] Since he had nothing to lose at this point, however, he took a calculated risk and announced his candidacies during the first week of August. Given his tremendous victory in the Nord in April, he felt reasonably sure of further success there. Inasmuch as the Somme and the Charente-Inférieure had

[26] *Le Patriote de l'Ardèche,* July 18, 1888.

[27] *L'Ardèche Républicaine,* July 22, 1888.

[28] A.N.F., C 5301 A 71; *Le Temps,* July 24, 1888.

[29] *La Justice,* July 24, 1888; *L'Autorité,* July 25, 1888; *Le Gaulois,* July 24, 1888.

[30] Monod, "Contemporary Life and Thought in France," *Contemporary Review,* LIV (Dec., 1888), 904.

each elected five Conservatives and only two Republicans to the Chamber in 1885, the General expected a firm electoral base in these departments as well. He certainly encountered no financial problems, since the Duchesse d'Uzès contributed 500,000 francs for the triple election campaign alone.[31]

In this frankly plebiscitary venture, Boulanger paid little attention to the Nord and concentrated on the Somme and the Charente-Inférieure. By August 10, he was fully recovered from his wound and embarked on a four-day speaking tour of the Charente-Inférieure, followed by one of equal duration in the Somme. In both departments his campaigns were based on the American whistle-stop technique, in which he gave essentially the same speech in several towns during the course of a single day. His now well-worn theme was centered on a condemnation of the present Chamber and a promise of a new Republic, open to all.[32] Thanks to the contribution of the Duchesse d'Uzès, publicity was not lacking. The preparations for Boulanger's visit to Amiens on August 15 were extremely thorough.

The walls of the city had been covered with proclamations and portraits of the General, who was represented sometimes on foot, sometimes on horseback, here in uniform, elsewhere as Christ (!!) crucified by the Opportunists and the Radicals. All the songs composed during the past year in honor of the General were posted, and there was a profuse distribution of cocardes, red carnations, and small illustrated brochures bearing the title: "Life of General Boulanger." [33]

In addition, Dillon hired newsboys to mingle with the crowds and lead cheers for Boulanger; for each cheer they were each

[31] Mermeix [Gabriel Terrail], *Les coulisses du boulangisme* (Paris: Cerf, 1890), pp. 132–133.
[32] *L'Intransigeant*, Aug. 16, 1888.
[33] *Le Temps*, Aug. 17, 1888.

promised twenty-five centimes. The same price was to be paid for insulting the opposition candidates.[34]

It was in the Somme that Boulanger's campaign was the most intense, and it was there also that circumstances seemed the most favorable. To begin with, he enjoyed widespread and active support among voters of the Right. Ten days before the election, the Conservative Committee of the Somme announced that the party would not present a candidate and advised its members to be guided by their patriotism in voting.[35] Their choice, in any case, was extremely limited. Boulanger's opponent, a moderate Radical named Achille Bernot, was sponsored by René Goblet, who was then a Deputy from the Somme. Goblet's high praise of Bernot as a champion of laicism carried no appeal to Conservative and Catholic voters.[36]

Bernot, who was vice-president of the Syndicate of French Sugar Manufacturers, appears to have won little favor from the department's workers and artisans. The Somme was then experiencing a severe economic crisis, traceable to declining sugar prices; agricultural hardship compounded that of the already ill-paid urban workers. Although Bernot, by favoring protective tariffs to exclude low-priced German sugar, appealed to the countryside, he had no program for the towns. Meanwhile labor discontent was growing. On August 1, a strike of construction workers broke out in Paris, followed six days later by a weavers' strike in Amiens. Protesting against the hiring of foreign workers, the weavers razed the home of their leading employer, thereby prompting the city's moderate mayor to declare Amiens under martial law. The newspaper which supported Bernot there bitterly reprimanded the strikers.[37]

---

[34] Mermeix, *op. cit.,* p. 279.   [35] *L'Autorité,* Aug. 11, 1888.
[36] *Le Mémorial d'Amiens,* Aug. 3, 1888.
[37] *Le Petit Progrès de la Somme,* Aug. 8, 1888.

The Boulangists, on the other hand, were quick to profit from the situation and hired striking workers to distribute leaflets and to post signs for the General.[38] Many workers came to welcome Boulanger on his arrival in Amiens; the more enthusiastic among them were manhandled and arrested by the local police.[39] Their enthusiasm for the General does not seem to have been based on any concrete economic proposals, for he did not address himself directly to such issues. The closest he came to doing so was in an open letter of August 11 to the voters of the Somme. Referring to the strikes in Paris, he accused the present government of having created "only disturbances and serious problems in agricultural, industrial, and commercial transactions." [40] More to the point was a "Letter to the Strikers" of Amiens by Mermeix, who blamed the Opportunists for not heeding workers' grievances and for serving only the interests of finance and industry.[41]

In the Charente-Inférieure, Boulanger was only slightly less fortunate than in the Somme. Besides Bonapartist favor, which was essential in this stronghold of the party, he also enjoyed that of the local Radicals. Their newspaper accused the General's Opportunist adversary of being an ally of the Orleanists.[42] There may have been some truth in this charge, inasmuch as the department's royalist committee issued a public statement early in the campaign "in order to release the monarchist party from any involvement in this adventure." The kind of revision represented by Boulanger, it observed, had nothing in common with that sought by the royalists.[43]

Lack of royalist support, however, was more than compensated for by the shortcomings of the opposition to Boulanger.

---

[38] *L'Echo de la Somme,* Aug. 11, 1888.
[39] *Ibid.,* Aug. 18, 1888.   [40] *L'Action,* Aug. 10, 1888.
[41] *Le Mémorial d'Amiens,* Aug. 10, 1888.
[42] *Le Rochefortais,* Aug. 12 and 19, 1888.
[43] *Le Progrès de la Charente-Inférieure,* Aug. 8, 1888.

As in most other departments, the moderate Republicans fell into a trap: instead of producing a positive program, they made Boulanger himself the issue. In the Somme, for example, Bernot published a manifesto predicting both civil and foreign war if the General happened to win. "That slavish imitator of Louis Napoleon could only lead us to a new Sedan," he warned.[44] By the same token, the Opportunist candidate in the Charente-Inférieure, one Joseph Lair, offered no concrete electoral proposals, save a promise to bring order and stability to the Republic. Rather, he spent most of his time attacking Boulanger as a would-be dictator.[45] Similarly, the department's Opportunist journal devoted the entire front page of two issues just before the election to charges against the General.[46]

In his manifesto to voters of the Charente-Inférieure, Boulanger avoided economic matters completely and spoke only of parliamentary corruption and the need for strong national defense. The whole document is Napoleonic in tone, as when Boulanger complained that the politicians "took from me my sword, which I had consecrated to the defense of the homeland." [47] To voters in the Nord, which he did not visit in person, he simply repeated his call to support the cause of revision. This, plus a declaration originally addressed to the Assumptionist newspaper, *La Croix*, in which he promised never to persecute religion, were his only messages to the Nord.[48] That department was not notified until August 12 of Boulanger's candidacy, which had been announced on July 31 in the Somme and on August 8 in the Charente-Inférieure.[49]

[44] *La République Française*, Aug. 17, 1888.
[45] *Courrier de la Rochelle*, Aug. 12, 1888.
[46] *Ibid.*, Aug. 16 and 19, 1888.   [47] *L'Action*, Aug. 13, 1888.
[48] *La Vraie France*, Aug. 15, 1888.
[49] *Le Petit Progrès de la Somme*, Aug 10, 1888.

Since there were two vacancies in the Nord, the workings of *scrutin de liste* made it virtually mandatory for Boulanger to have a running mate. The members of the Boulangist committee in Paris wisely decided not to nominate one of their own number, who might antagonize Conservative voters. Déroulède's example in the Charente was not an encouraging precedent. So they chose a little-known moderate Republican named Koechlin-Schwartz, who was an important contributor to the General's campaign fund.[50] Koechlin had served as mayor of a Paris arrondissement until relieved by Floquet for having officiated at the marriage of the daughter of the Duc de Chartres and the Prince of Denmark.[51] Unlike Boulanger, Koechlin campaigned personally in the Nord; besides reminding voters of his Alsatian origins, he adopted without qualification the General's position on revision.[52]

The existence of electoral lists in the Nord set that by-election off from the other two, even though each list contained only two names. Where Boulanger met the opposition alone, his personality could play an important role. Once he had to join forces with another candidate, however, a common position had to be agreed on if both were to be successful. By concentrating on the question of revision, rather than on personalities, Koechlin showed that he understood this principle. So did the Republican candidates, whose personal political views were most dissimilar. One was Desmoutiers, a sugar manufacturer of Left-Center (that is, just to the right of the Opportunist) persuasion, who was close to eighty years old. The other was Moreau, who had represented the dissident

---

[50] Adolphe Cohn, "Boulangism and the Republic," *Atlantic Monthly*, LXVII (Jan., 1891), 96.

[51] Charles de Mazade, "Chronique de la quinzaine," *Revue des Deux Mondes*, LXXXIX (Sept. 1, 1888), 229.

[52] *L'Intransigeant*, Aug. 13 and 18, 1888.

Radicals in April. Since these two candidates had nothing in common except their Republican label, they limited their public declarations to a defense of the Republic.[53]

Against such pallid opposition, Boulanger won in all three departments, but his victory in the Nord was far less impressive than on April 15. He received 130,303 votes, a drop of over 40,000 from the previous by-election. Koechlin's total was 126,639, nearly matching that of Boulanger, while Desmoutiers and Moreau mustered 97,409 and 95,023 votes respectively, an average increase of over 20,000 votes more than what Foucart had received. There were also two Socialists in the election of August 19: Delcourt received 6,347 votes, while his comrade, Delcluse, won 5,837.[54] Boulanger's loss since April was registered almost exclusively in the urban and industrial centers, while in the countryside and the Flemish towns his total vote remained about the same.[55] Final results from some of the department's largest towns show the extent of the change.[56]

	Boulanger	*Koechlin*	*Desmoutiers*	*Moreau*	*Delcourt*	*Delcluse*
Lille	9,731	9,723	14,007	13,578	2,577	2,636
Roubaix	6,332	6,376	3,879	3,605	1,371	1,364
Tourcoing	5,201	5,247	5,352	5,186	287	286
Dunkirk	6,572	5,408	2,320	2,323	2	1

Boulanger's overall losses in the Nord since April 15 can be explained partly by his absence in that department while he was campaigning actively from the other two. Most voters, moreover, did not understand why he had resigned in the first

[53] *La Vraie France,* Aug. 2, 1888.

[54] *Le Temps,* Aug. 21, 1888.

[55] Jacques Néré, "Les élections Boulanger dans le département du Nord" (unpub. complementary thesis, Doctorat ès Lettres, University of Paris, 1959), pp. 196–197.

[56] A.N.F., C 5306 A 76; Cf. *supra,* p. 129.

place.[57] An increase of some 25,000 abstentions since April indicates widespread lack of interest. The reasons for the General's failure to retain all his votes from Republicans are less apparent. Despite his talk of revision, he had accomplished nothing tangible while serving as Deputy. Before the by-elections of April 15, his connections with the Right were barely visible. By August, however, royalist leaders were talking openly of using Boulanger as a tool to restore the monarchy. Martimprey, who led the royalist Deputies from the Nord, wrote to Arthur Meyer just before the election to say that the General's role was that of a battering ram against the Republic. "Once the breach is made, the [different] principles will suffice to separate us—I do not say from our allies, since there can be no question of alliance—but from our auxiliaries of circumstance." [58] In view of such remarkable candor on the part of the royalists, it is not surprising that nearly all Boulanger's losses in the Nord were estimated to have come from Republican voters.[59]

In the strike-ridden department of the Somme, Boulanger appears to have owed at least an important minority of his votes to Republicans. His greatest margin of victory was in Amiens, where he received 10,282 votes to only 3,797 for Bernot. Here the support of strikers appears to have been an important factor in the General's success. Even in the more Conservative countryside, Boulanger led by a margin of as much as 2 to 1 in every canton but one. Totals for the entire department gave him 76,155 votes, whereas the leading Conservative candidate in 1885 had won 70,514. Bernot's decline was far greater than Boulanger's: in 1885 he had led the Republican list with 57,380 votes, but now he won only 41,422.[60] In the Charente-Inférieure, Boulanger's total vote

[57] *L'Autorité,* Aug. 25, 1888. [58] *Le Gaulois,* Aug. 16, 1888.
[59] *Le Temps,* Aug. 21, 1888. [60] A.N.F., C 5310 A 80.

of 57,242 was less than the 62,551 votes given to Jolibois, the leading Conservative candidate in 1885. Republican losses, however, were far greater: whereas the leading Republican candidate in 1885 had won 61,990 votes, Lair received only 42,449. The General's margin of victory was, moreover, greatest in the *arrondissement* of Rochefort, which had gone strongly Republican in 1885.[61]

Boulanger's three-fold success confirmed in most dramatic fashion the lesson of his previous victories: his interests and those of the Right were complementary. While it is most doubtful that he could have won in any of the three departments without Conservative support, his candidacy did add Republican votes to those of the Right. If the General's success continued, a coalition of royalists and Boulangists could possibly win a majority of seats in the next Chamber.

ANTI-BOULANGISM

The task of preventing a royalist-Boulangist victory in the general elections of 1889 fell to the Republicans supporting the government, and to this task they now gave their undivided attention. They were sorely divided, however, on what means to use against Boulanger. In the post mortems which followed the shock of August 19, *Le Temps* suggested a typically Opportunistic solution. Inasmuch as the General owed most of his votes to Conservatives, the journal argued, his attempted plebiscite could be rendered ineffective only if he were separated from his rightist allies. Since such a maneuver could lead to another entente between Conservatives and Opportunists, the Radicals quite logically objected. "The strength of Boulangism," Pelletan retorted, "is in the unpopularity of Opportunism." Boulanger could be defeated only by a policy

[61] *Ibid.,* C 5302 A 72.

of thoroughgoing Radicalism by which the Radicals hoped to detach his leftist voters from him.[62]

The tactic of winning Boulanger's leftist following away from him by espousing reform found its most perfect expression in the *Société des droits de l'homme et du citoyen*, which was founded on May 23, 1888. Not to be confused with the *Ligue* of the same name which was founded during the Dreyfus affair, this organization was formed to defeat Boulanger by strengthening democracy. Its leaders—Ranc for the Opportunists, Clemenceau for the Radicals, and Joffrin for the "possibilist" Socialists—were supposed to represent all sections of Republican opinion. The second of these was the organization's real leader, and he read a statement of its position to some four hundred anti-Boulangists (mostly Radicals) assembled at the Grand Orient, headquarters of French Masonry on the rue Cadet, for the *Société*'s first meeting.

We are devoted to the policy of revision, but we want the sincere application of this policy and not its exploitation by a general who poses as a pretender and who recruits his followers from all parties. . . .

But revision alone cannot suffice. We must take up the national movement of the French Revolution from where it has been halted and become its continuators. We must protect individual and public liberties, freedom of the press, of reunion, and of association, guaranteed by Republican institutions. We must continue the integral development of the Republic—that is, the progressive realization of all constitutional, political, and social reforms contained therein. Such is our goal.

We find the instrument for attaining it in our Republican tradition, in the rebirth of the great political association which, by grouping all the democratic forces of Paris and the departments, were the stimulant of the assemblies of the Revolution.[63]

[62] *La Justice,* Aug. 23, 1888.   [63] *Le Temps,* May 25, 1888.

Here is perhaps the ideal summation of the Radicals' attitude toward Boulanger. His success, they believed, came from a certain stultification in the Republic, whose leaders (read: the Opportunists) had abandoned their revolutionary vocation. Once the Republic resumed its revolutionary course, the masses, for whom the Radicals had nothing but esteem—in the abstract—would leave Boulanger. So they set out to form latter-day Jacobin clubs in order to revive the spirit of the French Revolution. Proudly, the directors of the *Société* insisted that it was not a vulgar "electoral association," but had been created in order to correct the political and social evils upon which the Boulangist movement fed.[64] This was the long-range approach, and it might have been successful had there been sufficient time to dig at the roots of such problems. But with the general elections less than eighteen months away, an "electoral association" or some other political remedy, however superficial, might have been better suited to the task of combatting Boulanger.

Actually, the *Société* could not have become a mass movement in the sense that Boulanger's was without laying all the political and social evils it opposed before the public. To do so would probably have given only more credibility to the General's claim that the Chamber had to be dissolved. The organization's sole venture in mass propaganda consisted of brochures which accused Boulanger of wanting to become a dictator.[65] By 1888, there was no scarcity of anti-Boulanger literature, which centered its message around two themes: the General had been a bad soldier and a dangerously incompetent War Minister [66]; now he was a mere tool of the

[64] *La Justice,* July 13, 1888.

[65] Société des droits de l'homme et du citoyen, *Le bilan de Boulanger* (Paris: Cusset, 1888), *passim.*

[66] Eugène Tenot, *La vérité sur M. Boulanger militaire* (Paris: Alcan-Lévy, 1888), pp. 15–16.

Right.[67] In so far as such pamphlets were intended to win Boulanger's mass following away from him, they appear to have met with negligible success.

True to its original plans, the *Société des droits de l'homme* devoted its efforts primarily to improving the conditions of the industrial masses. At its general meeting on July 12, Stephen Pichon read the report of the action committee, which had been organized into three sections: finance, propaganda, and political and social studies. To judge from the report, the last of these was by far the most active. It drafted resolutions on workers' demands, which were to be presented to municipal and departmental assemblies. Chief among the reforms it proposed were legal guarantees for adequate safety and hygiene measures in factories and workshops, and a national public health service.[68] By a unanimous vote, the members of the *Société* approved a resolution demanding repeal of the law of March, 1872, which had banned the International Workingmen's Association in France.[69] Another unanimous vote called for the replacement of state-operated employment agencies by union-controlled labor exchanges.[70]

During the strike of construction workers in Paris, the *Société* voted the strikers a contribution of 200 francs—hardly a large sum, but enough to provoke the *République Française* into calling the gesture "an encouragement of demagogy." The sum was only meant to be symbolic of the solidarity felt by the members of the *Société* for the strikers' aims.[71] Limited as it was, this gesture went far beyond the attitude of the Boulangists, who gave the strike little support morally and none materially. For the entire duration of the walkout, which

[67] Ligue républicaine antiplébiscitaire, *La république de M. Boulanger* (Paris: Jules Lévy, 1888), pp. 26–27.

[68] *La Justice,* July 13, 1888.   [69] *Le Radical,* July 31, 1888.

[70] A.N.F., F⁷ 12445, Dec. 22, 1888.

[71] *La Justice,* Aug. 2, 1888.

lasted nearly three weeks, *La Presse* carried only one editorial on the subject. Written by Francis Laur, who had vigorously supported the cause of the Decazeville miners in 1886, the article was devoted entirely to denying Opportunist charges that the Boulangist committee was subsidizing the strike.[72] The General himself made no public statement on the question.

Despite its advanced economic and social policy, the *Société des droits de l'homme* appears to have done Boulanger no real harm, while badly dividing the opposition to him. On learning of that organization's program, Boulanger predicted that it would split the Opportunists and remarked with evident satisfaction: "I hardly expected M. Clemenceau to aid my cause, and I thank him." [73] This prediction was entirely correct: although it included Ranc, the *Société* was shunned by most Opportunists, who considered it too exclusive (only nine hundred members). Worse still, it received no help from the left-wing Radicals in the *Fédération des groupes républicains socialistes*.[74] Nor did the "possibilist" Socialist leaders remain affiliated with the *Société* for long. They left it in August, 1888, under pressure from their party's rank and file, who objected to any collaboration with bourgeois politicians.[75] Even among its own members, the *Société* was plagued by serious division over tactics. Its meeting of December 21, 1888, ended in total deadlock over the question of restoring the single-member constituency.[76] Finally, because it was both anti-Boulangist and progressive, the *Société* made the rank-and-file royalists only more willing to collaborate with Boulanger.[77]

---

[72] *La Presse,* Aug. 11, 1888.   [73] *Le Temps,* May 25, 1888.
[74] A.P.P., B a/99, July 10, 1888.
[75] *Ibid.,* B a/497, Oct., 1888.
[76] A.N.F., F7 12445, Dec. 22, 1888.
[77] A.P.P., B a/976, Aug. 30, 1888.

As long as Floquet was Premier, no attempt was made to dislodge the Conservatives from Boulanger. The government put all its hopes into revision of the constitution as the means of wooing the masses attracted to the General's own revisionist program. But it was in no hurry. On June 2, 1888, Floquet appeared before the parliamentary commission charged with examining proposals for revision and explained the cabinet's stand on the question. All members of the government favored revision, he noted, but they refused to propose it to the Chamber under pressure from dictatorial elements. A bill for revision would probably be introduced at the end of the year.[78] The Premier had good reason not to rush the issue. His problem was that the commission then studying revision had been established by virtually the same Conservative-Radical coalition which overthrew Tirard. Floquet realized that it would take considerable time to muster a truly Republican majority behind his own revision bill.[79] The fact that this task proved to be impossible only justifies his caution.

Several months passed before the government was willing to commit itself to any particular form of constitution. Floquet addressed the Chamber on October 15, not to introduce a bill for revision, but to present the cabinet's views on a new constitution, which was to include the following articles:

A House of Representatives elected by direct universal suffrage, renewable by thirds every two years. This will permit the elimination of the right of dissolution and adjournment.

A Senate chosen by indirect universal suffrage, with special conditions of age and eligibility, authorized to pass on all laws and renewable by thirds every two years at the same time as the House of Representatives.

[78] Charles de Mazade, "Chronique de la quinzaine," *Revue des Deux Mondes,* XC (Nov. 15, 1888), 468.

[79] Raoul Frary, "Chronique politique," *La Nouvelle Revue,* LII (June 15, 1888), 991–992.

Ministers appointed by the President of the Republic for the duration of the period between legislative renewals, but who can be maintained by him in their functions beyond that time. These ministers are responsible to the House of Representatives, which can impeach them before the Senate and which can also demand their dismissal by a formal declaration that they have lost the confidence of the nation.

After reading this outline, Floquet asked for and received the Chamber's approval to refer it to the revision commission.[80] The government thus gained more time.

During his term as Premier, Floquet accomplished very little besides drafting a new constitution. Some anticlerical measures were enacted, such as a law requiring state authorization for religious congregations whose sees were outside of France and the dissolution of the order of Saint Joseph at Cîteaux.[81] In the economic and social field, however, the government's record was blank. On May 15, 1888, the Deputies Hanotaux, Jaurès, Millerand, and Poincaré—representing most segments of Republican opinion—proposed that the Chamber set aside Monday and Tuesday of every week to the discussion of questions in these areas.[82] Although Floquet approved of the proposal, it remained a dead letter.[83] By September, the Interior Ministry warned that many voters were losing confidence in the Chamber because of its inertia in enacting remedial legislation to ease economic hardships, especially to small business.[84] Without attempting to strike at the roots of all social ills, the cabinet would probably have

[80] *J.O.C.* (1888), pp. 2169–2171

[81] Antonin Débidour, *L'Eglise et l'Etat en France sous la Troisième République, 1870–1906* (3 vols.; Paris: Alcan, 1906), I, 393–395.

[82] *Le Radical,* May 17, 1888.

[83] *Année politique,* XV (1888), 25–26.

[84] A.N.F., F⁷ 12445, Sept. 3, 1888.

gained popular esteem by at least taking action on some of the more immediate problems. Instead, it spent many precious months preparing a new constitution.

It is doubtful that Boulanger was giving much thought to constitutional questions, even while proclaiming the dire need for revision. When he appeared before the parliamentary commission studying proposals for constitutional change in October, 1888, his ideas on the subject seemed even more vague and contradictory than during his speech before the Chamber in June. On being asked what kind of regime he foresaw for France, the General replied that he would leave that question for the constituent assembly to decide. As to what sort of constitution he preferred, he answered that he had no preference. Among the constitutional principles he enunciated were these: a Republic without a President. "We might have a committee composed of three or five directors." But if the constituent assembly decided to retain the Presidency, it alone would determine the mode of election. The President was to be "responsible," assured Boulanger. "The Assembly may, if necessary, depose the chief executive." But the executive branch must be fortified; it must not be subordinate to the legislature. The legislature, in turn, should be unicameral, the Senate no longer being necessary.[85] Just how the chief executive was to become stronger while being "responsible" to a unicameral legislature, which "may depose him," the General did not bother to explain.

Revision of the constitution was not the sole, or even the prime, reason for Boulanger's success. Before the Comte de Paris issued his manifesto of September, 1887, hardly anyone save a few dissident Jacobin leftists even discussed the question. By August, 1888, Boulanger's pronouncements on revi-

[85] Auguste Boucher, "Chronique politique," *Le Correspondant*, CIII (Nov. 10, 1888), 583.

sion were far more elaborate than they had been in April, yet his showing in the second by-election of the Nord was less impressive than it had been in the first. One reason for the General's continued good fortune was that his success fed upon itself: the more votes he won, the more he tended to attract. Starting out with a small circle of left-wing revisionists, he gained the support of the Bonapartists. Thanks in part to their favor, he won in the Dordogne and thereupon secured the backing of the Orleanists. Following his threefold victory of August, 1888, Boulanger enjoyed the following of many peripheral movements, whose leaders hoped to reap some benefit by their association with him. While not directly related to the Boulangist movement, the peripheral groups did, at least temporarily, add to the General's apparent strength.

8

The Peripheral Movements
1888-1889

~~~~~~

"Boulangism," noted Raoul Frary in the fall of 1888, "is a river with many tributaries." Using the term "Boulangism" to define all the varied elements that actually voted for the General, Frary recalled that Boulanger had won his early following as a War Minister active in the renovation of France. Other voters remembered him especially for having expelled the princes from the army; still others preferred to see him as the chief enemy of the Opportunists, if not of parliamentary government itself. Part of the electorate favored Boulanger in the hope that he would destroy the Republic, while another group expected him to re-establish it even more firmly. Wherever there were economic and social problems—for the capitalist, worker, or farmer—Boulanger could expect votes.[1] During the entire Boulanger affair, virtually every politician or journalist regarded the sum total of the General's following as "Boulangism," regardless of its source.

Those who voted for Boulanger were not all Boulangists, however. Contemporary observers generally agreed that only the dissident leftists who, for economic or ideological motives,

[1] Raoul Frary, "Chronique politique," *La Nouvelle Revue,* LIV (Sept. 15, 1888), 424.

favored the General as a means of obtaining revision of the constitution merited that label. Only their political philosophy —its contradictions momentarily obscured in a common desire for unity—can truly be called Boulangism. It was a philosophy shared by only a small portion of the French electorate and rarely invoked by the General himself, who was not by personal conviction a Boulangist. His belated conversion to revision of the constitution was in large measure a device to ensure the support of political elements outside Boulangism. It came only after the General's staggered plebiscite had already been launched. To the hard-core Boulangists in the so-called "National Committee," this was a minor fault; they did not look to Boulanger for his political convictions (if indeed he ever had any), but because he could get votes.[2] It was this quality which also recommended him to the fringe groups.

SOCIALISM

Disorganized and divided into several conflicting factions, French socialism of this period was obliged to remain on the sidelines of politics. From this position, the Socialists took little interest in Boulanger until his brilliant performance in the Aisne on March 25, 1888. That event split the Socialist groups still further as to what attitude to adopt toward the General and his political campaign. The so-called "possibilist" faction was quick to issue a warning to workers that Boulanger, who as a colonel had helped repress the Commune, would easily develop into another Cavaignac or Napoleon III unless he were checked. A group of possibilists, headed by Allemane, then left *Le Cri du Peuple* because of its relative sympathy toward the General and on April 8 founded a resolutely anti-Boulanger organ called *Le Parti Ouvrier*. In one of its first

[2] Mermeix [Gabriel Terrail], *Les coulisses du boulangisme* (Paris: Cerf, 1890), pp. 236–239.

issues, the new paper published the words to a song entitled: "We can well do without Boulanger." [3] At an anti-Boulanger rally, organized by the possibilists and attended by three to four hundred persons, one speaker drew loud cheers by suggesting that the government have the General tried before a war council and shot. [4]

Such bitter feelings were the exception, however. Boulanger's impressive victory in the Nord on April 15 won him the admiration of several Blanquists, who began to see in him the harbinger of their revolution. "Boulanger has been elected by national discontent," asserted Jacques Dest. "Whether he likes it or not, the General is now committed to the irresistible movement which is carrying our modern society toward a more perfect and more just organization." [5] It is not surprising that many Socialists were attracted to the General's politics. Their economic principles were in many ways similar to those of the more advanced economic thinkers in the Boulangist movement. As Jaurès noted in 1889, the quasi-socialism of some Boulangist leaders appealed to many "pure" Socialists. The Socialists also shared with the Boulangists an undying hatred of Ferry. [6]

At first, the Blanquist leaders decided that a position of neutrality between Boulanger and his enemies would best serve their cause. Séverine gave the word on the spring of 1888:

We are witnessing at this moment a curious duel between the Opportunists and the Boulangists: the former have power on their

[3] Alexandre Zévaès, *Au temps du boulangisme* (Paris: Gallimard, 1930), pp. 103–105.

[4] A.N.F., F⁷ 12445, April 25, 1888.

[5] *Le Cri du Peuple*, April 18, 1888.

[6] Maurice Dommanget, *Edouard Vaillant: Un grand socialiste* (Paris: La Table Ronde, 1956), pp. 90–92.

side; the latter, the crowd. In my humble opinion, there is no need for us either to ally ourselves with M. Ferry or to become the vassals of M. Boulanger; the Socialist party may cross its arms, remain an onlooker, and await the outcome of the struggle before reaping the benefits.[7]

The formation of the *Société des droits de l'homme,* with initial possibilist participation, encouraged the Blanquists in their neutrality. Referring to the rue Cadet, where the *Société* had held its first open meeting, Vaillant told his followers on June 2: "We shall be neither Caesarians nor Cadetists, simply Socialists; that is enough." At the party congress at Amiens on July 29, he persuaded the delegates to urge that Socialist voters abstain in elections where no Socialist candidate was entered.[8]

As Boulanger continued to increase his influence over the masses, the Blanquists gradually abandoned neutrality as a way of dealing with his popular movement. Although they favored revision of the constitution, they expected it to take place within the larger context of integral social change. When the General presented his plan for revision to the Chamber, Séverine expressed bitter pessimism. What could a new constitution do for the poor and the unemployed? It was just "another sonorous and empty word . . . a pretext for the rabble rousers—nothing for the poor and the underprivileged." [9] Vaillant elaborated on this theme in an address to his constituents of the Père Lachaise district, which he represented in the Paris city council. A new paper constitution, he told them on October 13, would mean nothing, being—like all its predecessors—of bourgeois origin. Only when the people took the

[7] Séverine [Caroline Rémy Guebhard], *Notes d'une frondeuse de la Boulange au Panama* (Paris: Empis, 1894), p. 27.

[8] Dommanget, *op. cit.,* p. 93.

[9] *Le Cri du Peuple,* June 8, 1888.

reins of government would the question of revision assume any real importance.[10] The General's proposed revision was just as reactionary as that of Floquet, charged Vaillant.[11] "M. Boulanger can stuff his speeches with Republican declarations as much as he likes; that does not affect us, any more than do his intentions." [12] The Blanquists were soon to present a candidate of their own against Boulanger in Paris.

Among the Marxists, opinion was sharply divided as to how to deal with the Boulangist movement. From London on July 15, 1888, Engels wrote to Paul Lafargue, Marx's son-in-law, that he considered the General's success at the polls merely "another form of Bonapartism." Now that Boulanger had lost a duel to Floquet, Engels looked forward to the former's imminent political demise.[13] His hopes unfulfilled, Engels became alarmed over Boulanger's by-election victory in Paris on January 27, 1889. "To put it mildly, Paris has, at least temporarily, abdicated as a revolutionary city," he wrote on February 4. German Marxists, he reported, were convinced that Boulanger was a future dictator of the Right.[14] What these Marxists were really admitting tacitly was that their deterministic ideology could not explain the Boulangist phenomenon. Inasmuch as Boulanger did not belong to *their* Left, they immediately classified him as a rightist.

In France, the General's leading Marxist adversary was Jules Guesde, who had campaigned against him from the very start of his plebiscite. When Boulanger was a candidate in the first by-election in the Nord, Guesde visited the department and asked everyone who opposed both Boulanger and his

[10] A.N.F., F⁷ 12445, Oct. 14, 1888.

[11] *Le Cri du Peuple*, Oct. 8, 1888.   [12] *Ibid.*, Dec. 6, 1888.

[13] Friedrich Engels and Paul and Laura Lafargue, *Correspondance* (3 vols.; Paris: Editions Sociales, 1956), II, 150.

[14] *Ibid.*, p. 209.

rivals to vote for the General's horse! Ballots printed with the horse's name, Tunis, were duly printed, and a few hundred voters actually cast them; but the reputation of Boulanger did not suffer from this attack.[15]

To Paul Lafargue, it seemed futile to oppose Boulanger once he had amassed such a broad following. At first, Lafargue simply expressed satisfaction that the General was causing so much difficulty for the Opportunists and the Radicals.[16] In a letter to Engels of April 24, 1888, Lafargue explained that the Socialists had nothing to fear from the General's mass following. "Boulanger is the man of the people in opposition to Ferry, Clemenceau, and the parliamentarians," he insisted. As a man of the people, Boulanger was in no danger of becoming a dictator, as foreign Socialists claimed. "With the people, he does not have the elements of a *coup d'état,* but of a revolution." [17] It was only a step from this opinion to urging that the Socialists use Boulanger to accomplish their revolution. Lafargue took this step after the General's three victories in August; on October 15, he wrote to Engels:

It is not we, but the Radicals who have created Boulanger; we cannot undo him, for the more he is attacked, the more powerful he becomes. But we can use him; and we would be very stupid to follow the Radicals' lead, as the possibilists have done, only to lose favor with the public.[18]

Actually, the kind of alliance of convenience suggested by Lafargue was sealed formally between Boulangists and So-

---

[15] *Ibid.,* p. 185.   [16] *L'Intransigeant,* May 1, 1888.
[17] Engels and Lafargue *op. cit.,* II, 123–124.
[18] *Ibid.,* p. 174.

cialists in only one part of France: Bordeaux. Raymond Lavigne wrote to Guesde on July 8, 1889, that before Boulanger's victory in Paris, he had hoped that the Socialists could wage their political battles in Bordeaux alone. Since then, however, the pro-Boulanger current in that southern city had grown so powerful that the Socialists decided to ride along with it.[19] They did, electing three of their number as Boulangists in the general elections of 1889. One of these was Henri Aimel, a friend of Rochefort, who called himself a "Socialist intransigent." In a newspaper article entitled "Boulanger's Nose," Aimel explained that for himself and other members of his faction, revision of the constitution was a prerequisite to any meaningful reforms. So they were going to ally themselves with the party most likely to accomplish revision, without questioning that party's credentials. "What does Boulanger's nose mean to us?" asked Aimel.[20] Neither his "nose" nor his methods prevented the Socialists in Bordeaux from collaborating with his organization in the hopes of achieving their own ends.

Like Aimel, Benoît Malon viewed revision of the constitution as being necessary for the realization of reforms in the economic and social spheres. He therefore welcomed Boulanger's electoral successes as a step in the direction of such reforms.[21] Now that certain Socialists had joined the mixed bag of dissident Radicals, royalists, and Bonapartists already clamoring for revision, Raoul Frary could write with some justification: "Revision looks a bit like a lottery in which

[19] Amsterdam, International Institute of Social History, Guesde Archives, 1889 (document graciously furnished by Mr. Thomas Moodie).

[20] *La France de Bordeaux,* June 23, 1889.

[21] Benoît Malon and Eugène Fournière, "Physiologie du boulangisme," *Revue Socialiste,* VII (May, 1888), 508.

several participants look forward to the drawing because each one is sure of holding the winning number." [22] Like the other factions associated with Boulanger, these Socialists were convinced that his success in the elections of 1889 would benefit their cause.

In face of the rising Boulangist tide, many individual Socialist voters were content to let the end justify the means and supported the General, even when their party leaders did not approve. Despite the steadfast opposition of Guesde, about two-thirds of his faction's delegates in Paris voted, late in September, 1888, to favor Boulanger should he decide to run in a by-election there.[23] Just how many Socialists joined Boulangist committees cannot be determined, but their presence was certainly welcome. At a Boulangist rally held in Paris on December 19, 1888, a speaker from the Cher named Garnier drew loud applause when he predicted, "We shall bore the hole through which Socialism will pass!" [24] Like the royalists and Bonapartists, many Socialists saw Boulanger as a battering ram against the regime.

ANTISEMITISM

Even more than the Socialists, French antisemites were attracted to the Boulangist movement, although they did not find a secure place in it. Like Boulangism, French antisemitism in this period was primarily a movement of the Left. The early secular antisemites condemned Judaism as the parent religion of Christianity, just as they accused the Jews of monopolizing high finance. Conversely, many Socialists were drawn into an anti-Jewish position as a result of their attacks

[22] Raoul Frary, "Chronique politique," *La Nouvelle Revue,* LII (June 15, 1888), 994.

[23] A.N.F., F⁷ 12445, Oct. 2, 1888.   [24] *Ibid.,* Dec. 20, 1888.

on monopoly.[25] The antisemitic utterances of Auguste Chirac were published in installments in the *Revue Socialiste,* which gave a favorable criticism to Edouard Drumont's vicious tract, *La France juive.*[26]

For the bulk of the Paris proletariat, unable to understand all the elaborate economic reasoning of the Socialist intellectuals, it was far easier to blame one's misery on the Jews. Populist Jew-baiting found a ready platform in *La Cocarde,* which regularly ridiculed the Jews' religious practices and cast doubts on their patriotism.[27] When Boulanger was released from active duty in the army, the journal claimed that German (!) Jews in France rejoiced and sent stock prices soaring.[28] A similar line was taken by Lucien Nicot, who was to run as a Boulangist in Paris in the 1889 general elections. As part of a polemic against German immigration into France, Nicot reserved a special tirade for what he called "the crowd of German Jewish financiers who run the Bourse and the banks." [29] The presence in Paris of many Alsatian Jews, who were often mistaken for Germans, lent credence to the charge that a wealthy German-Jewish fifth column was operating in France. Thus, the same leftist nationalism which prompted the Parisian masses to favor Boulanger also seems to have encouraged their hatred of the Jews.

In the official Boulangist committee, which continually refused to recognize the authority of *La Cocarde,* antisemitism

[25] Zosa Szajkowski, *Anti-Semitism in the French Labor Movement* (New York: S. Frydman, 1948), pp. 154–156; Cf. Robert F. Byrnes, *Antisemitism in Modern France* (New Brunswick, N.J.: Rutgers University Press, 1950), pp. 114 ff.

[26] A. Regnard, "Aryens et Sémites: Le bilan du Christianisme et du Judaïsme," *Revue Socialiste,* V (June, 1887), 499–515.

[27] Cf. "Les Juifs de Paris," *La Cocarde,* July 1, 1888.

[28] *La Cocarde,* March 16, 1888.

[29] Lucien Nicot, *L'Allemagne à Paris* (Paris: Dentu, 1887), p. 63.

received no hearing until 1889. The committee's dominant member was Naquet, who, though a confirmed atheist, never denied his Jewish origins and refused collaboration with anti-semites.[30] Another partisan of the General was Arthur Meyer, the son of an Alsatian rabbi and a convert to Catholi-cism. Although Meyer later became a militant anti-Dreyfusard and joined the *Action Française,* he also fought a duel with and wounded Edouard Drumont, the leading antisemite in France.[31] Meyer's royalist journal was well disposed toward the Jews, and it is doubtful that he would have appreciated an alliance between the Boulangists and the rabble-rousing anti-semites.

Another factor which influenced Boulanger not to seek a following among the Jew-baiters was the fact that several of the contributors to his campaign fund were Jewish. Foremost among these were the Baron de Hirsh and the Péreire brothers.[32] Even the Jews in the world of finance who op-posed Boulanger were not eager to antagonize him. During the campaign leading to the by-election in Paris of January 27, 1889, the French branch of the Rothschilds expressed confidence that Boulanger would lose, but they wisely did not aid his rival. Immediately before the election, Dillon asked the leading financiers of Paris, many of whom were Jewish, not to sell after the by-election if Boulanger won. At a time when German "bears" were unloading stock on the pretext that a victory for the General would precipitate a war, the French financiers received Dillon cordially. Neither they nor the gov-ernment desired a crash. On January 28, 1889, the house of

[30] Mermeix [Gabriel Terrail], *Les antisémites en France* (Paris: Dentu, 1892), p. 41.

[31] Lucien Corpechot, *Souvenirs d'un journaliste* (Paris: Plon, 1936), pp. 97–100.

[32] A.P.P., B a/974, Jan. 21 and Feb. 18, 1889.

Rothschild and its associates in the *Haute Banque* let the market alone; at the close of the day's trading, it had fallen by only twenty centimes.[33]

Boulanger's own coolness toward antisemitism did not change following the rise to prominence of Edouard Drumont, who did more than anyone else in France to make vilification of the Jews respectable. Prior to Drumont, the leading French antisemite had been a renegade Socialist, who was gradually moving to the Right, named Auguste Chirac. For Chirac, Boulanger was simply the incarnation of what he called "bourgeois chauvinism." [34] He saw the General as being completely surrounded by Jewish financiers and wanted nothing to do with him.[35] Drumont, on the other hand, differed from Chirac by combining populist Jew-baiting with praise of France's noble and Christian values, which he claimed were being perverted by the Jews. With such arguments, Drumont convinced much of France's stagnant aristocracy that the Jews were to blame for its relative decline in an increasingly commercial age. Drumont's best-selling book, *La France juive,* appeared only three months after Boulanger became War Minister. Since both men achieved, in their respective fields, an apparent reconciliation of the Right and Left, their careers present a curious parallel.[36]

Writing late in 1888, Drumont placed his greatest hopes in Boulanger to restore French civilization to what he called its pre-Jewish integrity. "Of all the available pretenders," he predicted, "the only one who has any chance of success is Boulanger." Yet Drumont refused to seek a place in the Boulangist organization (assuming that it would accept him) on the

[33] Mermeix, *Les antisémites,* pp. 44–46.

[34] Auguste Chirac, *L'agiotage sous la Troisième République, 1870–1887* (2 vols.; Paris: Savine, 1889), II, 166.

[35] *Ibid.,* p. 305.   [36] Byrnes, *op. cit.,* p. 137.

grounds that it was being run by Jews and freemasons. If the General could only shake himself free of them, Drumont was certain that he would win power. Because of Jewish influence, French society had become so decadent that even the royalists and the Bonapartists now lacked the courage to seize control from the country's Jewish overlords.[37] While hoping that Boulanger was brave enough to face his responsibilities, Drumont occasionally had doubts. He especially reproached the former War Minister for not having marched on the Elysée from the Gare de Lyon.[38]

By this reproach, Drumont drew a clear distinction between himself and the General's patrons. Except for Thiébaud and possibly Dillon, none of the members of the National Committee wanted Boulanger to become a dictator. The royalists and Bonapartists had no such desire, since they expected the General to prepare the way for their respective claimants. When Boulanger failed both to stage a *coup d'état* in 1887 and, later, to win office by democratic means, Drumont not unnaturally blamed the whole fiasco on the Jews. "How did this once obscure general rise to such heights that he nearly became the master of France?" he asked rhetorically. "He was promoted by a Jewish syndicate; that explains everything." [39] After such a simple explanation, one might suppose that Drumont would have rejoiced in the knowledge that a Jewish puppet had been foiled. But no! In virtually the next breath he asserted that the General was defeated because Rothschild had put his riches at the disposal of the government.[40] Presumably, the Jews were so powerful that they could create

[37] Edouard Drumont, *La fin d'un monde* (Paris: Savine, 1889), pp. 312–313.

[38] *Ibid.*, pp. 316–317.

[39] Edouard Drumont, *La dernière bataille* (Paris: Dentu, 1890), p. 163.

[40] *Ibid.*, p. 182.

Boulanger with one hand and destroy him with the other. Like many Socialists, Drumont believed momentarily that Boulanger's success could help his particular cause. Despite the General's personal opposition to the antisemites, some members of his committee were eager to meet them half way and began to seek their votes in 1889. During the January campaign in Paris, Maurice Vergoin made a violent speech against the Jews at a pro-Boulanger rally. Immediately afterward, a Jewish delegation visited the General and asked him if Vergoin spoke on his own account or for the party. Boulanger assured them with all his customary charm that Vergoin's speech was purely personal and that the Jews, like all other Frenchmen, had nothing to fear if he, Boulanger, won. On the contrary, the forthcoming "National Republic" would be open to all Frenchmen, regardless of religion. So the Jewish delegation left, apparently convinced of the candidate's sincerity. A few days later, however, Drumont announced to the press that on election Sunday he would go directly from mass to vote for Boulanger. Thus warned, the Jews of Paris appear to have voted as a bloc for the General's adversary. The third *arrondissement,* which had the capital's largest Jewish population, was the only one in which Boulanger failed to win a majority.[41]

As long as Boulanger was doing well politically, he did not need the support of the antisemites, who carried even less political weight than the Socialists and lacked a party organization. In the general elections of 1889, the antisemites presented their first candidate, a commercial artist named Willette, in the ninth *arrondissement* of Paris. He attacked both Opportunists and Radicals as puppets of the Jews, but reserved his heaviest barrage for Boulanger, whose success, he charged, was due entirely to Jewish funds. Willette received

[41] Mermeix, *Les antisémites,* pp. 43–44.

only a few hundred votes, not enough to hurt Boulanger polit-ically.[42] The elections' overall results, however, marked the end of the Boulangist movement as a national force.

It was the Boulangists' relative failure in the general elec-tions of 1889 that drew several members of the "National Committee" closer to the antisemites. Overnight, the General lost his royalist and Bonapartist allies, Arthur Meyer's support, and almost all his income, some of which had been contributed by Jews. Only the hard-core Boulangists remained; and now that the General was in exile, they were increasingly difficult to control. Never really hostile to the antisemites, the National Committee's Gentile majority eagerly sought whatever allies were now available. When Francis Laur, whose election as Deputy had been invalidated, sought to regain his seat in the Chamber, he openly accepted aid, both financial and political, from antisemitic circles. During a rally at Neuilly on January 18, 1890, Laur appeared on the same platform with the anti-semitic Marquis de Morès and launched into a bitter diatribe against Jews. Minutes later, his outcry was echoed by Déroulède, Laisant, and Susini.[43] Naquet immediately wrote to Boulanger, threatening to resign, and was persuaded to stay on only by the General's assurance that he had objected to Laur's speech before its delivery.[44]

After winning the election, Laur asked Boulanger to approve a formal alliance between Boulangist and antisemitic candidates in the Paris municipal elections, which were to take place on April 27 and May 4, 1890. Although the General would not allow any antisemitic candidates to campaign under

[42] Jean de Ligneau [François Bournand], *Juifs et antisémites en Europe* (Paris: Tolra, 1891), pp. 67–91.

[43] Raphaël Viau, *Vingt ans d'antisémitisme, 1889–1909* (Paris: Charpentier, 1910), pp. 14–16.

[44] Bibliothèque Nationale, N.A.F. 23783, no. 34, Jan. 22, 1890.

his name, there was *de facto* collaboration, similar to the kind formerly practiced with the Conservatives.[45] This time, neither party to the *entente* drew any benefit from it. The antisemitic candidates, Drumont and Morès, won barely six hundred and one hundred votes, respectively.[46] For the Boulangists, only two of whom were elected, there was no further hope. Their alliance with the antisemites had been an act of desperation; when it failed, they disbanded.

AMERICANISM

Americanism was more than a movement; it was a state of mind. In the late nineteenth century, Frenchmen of all parties seemed to view the United States as the principal source of everything liberal and progressive. A few years after the Boulanger affair, Pope Leo XIII was obliged to condemn a typically French heresy known as "Americanism," which had come to mean the relaxation of all hierarchical control over dogma. It was based on a misconception that, because the church in the United States accepted religious pluralism in practice, it must necessarily accept pluralism in the field of church dogma.[47] In reality, few Catholics—clergy or laity— were more inflexible on doctrinal questions than the Americans. The mere fact that such a misconception could arise indicates that when advanced elements in France wished to justify their own projects, they cited American precedent, real or imagined.

For the so-called "advanced Republicans" who supported

[45] Maurice Barrès, *L'appel au soldat* (Paris: Juven, 1911), pp. 225–228.

[46] Gabriel Monod, "French Affairs," *Contemporary Review*, LVIII (July, 1890), 22–23.

[47] Adrien Dansette, *Histoire religieuse de la France contemporaine* (2 vols.; Paris: Flammarion, 1951), II, 228–232.

General Boulanger, the United States held much the same mystical authority as for liberal Catholics. Not the least of the qualities which recommended Boulanger to his partisans was the fact that he had represented the French War Ministry at the ceremonies held in Washington in 1881 to mark the centennial of the battle of Yorktown. On his own accession to the post of War Minister, Boulanger replaced most of the Ministry's civilian employees with men of his own choosing. This move won high praise from Rochefort's newspaper, which compared it to supposed American practice. "In America," it explained, "when a new President is elected, his first duty is to replace all civil servants, high and low, who served the government of his predecessor." [48] A year after Boulanger himself was replaced as War Minister, Rochefort castigated "those suspicious Deputies, who would probably have dismissed Washington in order to prevent him from defeating the English at Yorktown." [49] Once he entered politics, Boulanger was called "the George Washington of France" by his more enthusiastic partisans. [50]

It was in the field of constitutional revision that the American example was cited most frequently. The United States Constitution, which was nearly a hundred years old when Boulanger began his staggered plebiscite, was widely revered among French Republicans, especially of the Left. To these critics of their own country's weak executive, the American Presidency was far more attractive. Proposing an American-type President for France, however, would have run counter to an established Republican prejudice against strong rulers. To avoid charges of attempting to create a dictatorship, Naquet proposed a directory as an alternative to a strong President. The important thing, he argued, was that France's new

[48] *L'Intransigeant,* Jan. 12, 1886.   [49] *Ibid.,* March 23, 1888.
[50] *Le Clairon,* March 26, 1889.

constitution provide for separation of powers as in the United States. Only this solution would avoid the Scylla of one-man rule and the Charybdis of legislative omnipotence.[51]

Louis de Belleval, who was elected Deputy from Sceaux as a Boulangist in 1889, averted the problem of a one-man or committee-type executive simply by not discussing it. He did insist, however, that the present system, by which governments succeeded one another without consulting the people, be eliminated. "In the United States," he asserted, "as soon as the results of the general elections are known, everyone knows who the ministers will be. At the same time, one can be certain that they will stay in power for four years."[52] Actually, of course, none of this is true. There are no general elections in the United States by which ministers are chosen to rule. Nor is it certain that American cabinet members will enjoy the same uninterrupted term of office as the President. Rather, Belleval's simplistic view of the American Constitution illustrates how French critics of the 1875 laws projected their own ideas on existing American reality.

More sophisticated remedies to France's political ills included not only constitutional, but political changes as well. Here too, the United States was often cited as a model. When Portalis, the publisher of *Le XIXe Siècle,* suggested that his country simply adopt the American Constitution without any modifications, *La Cocarde* offered some cogent qualifications. In an unsigned editorial, the paper noted that the success of the United States Constitution was due less to the text itself than to the federal system in which it operated and to the public spirit of the American people. "With the organically democratic, federalistic institutions which contribute to the

[51] *La Presse,* Oct. 20, 1888.
[52] Louis de Belleval, *Le complot contre le suffrage universel* (Paris: Rousseau, 1888), p. 10.

greatness of the American republic, the freedom and the strength of its people . . . all regimes—even parliamentary —would be, if not good, at least acceptable." [53] Although the Boulangists never publicly admitted that the parliamentary system might be made to work, they promised that American political mores as well as the American Constitution would serve as the foundation of their new regime. As Boulanger himself assured French voters: "It is the application of America's great freedom which is advocated by the National Republican Party." [54]

Boulanger even went as far as to seek the sympathy of Americans for his revisionist program. In a press statement for release in the United States he argued that France's existing constitution, based as it was on a hybrid English model, was unsuited to the French character. He hoped instead to make his country's political institutions correspond to those of America. Such plans, however, found little favor in the United States, where it was noted that the American Constitution itself was based largely on supposed English precedent.[55] The General's proposal for revision, laid before the Chamber on June 4, 1888, was sneered at as an "elaborate and barren statement" by one American journalist.[56] Criticism from the United States did not, however, prevent the Boulangists from claiming American inspiration for their political projects.

Admiration of the American system was by no means limited to Boulanger's party. Before the General entered politics, even moderate Republicans had been known to make comparisons of French and American politics to the detriment of the former. One such critic proposed giving the French executive greater freedom in foreign affairs, but did not feel that any

[53] *La Cocarde,* June 12, 1888.
[54] *L'Intransigeant,* April 2, 1889.
[55] *New York Herald,* April 30, 1888. [56] *Ibid.,* June 15, 1888.

change in the constitution was necessary.[57] Once Boulanger openly favored revision, the Radicals tried to outdo him in offering a solution based on American precedent. No better example of Americanism in this period can be found than in the outline of a proposed constitution which Floquet submitted to the Chamber on October 15, 1888. With its Senate and House of Representatives renewable by thirds every two years and its cabinet ministers appointed by the President, this imaginary regime drew heavily on both the experience and the prestige of the United States.[58]

Once emulation of American practice became associated with revision, the Opportunists began to cast doubt on such practice. The party's chief organ did so, rather timidly, by noting that Boulanger had spent only a short time in the United States, during which he lacked the opportunity to study the American system thoroughly. Despite its many fine qualities, the United States Constitution was not suited to France. The paper expressed anger, moreover, that the General was trying to "Americanize" his own country. As if to emphasize its point on the defects of American methods, the journal published on the same page an article entitled: "Democracy in the United States." Here was told the shocking story of how, in American election campaigns, votes were actually bought out of enormous party funds.[59] The implication was clear that Boulanger was intent on perpetrating similar frauds in France.

Without really buying votes, the General was able to win many votes as a result of the tremendous campaign funds at his disposal. Here too, American influence played a role. Dillon used his business connections to solicit contributions from

---

[57] E. Masseras, "Nos essais parlementaires et la constitution américaine," *La Nouvelle Revue*, XLV (April 15, 1887), 657–660.
[58] Cf. *supra*, pp. 163–164.
[59] *La République Française*, Feb. 11, 1889.

the American cable magnate Mackay, who responded with two checks of 400,000 francs in mid-August, 1888.[60] More funds came from James Gordon Bennett, a business associate of Mackay and publisher of the *New York Herald,* who reportedly promised to help create a new French newspaper favorable to Boulanger if the latter's party won in the 1889 elections.[61] Whatever the extent of Bennett's financial commitments to the General, his paper was openly anti-Boulangist until the triple by-election victory of August, 1888, whereupon it assumed a posture of strict neutrality. Following the Boulangists' massive defeat in the fall of 1889, however, the American journal did not hesitate to express its immense satisfaction.[62] Although by far the greater part of the General's campaign contributions came from French royalist sources, his opponents made occasional references to his "American and English sponsors" in order to cast doubt on his patriotism.[63]

More than money, Boulanger owed much of his electoral methods to American example. His middle-class and aristocratic critics accused him of vulgarity because he resorted to modern advertising techniques in his appeal to the masses. "For the first time," lamented Gabriel Monod, "we see politics degraded into a commercial enterprise, an enterprise of puffs and quackery." [64] Thanks in part to his American-style publicity, Boulanger was able to mobilize the support of what Séverine derisively called "that irresolute and floating mass . . . which can be found wherever a rumpus is being raised. . . . But that is the mob; it is not the people!" [65]

[60] A.P.P., B a/977, Aug. 22, 1888.
[61] *Ibid.,* B a/974, Jan. 20, 1889.
[62] *New York Herald,* Oct. 7, 1889.
[63] *La Lanterne,* April 19, 1889.
[64] Gabriel Monod, "Contemporary Life and Thought in France," *Contemporary Review,* LII (June, 1888), 910.
[65] Séverine, *op. cit.,* pp. 12–13.

On the French Left, it was not uncommon to distinguish between an idealized conception of "the people," who were expected to vote for leftist candidates, and the grim reality of "the mob," which voted otherwise. "Like the *Société des droits de l'homme,* which refused to engage in electoral activity, Séverine boasted: "We are not politicians." [66] But Boulanger was. The potential danger lay not in his use of American methods, but in his attacks on France's political system. In the United States, both the Constitution and the essential party structure are generally unquestioned both before and after each election. Boulanger campaigned outside the basic political framework of his country. His American-inspired appeal for votes had, therefore, a far more disruptive effect than if he had respected the system.[67] His chief accomplishment, one which failed to survive him, was to have created in France a mass movement along modern lines. Nowhere was his success greater than in Paris.

[66] *Ibid.,* p. 27.

[67] Raoul Frary, "Chronique politique," *La Nouvelle Revue,* LIV (Sept. 1, 1888.), 193.

9

Triumph in Paris

1889

More than any other part of France, the city of Paris was greatly cherished by Republicans and especially by the Radicals. A commercial and administrative as well as industrial center, the capital had traditionally been the cradle of democratic revolution; more recently, it had voted heavily for the Radicals in the general elections of 1885. That party therefore considered Paris its rightful stronghold. When Boulanger won his stunning victory in the Nord on April 15, 1888, the Radicals boasted that he could never be elected in the capital. The Parisians, they claimed, were too democratic to be taken in by the demagogy of a general on horseback.

On learning of the Radicals' boast, Henri Rochefort sent them a challenge: the Radicals of Paris were to draw up a slate of candidates there to be opposed by one of what he called "socialist republicans," endorsing Boulanger's platform of revision and dissolution. The Radical Deputies in the capital were then to resign, thereby precipitating new by-elections. This would settle the issue once and for all, said Rochefort.[1] Not unnaturally, the Radical Deputies were loath to put their hard-won seats to an unnecessary test. Only Anatole de la

[1] *L'Intransigeant*, April 26, 1888.

Forge accepted Rochefort's challenge by offering to resign his seat in the Chamber and face Boulanger himself in the ensuing by-election. He made his resignation subject to two conditions, however: the General must agree to participate in open debates with him and must, before the campaign, state his views in detail on all the important political, economic, and social questions of the day. Rochefort rejected la Forge's offer with the rather lame excuse that the election should be a contest of programs, not personalities. More to the point was the fact that Boulanger had recently promised his constituents in the Nord that he would represent them faithfully.[2]

These matters rested until after the General's threefold triumph of August 19, by which he clearly demonstrated his intent to seek a plebiscite. Now Rochefort called for a single by-election in the capital with Boulanger as one of the candidates. He first asked the Radical Deputy, Sigismond Lacroix, to resign, but without success.[3] Next, he requested the Minister of the Interior to force the resignation of Villeneuve, who had long been confined to a sanatorium. Here again, his request was refused.[4]

By the fall of 1888, Boulanger's election in Paris had become a leading aim of his lieutenants. During his second campaign in the Nord, he had promised to remain a Deputy from that department only as long as no vacancy existed in Paris. Early in December, 1888, Naquet predicted that should such a vacancy appear, "the General is certain to be elected by a formidable majority." [5] There was good reason for confidence. Nowhere was the Boulangist movement—its local committees and propaganda—better organized than in the capital. The General had enjoyed a large following in Paris ever since his days as War Minister, and his leading spokes-

2 *Ibid.,* April 28, 1888.　　3 *Ibid.,* Aug. 23, 1888.
4 *Ibid.,* Oct. 26, 1888.　　5 *La Presse,* Dec. 8, 1888.

men in the Chamber had been elected there. The Boulangist Deputies were convinced, moreover, that their party presented to the Paris proletariat an image of pure and sincere Republicanism. They were given ample opportunity to prove their devotion to the Republic in the by-election held in the Ardennes on December 9, 1888.

THE ARDENNES ELECTION

Traditionally Republican, the department of the Ardennes had elected a full slate of Republican Deputies in the general elections of 1885. One of the defeated Conservative candidates was Georges Thiébaud, who blamed his loss on royalist control of the department's Conservative organization. In the eastern regions of France, Thiébaud argued, the royalists could not hope to win majorities because of the militant patriotism of the inhabitants. Disregarding Boulanger's earlier pledge not to resign from the Nord unless a vacancy appeared in Paris, Thiébaud tried to enter the General in the Ardennes by-election. Boulanger was saved the painful choice between accepting this candidacy and keeping his promise to his constituents of the Nord by the royalists' decision to present their own candidate.[6] Their nomination went to Jules Auffray, an Orleanist who had been badly defeated in 1885 on the Conservative list for the Seine-et-Oise.

As candidate in the Ardennes, Auffray did his best to imitate Boulanger's style. Attacking "the constitution of 1875, which rivets France to a bastard parliamentarism," he invited all voters—monarchists, Bonapartists, and Republicans—to support his so-called "program of patriotic union." This program, he predicted, would soon be adopted by all of France. "It has already brought success to all who have adopted it. It is the reason behind General Boulanger's triumphal elec-

[6] *La Cocarde,* Dec. 12, 1888.

tions." [7] Since revision had brought success to Boulanger, Auffray reasoned, could it not bring success to him? In this opportunistic vein, the Orleanist tried to conceal his true identity by running as a "revisionist candidate." [8]

At first, Auffray's tactic seemed to work well, since *La Presse* informally favored his candidacy. What he did not foresee was opposition from within the Boulangist committee. Henri Michelin, who had always been the committee's most idealistic member, called a special meeting at which he obliged his colleagues to withdraw their endorsement of Auffray unless the latter declared himself to be a Republican.[9] In the absence of such a declaration, Georges Laguerre issued a statement for the committee, saying that Auffray's candidacy was purely personal and did not have the support of the National Committee. "M. Auffray has not adopted the Republican formula; he uses the label *Revisionist,* but that is not enough for us." [10]

To make sure that there was no misunderstanding as to the Committee's position, Naquet published a warning against collaboration between Boulangists and Conservatives. He saw a great danger in the tactics of royalists and Bonapartists, who "are trying to use the General, in spite of himself, to assure themselves of a majority in the Chamber of 1889." Naquet closed his diatribe against the Right with a ringing cry: "Orleanism, there is the enemy!" [11] Inasmuch as Orleanism was the chief source of funds for the Boulangist party, one might have expected the Orleanists to call their associates of the far Left to order. Yet no such reprimand was forthcoming. The Orleanists did not prevent the Boulangists from making

[7] *Le Gaulois,* Dec. 5, 1888.
[8] *Le Courrier des Ardennes,* Dec. 7, 1888.
[9] *L'Action,* Dec. 3, 1888.   [10] *La Presse,* Dec. 6, 1888.
[11] *Ibid.,* Dec. 8, 1888.

antiroyalist declarations in the belief that the Republican votes won in this fashion would eventually serve the Orleanist cause.

While his partisans were reaffirming their loyalty to the Republic and its principles, Boulanger was busy repairing any possible damage done to Auffray's campaign. In a newspaper interview, he repeated his committee's policy statement that no one who did not declare himself a Republican could receive their official endorsement. He noted, however, that he was in complete accord with Auffray on all other points. Besides, added Boulanger, "I recognize . . . that he is superior to all his rivals." [12] If there was any embarrassment in the Boulangist camp over the General's equivocation, it was quickly dissipated by the election results, in which Auffray ran a poor second to the Radical candidate.[13] Since the Orleanist's attempt to use the issue of revision for his own ends had failed, no dishonor fell on the Boulangist committee.

THE CAMPAIGN IN PARIS

The death on December 23, 1888, of a rather obscure Radical Deputy from Paris named Hude set the stage for the ultimate test of strength between Boulangism and Radicalism. Immediately after Hude's passing, the government set January 27, 1889 as the date for the by-election in Paris. If this was an attempt to catch Boulanger off guard, it failed, for he announced his candidacy on December 25. "Ever since I entered political life, I have been a candidate in Paris," he boasted. By the way, who would be the official candidate? Boulanger predicted that the government would have difficulty in finding one.[14] He was correct; not until January 6 did he have a rival.

On entering the Seine by-election, the General already en-

[12] *Le Figaro,* Dec. 5, 1888.   [13] *Le Temps,* Dec. 11, 1888.
[14] *La Presse,* Dec. 27, 1888.

joyed the aid of several organizations which were similar to modern front groups in that they had been founded supposedly for other purposes than merely furthering Boulanger's political fortunes. The oldest of these was the *Ligue des patriotes,* which Déroulède had tried to transform into a pro-Boulanger organization in 1887. Immediately after the rally at the Cirque d'Hiver,[15] articles by Naquet, Millevoie, and Nicot began to appear in *Le Drapeau.* During the presidential election of December, 1887, Déroulède tried to involve the *Ligue* still further in politics by organizing a demonstration against Ferry. Although favored by some of the rank and file in Paris, this maneuver was strongly condemned by the *Ligue*'s board of directors.[16] Déroulède then resigned as honorary president of the organization, citing pressing family matters.[17]

For several months thereafter, the *Ligue des patriotes* resumed its former attitude of political neutrality. Déroulède, however, refused to remain on the sidelines. Shortly after resigning, he formed a so-called "Action Group," composed of *ligueurs* favorable to Boulanger. At its inception, the Action Group numbered only fifteen members, but these grew to nearly three hundred by mid-April, 1888.[18]

By this time, Déroulède felt strong enough to wrest control of the *Ligue* from its existing leadership. With the open support of the Action Group, he was reinstated as honorary president of the *Ligue* at a meeting of the board of directors on April 16, 1888. Ten directors had voted for his return to office and seven against.[19] When, on April 22, the delegates of the *Ligue's* local committees were summoned to ratify Dé-

---

[15] Cf. *supra,* p. 72.
[16] A.P.P., B a/1337, Dec. 2 and 3, 1887.
[17] *Le Drapeau,* Dec. 10, 1888.
[18] A.P.P., B a/1496, April 4, 1889.
[19] *Le Drapeau,* April 22, 1888.

roulède's election, they refused, by a vote of 21 to 18. This left the board of directors in a most embarrassing position. The *Ligue des patriotes* already owed Déroulède more money than it could possibly pay; he had been subsidizing it from the start and owned its newspaper, *Le Drapeau,* outright. Accordingly, the directors voted to turn over to Déroulède as his personal property the offices and lecture hall of the *Ligue,* whereupon they themselves resigned as a group.

Déroulède was now free to run the *Ligue*—or what was left of it—as he wished. On April 25, 1888, some 250 members of the "Action Group" met at the *Ligue*'s lecture hall and unanimously approved Déroulède's proposal that "the *Ligue des patriotes* enter the revisionist movement." [20] The organization's former directors and dissident members formed the *Union patriotique de France* early in May, 1888 in order to continue the original apolitical program of the pre-1885 *Ligue*. At a meeting on May 7, 1888, Déroulède's organization decided to admit partisans of Prince Jérôme to membership.[21] A declaration issued in July, 1888, in favor of revision confirmed the new *Ligue*'s policy; it was signed by the directors, who now included Naquet, Laisant, Turquet, and Laguerre. They had joined the organization after Déroulède assumed control.[22] From this point until the general elections of 1889, the *Ligue des patriotes* was to be subsidized by the Boulangist central committee.[23]

When other pro-Boulanger groups were formed independently of the National Committee, some of its members joined them in order to maintain a minimum of unity within the Boulangist movement as a whole. Such was the case of the

[20] *Ibid.,* April 29, 1888.
[21] A.N.F., F⁷ 12445, May 8, 1888; A.P.P., B a/976, June 23, 1888.
[22] A.N.F., F⁷ 12446, July 17, 1888.
[23] A.P.P., B a/1465, Oct. 3, 1889.

Ligue d'action républicaine, which was founded on April 23, 1888, by a lawyer named Alfred Martineau, who had been expelled with several of his associates from the *Union de la jeunesse française,* when they tried to turn it into a Boulangist front group. Within a week after its creation, Martineau's new organization accepted several leading Boulangists as members. With their help, Georges Laguerre was elected president on April 30; Déroulède, Laisant, and Ménorval became vice-presidents, while Martineau was given the post of secretary-general.[24]

The program of the *Ligue d'action,* which was drafted in the presence of Laguerre, was exactly the same as Boulanger's. While the new *Ligue des patriotes* accepted Bonapartist members and organized provincial branches, the *Ligue d'action* tried to win Socialist support and confined its activity to the capital. At its peak early in 1889, the latter numbered some four hundred members in a dozen *arrondissement* committees.[25] Shortly after having formed the *Ligue d'action,* Martineau tried to create a pro-Boulanger student movement, but had to abandon the project for lack of members.[26] Most of the students in the Latin Quarter were firmly opposed to Boulanger.[27]

In addition to front groups, the National Committee organized branches on the *arrondissement* level throughout Paris. These sections held public meetings at which members of the National Committee spoke in favor of revision. Before the death of Hude, little was said about Boulanger, who was still Deputy from the Nord and not yet a candidate in Paris. The purpose of these meetings, which were first held regularly in

[24] A.N.F., F⁷ 12447, May 1, 1888.
[25] A.P.P., B a/976, Feb. 6, 1889.   [26] *Ibid.,* Sept. 23, 1888.
[27] Léon Daudet, *Devant la douleur* (Paris: Nouvelle Librairie Nationale, 1915), pp. 183–184.

the fall of 1888, was apparently to prepare public opinion for a possible by-election there, as well as for the coming general elections. The fact that the *arrondissement* committees were called revisionist, rather than Boulangist, indicates that the support of all the discontented was sought, not just that of the General's admirers.[28] At a meeting in the fourteenth *arrondissement* on December 21, 1888, Ménorval was asked to explain Boulanger's role in the event of the party's victory in 1889. He replied somewhat evasively that Boulanger would be whatever the people wanted him to be.[29]

Once the General had announced his candidacy in Paris, the task of his organization changed from preparing public opinion to ensuring his election. There were the usual campaign declarations, more numerous than in previous contests. The first, issued on January 3, 1889, presented Boulanger as the champion of democracy. Attacking what he called "the parliamentarians," the General charged: "In reality, they are not afraid of me, but of universal suffrage." If he had ever wanted to become a dictator, the time to have done so was when he was War Minister.[30] An appeal addressed "to the Workers of the Seine" reminded them that workers in the Nord and the Aisne had voted for him. (No other departments were mentioned.) "By voting for me, you will show your exploiters that you are no longer willing to give them your sons for useless and dangerous conquests, nor your taxes for their sinecures." [31] The exploiters to whom Boulanger refers are the same parliamentarians of his earlier manifesto, not the capitalists. While seeking votes from workers, he did not try to foment class war. To do so would be to repudiate Naquet's

[28] Cf. A.N.F., F⁷ 12445, Sept. 23, 1888; F⁷ 12447, Dec. 18 and 20, 1888.

[29] *Ibid.*, F⁷ 12447, Dec. 22, 1888.

[30] *L'Intransigeant*, Jan. 5, 1889.   [31] *La Cocarde*, Jan. 20, 1889.

political philosophy, which proposed political solutions to social problems and even refused to recognize the existence of
social classes.[32] Finally, Boulanger promised suburban voters
greater representation in the general council of the Seine.
Decentralization in government, he recalled, was an idea he
had acquired in America.[33]

These manifestoes were posted in every available space,
and the 450,000 francs spent on the General's campaign in
Paris assured their widest possible diffusion.[34] As the election
approached, however, the public had increasingly less opportunity to read the billboards. No sooner was a pro-Boulanger
poster put up, when one for his opponent was stuck on top of
it, only to be followed by another for the General, and so
on.[35] Other means of publicity had to be used. They included
leaflets, distributed by newsboys of the Boulangist papers, who
received an extra two francs a day for this work. Sandwich
men carrying the General's declaration earned six francs a
day.[36] The most original scheme in the propaganda war came
from Georges Laguerre, who sent his newsboys over to opposition headquarters, where they asked to distribute leaflets. As
soon as they received this material, they brought it to the
offices of *La Presse*. Close to 10,000 flyers and brochures
were diverted in this way.[37]

For the Republican opposition, electoral propaganda had
to wait until a candidate was found; and the long delay helped
only Boulanger. On learning of the General's candidacy,
Alexandre Millerand predicted that the Republicans would

[32] Cf. *supra*, p. 74.   [33] *L'Intransigeant*, Jan. 22, 1889.

[34] Mermeix [Gabriel Terrail], *Les coulisses du boulangisme* (Paris:
Cerf, 1890), p. 281.

[35] Edouard Millaud, *Le journal d'un parlementaire* (4 vols.; Paris:
Oudin, 1914–1925) II, 203–204.

[36] A.P.P., B a/971, Aug. 23, 1889.

[37] *Ibid.*, B a/976, April 17, 1889.

have to agree on a single candidate. Inasmuch as Boulanger was certain to receive Conservative support, the presence of more than one Republican candidate could well divide votes for the opposition seriously enough to assure his victory. Speaking for the Republican Left, Millerand promised: "Whatever our preferences, we are ready to bow to the final decision of the Republican party." [38]

Millerand's foresight proved to be deadly accurate: not only was a single candidate chosen, but it was the Left which had to forego its preferences. In previous general elections, the Opportunists had largely conceded Paris to the Radicals because of the capital's well-deserved reputation for leftist leanings. For the advanced Radicals and Republican Socialists, it seemed only logical to choose as Boulanger's rival someone with a sufficiently progressive record to win votes from the discontented proletariat. They therefore proposed the nomination of Hovelacque, a former Communard with socialistic tendencies.[39] At the *Société des droits de l'homme,* however, it was informally agreed that Jacques, president of the general council of the Seine, was the most appropriate choice. As a distiller and a suburbanite, Jacques was said to wield great influence among important segments of the population.[40]

Actually, there was a more fundamental reason for choosing Jacques: as a Radical of the palest possible hue, he was unlikely to excite animosity within the Republican camp, particularly among the Opportunists.[41] When the so-called "Republican Anti-Boulangist Congress" met on January 6 to choose a candidate to represent all Republican factions, Hovelacque was criticized for not having opposed Boulanger

[38] *La Justice,* Dec. 28, 1888. [39] *Ibid.,* Jan. 3, 1889.
[40] Charles Chincholle, *Le général Boulanger* (Paris: Savine, 1889), pp. 312–313.
[41] *L'Autorité,* Jan. 6, 1889.

from the very start. Jacques easily won the nomination with the votes of 239 delegates; Hovelacque received 69 votes, while the writer, Auguste Vacquerie, ran third with 58.[42] Camille Pelletan, who would have preferred either Hovelacque or Vacquerie, did not try to conceal his disappointment at the outcome. In the name of Republican unity, however, he urged all Radicals to vote for Jacques.[43]

In retrospect, it is difficult to imagine a more unlikely choice of a candidate to win the Paris electorate away from a popular general of the Left. A journalist favorable to Jacques noted with pride that the official Republican candidate belonged to the "middle bourgeoisie." Given the social composition of the Paris electorate, however, this was probably a disadvantage. Another was Jacques' personality, which his admirer admitted to be rather colorless. But no matter! That would only make his victory more convincing as a vote of confidence in the Republic.[44] In other words, the moderates who favored Jacques were somehow convinced that the mere label "Republican" would persuade the Parisians to vote for him. The suburban distiller had little else to recommend him, as Jules Simon pointedly admitted. "For my part," wrote the Left-Center chieftain, "I shall put the name of M. Jacques in the ballot box. This will not mean, 'Long live Jacques!'—something that would make everyone laugh, including the candidate's friends. It will mean, 'Down with Boulanger!' "[45]

With its purely negative approach, the opposition to Boulanger was not making a very impressive showing. It allowed

[42] Chincholle, *op. cit.*, pp. 318–322.

[43] *La Justice,* Jan. 7, 1889.

[44] Henry Fouquier, "L'élection de Paris et M. Jacques," *Revue Bleue,* 3ème série, XXVI (Jan. 12, 1889), 35.

[45] Jules Simon, *Souviens-toi du Deux-décembre* (Paris: Victor-Havard, 1889), p. 358.

him to campaign unopposed for almost two weeks before it chose a rival more favorable to the bourgeoisie than to the masses. The very name of the nominating convention indicates that, as in previous by-elections where the General had been victorious, the Republicans again let him become the sole issue. Lacking a positive program, they were reduced to conjuring up imaginary disasters that would befall France if Boulanger were elected. It is unlikely that Jacques' favorite slogan, "No dictatorship! No Sedan!" frightened many Parisians away from the General. As in 1887, Boulanger was the symbol of military readiness, which was supposed to avert further defeats. In his answer to Jacques, Boulanger accused the Opportunists of neglecting national defense.[46]

In addition to warning of military disasters, Jacques also raised the clerical issue. As a champion of secular education, the Republican candidate claimed that he belonged to "the advanced faction" of the party. "Once again," he warned, "clericalism is leading into battle all the enemies of the Republic. Boulanger is their standard-bearer." Cornély then predicted that all royalists and Catholics would oppose Jacques.[47] The royalists' official position was ambiguous. On January 4, the Comte de Paris instructed the monarchist committee of the Seine not to present a candidate. In practice, this amounted to a tacit endorsement of Boulanger.[48] The committee's important Legitimist minority insisted, however, that these instructions be taken to mean complete abstention from voting for either of what it called "the two Republican candidates." A resolution to this effect was drafted, but it was not posted anywhere.[49] From the Bonapartists came a declaration of official neutrality, followed by expressions of unofficial

[46] *L'Intransigeant,* Jan. 13, 1889.   [47] *Le Gaulois,* Jan. 8, 1889.
[48] Chincholle, *op. cit.,* p. 316.   [49] *Ibid.,* pp. 333–334.

support for Boulanger. As Cassagnac explained: "We advise our friends to vote AGAINST Jacques, more than FOR Boulanger." [50]

Since the Conservatives were only a minority in Paris, Jacques could derive no political advantage by defying tradition and subduing his attacks on the Right. So he addressed his entire campaign to Republican voters, hoping to identify himself with them through appeals to anticlericalism. In most provincial departments, where the clerical question was the only one—aside from that of the regime—to separate Republicans from Conservatives, such appeals might have been sufficient. In revolutionary Paris, however, social problems were also political issues; yet Jacques did not even discuss them, as he surely had to do in order to win the votes of workers away from Boulanger. Indeed, some of the Republicans' anticlerical measures, such as the expulsion of nursing nuns from the public hospitals of Paris, may have hurt the party's position with the masses. It was the poor who suffered from the ensuing reduction in hospital service.[51]

As for Boulanger, his increasingly evident ties with the Right do not appear to have diminished his popular appeal. He defended Conservative support by the claim that he was bringing former royalists and Bonapartists into the Republic—*his* republic.[52] To Charles de Mazade, it appeared that the General would draw his political strength from the same nationalistic and revolutionary feelings that dominated the Commune of 1871. The moderate journalist took some comfort in the assurance that, as the experience of the Commune

[50] *L'Autorité,* Jan. 18, 1889.

[51] W. T. Stead, "Madame France and Her 'Brav' Général,' " *Contemporary Review,* LV (June, 1889), 924–925.

[52] *L'Intransigeant,* Jan. 27, 1889.

itself showed, Paris could no longer speak for all of France. A Boulangist victory in the capital would not necessarily be repeated throughout the country.[53]

The General's success at the polls on January 27 was, in fact, tremendous. He won with 245,236 votes, as against only 162,875 for Jacques, who was defeated even in his own *arrondissement*. Boulé, the Blanquist candidate, who had led the construction workers' strike of August, 1888, received a mere 17,039.[54] In a relatively unimportant Paris by-election in 1886, the Socialist-Revolutionary candidate had received some 100,000 votes. It is possible, therefore, that as many as 80,000 Socialists voted for Boulanger in Paris.[55] Indeed, the General did not merely win a handsome majority in Conservative districts, such as Passy, the Louvre, and the Luxembourg; his margin of victory in such Radical strongholds as the Gobelins and Vaugirard was almost as great. Even more impressive majorities came from the working-class districts of Montmartre (which had once been Clemenceau's fief), Buttes-Chaumont, and especially the industrial suburbs of the North and South.[56] Boulanger was most successful in the newly industrialized fifteenth *arrondissement* and made his poorest showing in the third and tenth, both of which were dominated by middle-sized commerce and independent artisans.[57] In modern terms, he had won his "base"—the Paris proletariat.

Although the election results had no immediate effect on

[53] Charles de Mazade, "Chronique de la quinzaine," *Revue des Deux Mondes*, XCI (Jan. 15, 1889), 466.

[54] A.N.F., C 5309 A 79.

[55] Raoul Frary, "Chronique politique," *La Nouvelle Revue*, LVI (Feb. 1, 1889), 705.

[56] Chincholle, *op. cit.*, pp. 352–353.

[57] Cf. D. R. Watson, "The Nationalist Movement in Paris, 1900–1906," *The Right in France, 1890–1919*, ed. David Shapiro (London: Chatto & Windus, 1962), pp. 83–84.

the rest of the nation, they were highly embarrassing to the Republican leaders. Except for Lille and Marseilles, no demonstrations were reported in any of the most important provincial cities.[58] If the Republic itself seemed less secure after the election, the Republican politicians had only themselves to blame. By heralding Jacques as "the candidate of the Republic," they had tried to make it appear as if the fate of the regime itself depended on his victory. After his defeat, they blamed the fiasco on everything and everyone but themselves: the Right, the revolutionary tradition of Paris—even universal suffrage itself.[59] It was the Republicans, not Boulanger, who claimed that the regime was in danger. By draping themselves in the banner of the Republic, they had admittedly soiled it somewhat. Yet in the final analysis, the vote of January 27, 1889, was directed more against Republican politics than against Republican institutions.

A "COUP MANQUÉ"?

As if to add substance to the theory of the Republic in danger, a legend worthy of the highest French tradition of intrigue has grown out of the Paris by-election. The story goes that on the night of January 27, as the election returns indicated a victory for Boulanger, a crowd of some 100,000 persons gathered near Durand's restaurant, Place de la Madeleine, where the General was celebrating his triumph in the company of his closest associates. By ten o'clock, shouts of "To the Elysée!" could be heard from the crowd; within an hour, these shouts had become a mighty roar. It was the perfect opportunity for a *coup d'état*. Since the police and the Garde Républicaine were now thoroughly Boulangist, all that the General had to

[58] *Le Temps,* Jan. 29, 1889.
[59] Charles de Mazade, "Chronique de la quinzaine," *Revue des Deux Mondes,* XCI (Feb. 1, 1889), 708–710.

do to seize control of France was to let the enthusiastic crowd carry him in triumph to the Elysée Palace, where it would be a simple matter to expel President Carnot.

But—so goes the legend—Boulanger hesitated. Leaving his cohorts for a moment, he sought the advice of his mistress, Mme. de Bonnemains, who was waiting in an adjoining room. In her arms, the General temporarily lost his political ambition. When he returned to the table, Boulanger resisted the pressing invitations of his lieutenants to leave for the Elysée. At the Presidential Palace itself, Ernest Constans, the future Minister of the Interior, glanced at his watch and announced: "Five past midnight, Gentlemen. For the past five minutes, Boulanger's stock has been falling!" [60] Having failed to seize this opportunity, the General progressively lost his popular following.

The source of the legend of a *coup manqué* cannot be traced to contemporary accounts. None of the Paris dailies published on January 28, whether Boulangist or not, mention shouts of "To the Elysée!" as having been uttered by anyone in the crowd of the previous night. Cries of "Long live Boulanger!" and "Long live France!" could be heard from the estimated 30,000—not 100,000—people gathered in front of the restaurant, but nothing that would suggest an invitation to a *coup d'état*.[61] Rather, the eyewitness account of Chincholle, who was present at the restaurant on election night, relates that when a crowd did assemble outside, Déroulède asked the people to disperse.[62] This version is corroborated by the diary of Romain Rolland, who, like the vast majority of his classmates at the Ecole Normale Supérieure, was hostile to Bou-

[60] Adrien Dansette, *Le boulangisme* (Paris: Fayard, 1946), pp. 243–251.

[61] *La Presse and L'Intransigeant,* Jan. 29, 1889.

[62] *Le Figaro,* Jan. 28, 1889.

langer. He wrote of the "very great joy of the people in the streets," but quickly added that those who celebrated the General's victory were well behaved. "Whatever disorder there was came from the anti-Boulangists," he noted.[63] No mention of a possible coup can be found in press dispatches or police reports of the week following the by-election.

Not until after the Boulangists had failed to win political control of France by democratic means in the general elections of 1889 did stories of a *coup manqué* begin to circulate. It is not uncommon for a defeated party to indulge in post mortems on the nature of its failure. For Francis Laur, who tried to analyze the defeat a few days after the elections, the problem was simple: Boulanger was just too ethical. The General could have seized power on at least three occasions: the Gare de Lyon demonstration, Rouvier's fall from office, and the Paris by-election of January 27.[64] Laur's explanation was eagerly adopted by the rightist leaders whose association with Boulanger had failed to bring them any benefits. It was inexcusable, said Cassagnac, that the General did not avail himself of such propitious occasions to stage a *coup d'état*. The Bonapartist chief blamed such inaction on the General's close friends, who supposedly prevented him from doing his duty.[65] With this analysis the royalists heartily concurred.[66]

The legend more closely assumed its present form when the General's death by suicide momentarily revived interest in his meteoric rise and fall. *Le Figaro* obligingly fed the speculative curiosity of its readers by providing what it called "Two judgments on January 27." According to the first of these, Boulanger and his immediate entourage were deliberating at

---

[63] Romain Rolland, *Le cloître de la rue d'Ulm* (Paris: Albin Michel, 1952), p. 273.

[64] *La Presse,* Oct. 11, 1889.   [65] *L'Autorité,* Oct. 14, 1889.

[66] *Le Gaulois,* Oct. 14, 1889.

Durand's as to how best to take advantage of the victory, when Rochefort suddenly took out his watch and exclaimed: "General, it is ten past midnight! Your popularity has been declining for the past ten minutes!" The second version relates that Constans strolled over to the Faubourg Saint-Honoré on the night of January 27, "to see how he [Boulanger] would enter the Elysée. . . . When, at midnight, I saw that he had done nothing, I said to myself: 'He is finished,' and I went home to bed." [67]

From there, the story took on new breadth and scope with the publication of Paul Déroulède's autobiography in 1900. That was the year after his pathetic attempt at a *coup d'état* on the occasion of President Faure's funeral. Having failed to enlist the support of General Roget, Déroulède now charged that Boulanger too had lacked courage. The nationalist leader recounted (without fear of contradiction, since Boulanger was now dead) that on January 8, 1886, the day after the General entered the War Ministry, he had offered the aid of his "300,000 [*sic*] *ligueurs*" to enable the latter to seize the office of President of the Republic. Boulanger is said to have listened attentively and, once Déroulède had exposed his plan, to have said only, *"Au revoir."* [68] Déroulède further states that on the night of January 27, 1889, he was the only member of Boulanger's entourage to suggest a *coup d'état*—the others having been too timid.[69]

After the death of Déroulède in 1914, his biographers embellished this theme to the point where he became the guiding spirit behind the entire Boulangist movement. In one account, Déroulède even jumped on Boulanger's carriage as the latter

[67] *Le Figaro*, Oct. 1, 1891.

[68] Henri Galli [Gallichet], *Paul Déroulède: Raconté par lui-même* (Paris: Plon, 1900), pp. 71–74.

[69] *Ibid.*, pp. 85–86.

was leaving Durand's in a vain attempt to have him change his direction and head for the Elysée.[70] Other participants in the affair, seeking, no doubt, to excuse their own failure, joined in condemning Boulanger's lack of boldness. Rochefort puts himself at the head of those associates who proposed a *coup d'état*. In almost the same breath, however, he praises the General's high sense of legal and moral scruples.[71] According to Barrès, Boulanger rejected proposals for a coup because he was afraid that it would fail. At the same time, he believed that such a drastic move was unnecessary in view of certain success in the forthcoming general elections.[72] Of all the apologetic versions of the affair, that of Barrès seems to be closest to the truth. As for the Duchesse d'Uzès, who had little regard for legal conventions, Boulanger's cowardice on the night of January 27, 1889, sufficed to explain his subsequent failure.[73]

To judge from contemporary sources, it seems clear that no one in the General's immediate entourage wanted to stage a *coup d'état* following his victory in Paris. Later that same year, when Boulanger was tried *in absentia* for having plotted against the state, he, Dillon, and Rochefort were accused of having prepared a *coup d'état* on three occasions: the first was the demonstration at the Gare de Lyon on July 8, 1887; the next was the military review of July 14, 1887; and the third, Boulanger's meetings with royalist leaders on December 1 and

[70] Jean and Jérôme Tharaud, *Paul Déroulède* (Paris: Emile-Paul, 1914), p. 51; *La vie et la mort de Déroulède* (Paris: Plon, 1925), p. 67. Both works give the date of the Paris election as 1887, not 1889. For other versions, see Camille Ducray, *Paul Déroulède, 1846–1914* (Paris: Ambert, 1914), p. 172; also, Florent Matter, *Paul Déroulède* (Paris: Sansot, 1919), p. 29.

[71] *Les Aventures,* V, 161–163.

[72] *L'appel au soldat* (Paris: Juven, 1911), p. 208.

[73] Anne de Mortemart, duchesse d'Uzès, *Souvenirs de la duchesse d'Uzès* (Paris: Plon, 1939), p. 89.

2, 1887. Nothing whatsoever was said about January 27, 1889.[74] At all events, the legal basis of the trial was fundamentally unsound,[75] and it is highly probable that no such plots against the state were ever formulated. Boulanger's apologists may well have been inspired by the plot theory of the trial as they elaborated the *coup manqué* legend.

All public statements by the General and his associates both before and after the Paris by-election indicate a desire for absolute calm on the part of the voters. On January 26, Boulanger issued a declaration to the press, asking his partisans to refrain from creating any disorder, lest the government use it as a pretext to outlaw or otherwise hinder his movement.[76] Only one mention of a possible march on the Elysée appeared in the Paris press before the election. It came from *La Lanterne,* a journal which had favored Boulanger until he began to enter by-elections, and thereafter bitterly opposed him. In 1887, the paper had excused the demonstration at the Gare de Lyon as a manifestation of patriotism.[77] Now it claimed that a march on the Elysée, led by the *Ligue des patriotes,* was being planned—not to profit from Boulanger's victory, but to protest his certain defeat.[78] To this accusation came a swift reply from *La Presse,* which categorically denied that such a march had ever been considered; it once more impressed upon the voters the necessity of avoiding disorder. "Remain calm despite all provocations! Answer insults only with disdain!" [79]

Following the General's triumph, his lieutenants again emphasized the democratic nature of his movement. A message to this effect, signed by Naquet, Laisant, and Michelin, appeared on February 4. It argued that popular disgust with

[74] France, Haute Cour de Justice, *Affaire Boulanger, Dillon, Rochefort: Procédure générale,* p. 60.
[75] Cf. *infra,* p. 225.   [76] *La France,* Jan. 27, 1889.
[77] Cf. *supra,* p. 68.   [78] *La Lanterne,* Jan. 28, 1889.
[79] *La Presse* (2nd ed.), Jan. 28, 1889.

parliamentarism was so great that if Boulanger were not there to channel this feeling into legal, constitutional action, violent revolution might erupt.

General Boulanger does not want to become a dictator. But even if he wanted to, he would not be able to do so, for he would find in front of him all of French democracy ready to block his way and to oppose any move against our liberties.

Voters were then asked to "help us avoid a new violent revolution" by voting Boulangist in the general elections.[80]

Police reports of this period corroborate the claim that the Boulangists did not plan any violent action against the regime. A dispatch marked "confidential" relates that, in conversations with his partisans, Boulanger expressed confidence that time was on his side. Any public agitation by his party would only help the government, he added.[81] At a meeting of Boulangist groups of the seventh and fifteenth *arrondissements,* Le Hérissé assured his audience that the ballot was the only weapon they needed.[82] The General himself repeated this assurance on March 24 to delegates visiting him from various *arrondissements* in the capital and its suburbs. Once again, he cautioned against impatience, predicting that in six months, victory would be theirs.[83]

Had Boulanger and his cohorts really wanted to stage a *coup d'état,* they would have had to do far more than simply occupy the Elysée Palace. Control over the ministries, especially that of the Interior with its special telegraph, was a prerequisite. Saussier, the military governor of Paris, would have had to be arrested, along with leading Republican politicians. Finally, the complicity of the army was necessary before a government could be designated.[84] Given the firm opposi-

[80] *L'Action,* Feb. 5, 1889. [81] A.P.P., B a/969, Jan. 30, 1889. [82] A.N.F., F⁷ 12445, Feb. 7, 1889. [83] *Ibid.,* March 25, 1889. [84] Dansette, *Le boulangisme,* p. 245.

tion to Boulanger on the part of the high officers,[85] such complicity was far from assured. In view of these major obstacles, it is not surprising that Lépine posted no extra police squads near Durand's restaurant on the night of Boulanger's victory in Paris.[86]

In the final analysis, what prevented the Boulangists from resorting to force was the nature of their electoral strategy. As the self-proclaimed party of universal suffrage, they would have been hard put to explain to their followers why they bypassed the ballot box to assume power. Francis Laur explained in April, 1888, that the Boulangists expected the parliament elected in 1889 to assume constituent authority.[87] The creation of electoral committees in the departments testifies to their desire to attain such ends by legal means in the general elections of 1889. Preventing the Boulangist Conservative coalition from winning these elections now became the major task of the Republicans in government.

[85] Cf. *supra,* p. 31.
[86] Louis Lépine, *Mes souvenirs* (Paris: Payot, 1929), p. 71.
[87] *La France,* April 18, 1888.

10

Boulanger Is Defeated

1889

~~~~~~

As a direct result of Boulanger's triumph in Paris, the government adopted a new method of dealing with him. Under Floquet, there had been a hesitant attempt to outbid him by espousing the principle of constitutional revision. Although the ministry accomplished few practical reforms, it was meant to be the embodiment of Radical policy. Whether or not it actually did embody this policy need not be argued here. The fact is that Floquet's program obviously had not won over that element of the French electorate at which it was principally directed: the Parisian masses. It was the "little people'" of the capital who had voted in greatest numbers for Boulanger, thereby throwing discredit upon the entire Radical strategy. Henceforth, the General would be opposed not by reforms— real or imagined—but by repression.[1]

Ironically, it was Floquet himself who took the first step in the direction of a new policy. On January 31, 1889, he asked parliament to have the re-establishment of the single-member constituency studied in commission. That such a change would be welcomed by the Opportunists was hardly a secret. As early

[1] Joseph Reinach, *Les petites catilinaires,* Vol. II: *Le cheval noir* (Paris: Victor-Havard, 1889), pp. 336–341.

as June, 1887, before Boulanger had embarked on his political career, Grévy confided to Münster that he viewed the *scrutin de liste* as "an unfortunate legacy from Gambetta" and would welcome its imminent replacement by the former system.[2] After Boulanger's first victory in the Nord, pressure to return to the *scrutin d'arrondissement* became increasingly vocal. At an informal meeting of Opportunist Deputies in July, 1888, a motion for the restoration of the single-member constituency was approved unanimously. The General could still try to run his "electoral steeplechase" by *arrondissements*, but the Opportunists considered this unlikely.[3] Jules Ferry was even more positive: in a letter to Reinach on September 5, 1888, he predicted certain defeat for Boulanger if the former system of voting were re-estabished.[4]

For a Radical to favor such a restoration, however, was an open betrayal of the party's long-established position. On being questioned as to his purpose, Floquet admitted that the single-member constituency would prevent one by-election from assuming national importance to the point of threatening the government. With obvious relish, Cassagnac then drew attention to the Radicals' complete reversal on this question. He quoted an earlier remark by Goblet, who had argued that the *scrutin de liste* was "the only way to avoid electoral corruption and official candidacies." On a vote of confidence, the Premier won approval for his motion by the respectable majority of 300 to 240. As expected, he was opposed by Conservatives and Boulangists, but he still had the support of his own party, plus most of the Opportunists.[5]

---

[2] *Grosse Politik,* VI, 197.

[3] Charles de Mazade, "Chronique de la quinzaine," *Revue des Deux Mondes,* LXXXIX (July 1, 1888), 233–234.

[4] Ferry, *Lettres* (Paris: Calmann-Lévy, 1914), p. 489.

[5] *J.O.C.* (1889), pp. 250–268.

The Premier's parliamentary majority emerged drastically reduced on February 11, when he introduced a bill to restore the *scrutin d'arrondissement*. It passed by only 283 to 274 votes, thanks mainly to the Opportunists, who voted almost to a man for the measure. Floquet's own party, however, was badly split. Although Barodet and Pichon did vote for the Premier's bill, those two pillars of Radicalism, Clemenceau and Pelletan, could not bring themselves to abandon their cherished faith in the existing method.[6]

This slim majority was Floquet's last. On February 14, now that the constitutional issue could be postponed no longer, he finally fulfilled his mandate as Premier by calling for discussion on revision. At once, Baron de Mackau objected that a constituent assembly would have to be elected before the question could be taken up. He therefore asked Floquet to have the parliament dissolved by the President of the Republic. When the Premier refused, another royalist Deputy, Douville-Maillefeu, moved that the question of revision be deferred indefinitely. By a vote of 307 to 218, the Chamber passed the motion, thereby obliging Floquet to resign. Along with the Boulangists and the Conservatives, more than half the Opportunists—including Ferry, Rouvier, and Steeg—voted against him.[7]

Since these Center politicians never had had any real sympathy for revision, it was only natural that they should vote to bury it. That the royalists and Boulangists voted along with them, however, raised some questions. Were the so-called "revisionist" parties afraid that a thorough discussion of revision in the Chamber might reveal their profound differences on the subject? Indeed were they truly interested in revision or simply in attaining power? Reflecting apparent embarrassment, Boulanger felt obliged to explain his vote and that of his

[6] *Ibid.*, pp. 394–395.   [7] *Ibid.*, pp. 400–404.

cohorts. He charged that Floquet had proposed revision in the full knowledge that it it would be rejected by the Senate; since the Premier presented his motion with the sole purpose of keeping himself in office, it was the Boulangists' solemn duty to oppose it. Similarly the General attacked the bill to restore the *scrutin d'arrondissement* as "a law which, in the minds of its authors, is just another blow struck against universal suffrage." Yet he claimed that it would not hurt him.[8]

TIRARD RETURNS

In the minds of its authors, the return to the single-member constituency was a blow against Boulanger. To the Opportunists it announced the beginning of a new counteroffensive against the coalition of Boulangists and royalists. Now that Floquet was out of the way, Joseph Reinach set the new political tone by demanding "a government of action, energetic and vigorous action against the Caesarian venture." [9] That government was installed under Pierre Tirard on February 23, 1889. In his ministerial declaration, the new Premier made no mention of revision, but pledged to restore order and respect due to the Republic.[10] Tirard was in a far better position to act decisively now than he had been during his first term as head of government. At that time, the Radicals, feeling betrayed by Rouvier and anxious to form a ministry of their own, had given him only wavering support. They were, to be sure, less than enthusiastic about the second Tirard cabinet— its sole Radical member, Yves Guyot, having been chosen only to satisfy the formal requirement for "Republican concentration." [11] This time, however, their loyalty to the gov-

[8] *La Cocarde,* Feb. 16, 1889.
[9] *La République Française,* Feb. 21, 1889.
[10] *J.O.C.* (1889), p. 413.   [11] *La Justice,* Feb. 23, 1889.

ernment was more nearly assured. Now that the Radicals had so conspicuously failed to stop Boulanger by their own methods, they had little choice but to step aside and let the Opportunists try others.

The Tirard ministry immediately mounted a two-pronged assault on Boulanger. It first made a frontal attack on his movement by a series of exceptional, repressive measures. Then it tried to cut off his financial support by making the regime more acceptable to Conservatives. Leading this assault was the new Minister of the Interior, Ernest Constans, whose first act on assuming office was to issue a directive banning all outdoor political demonstrations in Paris. Besides depriving the Boulangists of an opportunity to amplify their views, this edict also served to reassure the more conservative elements of French society, who abhorred mass demonstrations. As noted by Francis Magnard, the solid bourgeois of Paris, regardless of party, wanted order above all else.[12] The new government was more than willing to put him at ease.

To placate the Right further, the government issued a decree on March 9, allowing the Duc d'Aumale to return from exile. Although Constans insisted under questioning from the Left that this was an act of a personal, not political, character, the Radicals were not fooled. They realized that the government went out of its way to court the Conservatives.[13] Yet once the Duc d'Aumale did return, no serious objection was raised from any quarter. Most politicians viewed the government's decree as an act of justice and enlightened self-interest at the same time. It certainly presented no danger to the regime, since the Duc himself had never participated in any subversive movement and had accepted his exile gracefully. Even Floquet, as Premier, was said to have favored ending

[12] *Le Figaro,* Feb. 24, 1889.   [13] *La Justice,* March 10, 1889.

that exile, but he did not want to offend his Radical friends before the by-election in Paris and had therefore let the matter rest.[14]

Most important of all, the decree ending the exile of the Duc d'Aumale put the Boulangists in a most awkward position. As so-called "advanced" Republicans, they could make no public statement to give the impression of favoring royalism. At the same time, however, they also promised a national Republic, open to everyone regardless of political persuasion. After some hesitation, therefore, various Boulangist committees in the departments issued declarations approving the government's decision.[15] Laguerre went even further and predicted: "In six months, when we come to power, we shall bring back all the princes, without exception." The General himself was quoted as saying: "I have always been opposed to exile laws." [16] Coming from one who, in 1886, had helped carry out the very decree that exiled the Duc d'Aumale in the first place, here was news indeed. Yet if Boulanger had always opposed laws of exile, as he claimed, he had nonetheless waited for the government to repeal one such law before revealing his deep-seated opposition. Like the Radicals who favored Floquet's bid to revise the constitution, the General now assumed the weak posture of "me-tooism."

In other words, the government had seized the initiative. Boulanger was never to recover it.

By allowing the Duc d'Aumale to return to France, the new ministry weakened, if only slightly, the alliance between Conservatives and Boulangists. This may explain why the General

[14] Charles de Mazade, "Chronique de la quinzaine," *Revue des Deux Mondes*, XCII (March 15, 1889), 467–468.

[15] A.N.F., F7 12446, March 14, 1889.

[16] Joseph Reinach, *Les petites catilinaires*, Vol. III: *Bruno-le-fileur* (Paris: Victor-Havard, 1889), pp. 89–90.

now began to pay public court to voters of the Right. He did so as the last of seven speakers at a great political banquet held at Tours on March 17. The place was well chosen. Its Boulangist committee, formed in December of 1888 mainly by Conservatives, was allied after February, 1889, to Jules Delahaye, a powerful royalist Deputy and publisher of the ultraroyalist and clerical *Journal d'Indre-et-Loire*.[17] Among the speakers at the banquet were a royalist, a Bonapartist, two Socialists, Delahaye, and Boulanger.

It was Alfred Naquet who did most of the talking, however. The Jewish positivist set the tone for the entire assembly by denouncing the Republic's current anticlerical policy. He proposed that the Church-state question be settled by a national referendum. If there was to be separation, as Naquet personally wished, he would not allow it to be used as a weapon against the Church. In any case, he wanted a law explicitly permitting religious associations, so that they could not be dissolved by mere governmental fiat. So striking was the difference between these views and those normally expressed by the speaker that Pelletan referred to the banquet as "Naquet's first communion." [18]

When Boulanger rose to speak, it was to bow graciously: "My friend, M. Naquet, has left me very little to say." The General objected, though, to being called "the ally of the old royalist and Imperialist parties . . . who is to lead them in the assault on the Republic." Far from wishing to destroy the Republic, Boulanger proclaimed his desire to reaffirm its existence by inviting loyal Frenchmen of all parties to join it. This is why he spoke of the royalists and Bonapartists in the past tense; his movement had already won them over to the "national" Republic. To make it perfectly clear that he did not

17 A.N.F., F⁷ 12446, Dec. 10, 1888, and Feb. 25, 1889.
18 *La Justice*, March 19, 1889.

intend to restore the monarchy, he pointed out in conclusion that most Frenchmen no longer wanted one. "It would leave the nation as divided as it is now, perhaps even more so." [19]

Reaction to Boulanger's speech varied widely. In Tours itself, the General's popularity among Conservative voters appears to have reached a new peak, while Republicans of all tendencies chanted in unison that he had become a prisoner of the Right.[20] Since they had made this charge before, one cannot conclude that the banquet at Tours marked a decisive change in Boulanger's political course. It certainly left Conservative leaders in Paris with no illusions as to where he stood. Paul de Cassagnac accused Boulanger of trying to make the Right his instrument. The General, he charged, took its support for granted, "and he is strangely mistaken if he imagines . . . that all the Conservatives who have voted for him are sighing for his Republic. . . ." [21] Francis Magnard reported that by inviting royalists to join *any* Republic, Boulanger had angered them.[22] Yet by calling on the present regime to "repudiate its Jacobin heritage," he reduced his own partisans to silence.[23]

Even as Boulanger sought to reinsure his coalition with the Right, the net around him was drawing tighter. When the Tirard ministry took office, many wild proposals were made by the Opportunists, who looked for any means of defeating the General, without regard to propriety. One solution offered was to classify as a prince subject to exile any French citizen who aspired to "personal power." [24] Constans had a better

---

[19] *Le Gaulois*, March 20, 1889.

[20] A.N.F., F⁷ 12447, March 19, 1889.

[21] *L'Autorité*, March 19, 1889.   [22] *Le Figaro*, March 19, 1889.

[23] Cf. *La Presse, L'Intransigeant,* and *La Cocarde,* March 19–20, 1889.

[24] Charles de Mazade, "Chronique de la quinzaine," *Revue des Deux Mondes,* XCII (March 1, 1889), 230–231.

idea: he struck at Boulanger through the *Ligue des patriotes.* On March 10, the state prosecutor of the Court of Appeal in Paris announced that the *Ligue* was going to be prosecuted for being what he termed "a secret organization." He explained that at its inception, the organization had had only a patriotic purpose, which transcended politics. In 1887, however, its leaders had staged antigovernmental demonstrations and publicly insulted the nation's military command. The prosecutor concluded that the *Ligue* had abandoned its original aims and become a political organization.[25]

Since there was nothing illegal about an organization's becoming political, the charge to that effect seems to have been aired merely to sway public opinion. It did not appear in the official accusation, which confined itself to one specific contention: that the *Ligue des patriotes* was a secret society. To buttress its case, the government invoked two laws, promulgated respectively in 1834 and 1848, plus articles 291 and 292 of the Penal Code. The former, which forbade the creation of political or other organizations of more than twenty members, had been the object of considerable legal criticism during the July Monarchy. Since then, both laws had fallen into disuse. That the government had to resort to such obsolete and plainly inappropriate statutes illustrates the fundamental weakness of its case.[26] Using them in conjunction with articles 291 and 292, which dealt with plots against the state, appeared like a dictatorial measure to the Radicals. A republic, warned Pelletan, must respect all political associations; otherwise, it ceases to be a republic.[27]

For Constans, on the other hand, the end fully justified the

[25] Reinach, *Bruno-le-fileur,* pp. 94–97.

[26] Charles de Mazade, "Chronique de la quinzaine," *Revue des Deux Mondes,* XCII (March 15, 1889), 469–470.

[27] *La Justice,* March 8, 1889.

means. The end was Boulanger, and the means in this instance turned out to be only a slight inconvenience to the *Ligue*. On April 3, 1889, Déroulède was brought to trial along with Laguerre and Laisant on charges of leading a secret society. The organization's cellular structure and some secret instructions sent by Déroulède to his subordinates were cited as proof. Déroulède defended himself by noting that meetings of the *Ligue* were open to all, even if its inner directives were secret. Laguerre reminded the court that France was literally covered with secret societies, such as the Masonic orders, which had never been molested.[28] In view of the public demonstrations organized by the *Ligue* (and cited by the prosecution to prove that it was secret!), the court ruled that the defendants were not guilty of belonging to a secret organization. They were, however, fined one hundred francs each for belonging to an unauthorized one.[29]

BOULANGER FLEES

Clearly, French jurisprudence was not well served by the prosecution of the *Ligue des patriotes*. The very nature of the verdict and the relative leniency of the fines imposed amply show that there was no judicial purpose in bringing Déroulède and his associates to trial. There was a political purpose, however, and it was admirably served by the entire incident. As an Opportunist journalist noted late in March: "If MM. Déroulède, Laguerre, and Laisant are guilty, how can M. Boulanger, their lord and master, be innocent?" [30]

Boulanger was asking himself the very same question. As early as March 10, the General and some of his lieutenants

[28] Albert Bataille, *Causes criminelles et mondaines de 1889* (Paris: Dentu, 1890), pp. 10–14.

[29] *Ibid.*, pp. 42–43.

[30] *La République Française,* March 27, 1889.

were reported to fear imminent arrest. Most frightened of all was Naquet, who urged Boulanger to flee to Belgium immediately.[31] So on March 13, the General went alone to Brussels, where he waited for news that a warrant for his arrest had been issued in Paris. Since none was forthcoming, he returned to France unhindered two days later. By March 20, however, it was being rumored that he had decided to leave the country again.[32] On returning from his two-day sojourn in Brussels, Boulanger had been warned by Dillon that a plot was being prepared against him.[33] Yet the General remained in France, perhaps because the last warning had proved to be unfounded.

A "plot" of sorts was indeed being concocted by Constans against Boulanger, but its execution encountered so much difficulty that the General did not sense any immediate danger. Having already moved against the *Ligue des patriotes,* the government now sought to bring charges against Boulanger. Its legal arguments for doing so were so weak, however, that the chief state prosecutor, Bouchez, simply refused to take the case. As the Interior Minister looked about for some other way to proceed legally against his prey, Boulanger continued to receive both friends and journalists at his home. To one and all he said that in view of the legal problems now facing the government, he did not believe that its plan would be carried out. He further assured them that, come what may, he would not think of leaving his beloved France.[34]

The situation changed radically on April 1, when Bouchez abruptly resigned, following a dispute with Constans and the Minister of Justice, Thévenet, who had drafted the charges against Boulanger. On leaving his post, Bouchez told the

---

[31] A.P.P., B a/909, March 11, 1889.
[32] *La Nation,* March 22, 1889.
[33] A.P.P., B a/969, March 19, 1889.
[34] *Le Figaro,* March 31 and April 1, 1889.

assembled reporters that had he been a politician, he would have been only too happy to have Boulanger brought to trial. As a magistrate, however, he could not do so in good conscience. Bouchez was replaced by Quesnay de Beaurepaire, who was both a magistrate and a politician.[35] As soon as this news reached the press, Boulanger realized that the replacement of Bouchez cleared the way for a trial. He left his home in disguise, and with Mme. de Bonnemains at his side took the midnight train for Brussels.[36] The government, informed of the General's movement, made no effort to intervene.

Boulanger's decision to leave France was taken after consultation with Dillon and Arthur Meyer; but none of the leftist members of his committee—who, after all, did form the majority—had even been informed of his plans. As reported by the police, Dillon wanted Boulanger out of the country in order to exercise greater influence over him. In Paris, the General would have remained exposed to the views of his leftist associates. Meyer, in turn, did not want him to overshadow the Right at the approach of general elections. With Boulanger in exile, the Conservatives could use his name without having to suffer through any more of his speeches on the future "national republic." [37]

The General's sudden flight to Brussels took his most loyal supporters completely by surprise. On April 2, all the members of the National Committee—minus Dillon, who was in exile with Boulanger—arrived as scheduled at the Paris restaurant where they were supposed to have lunch with him. When he failed to show up, no one could explain his ab-

[35] *Le Gaulois,* April 1, 1889.
[36] Charles de Mazade, "Chronique de la quinzaine," *Revue des Deux Mondes,* XCII (April 15, 1889), 947–948.
[37] A.P.P., B a/972, April 3, 1889.

sence.[38] So the Boulangist press of that evening was probably sincere in denying, most vigorously, reports by other journals that he had fled.[39] Once Boulanger published a manifesto from Brussels condemning the French government for cowardice and dictatorial action, his committee could no longer claim that he was still in Paris. To keep from losing face, it issued a declaration of its own, approving completely of his conduct. Had he remained in France, it claimed, he would have been arrested the next day.[40]

Despite this brave front, the unity of the Boulangist movement was momentarily weakened by the sudden departure of its titular head. Georges Thiébaud promptly resigned from the National Committee, giving as his reason the argument that the movement had been taken over by the same reactionaries who had advised Boulanger to flee.[41] Since Thiébaud was no great progressive, it is more probable that he left because the General's absence reduced his usefulness as a vote getter. Another resignation was tendered by Susini, who approved of Boulanger's leaving the country, but claimed that the National Committee's growing monarchist tendencies compelled him to withdraw.[42] Whether or not these were Susini's true motives, his resignation was at least occasioned by Boulanger's flight.

Of the several defections from the Boulangist movement, the most serious in ideological terms was that of Henri Michelin. Unlike the other members of the National Committee, Michelin never had let strategic considerations keep him from trying to promote his own particular form of consti-

[38] *Le Figaro*, April 3, 1889.
[39] Cf. *La Presse, La Cocarde,* and *La France,* April 3, 1889.
[40] *La Presse,* April 7, 1889.   [41] *Le Matin,* April 4, 1889.
[42] *Le XIXᵉ Siècle,* April 7, 1889.

tutional revision. When a commission of the Chamber was holding hearings on the question, Michelin had been the only leading Boulangist to present a memoir distinct from that already presented by the General.[43] Now he left the movement altogether and announced that he was forming what he called a "Central Revisionist Committee." Members of all existing revisionist groups were invited to help in the drafting of a minimum program. New memberships were being received at the offices of *L'Action* and *Le Clairon,* another Boulangist newspaper which withdrew its support for the General after April 1.[44]

A week after leaving the Boulangists, Michelin announced that his new organization was forming committees throughout the Paris area. Only bona fide Republicans without a Conservative past were being accepted for membership, he declared. "There will never be an alliance with the so-called *ralliés* to the Republic."[45] At its first meeting on May 16, 1889, the new group elected Michelin president and adopted his political philosophy without hesitation. All speakers promised to work for "the triumph of the social and impersonal Republic [i.e., one not dependent on a particular leader], which alone is worthy of all the children of 1789."[46] So great was the attraction of Michelin's new group that the influential daily, *La France,* became its ally on May 21.[47] This was the most important Boulangist newspaper to quit the General's campaign organization.

That the government had scored an immediate victory over Boulanger could not be denied, even by those who disapproved of its methods. By having the Senate constitute itself as a High Court, Constans only added to the prestige of an institution

[43] *J.O.C.* (1889), pp. 357–358.   [44] *L'Action,* April 6, 1889.
[45] *Ibid.,* April 13, 1889.   [46] *Ibid.,* May 17, 1889.
[47] *La France,* May 22, 1889.

which the French Left wanted either to weaken or to eliminate altogether. Yet the same Radicals who criticized the Interior Minister's actions on legal grounds were the first to cheer his policy when it brought results. At the news that Boulanger had fled the country, *La Lanterne* cried: "The adventure is over." [48] Pelletan concurred, saying that the General's flight was an act of political suicide.[49] He rebuked Constans, however, for lack of scruples in the juridical aspects of the episode.[50]

In dealing with Boulanger, the government was on just as weak a legal footing as it had been with Déroulède. Its case rested on articles 87 through 89 of the Penal Code, which concerned the crimes of *complot,* plotting against the state, and *attentat,* attempting to execute the plot. According to Pierre Rigot, an advocate at the Court of Cassation, the Senate had no competence to try Boulanger. Only a jury could try a case of plotting against the state; and although the Senate was competent to try a plot followed by an actual attempt to carry it out, no such attempt was, in fact, made.[51] Regardless of possible improper venue, the Senate voted, 207 to 62, for the enabling act to transform itself into the High Court on March 30; the Chamber ratified the act by a vote of 333 to 199 on April 4.[52]

When the trial actually began on August 8, Quesnay de Beaurepaire demonstrated only too well the weakness of the government's case against Boulanger. Unable to prove that there had actually been an attempt to overthrow the regime, the prosecutor digressed into the claim that, as War Minister, Boulanger had misused the secret funds of his ministry. Some of the less savory aspects of the General's private life, such as

---

[48] *La Lanterne,* April 15, 1889.   [49] *La Justice,* April 4, 1889.
[50] *Ibid.,* April 5, 1889.   [51] *Le Figaro,* April 9, 1889.
[52] *La République Française,* March 31 and April 5, 1889.

an old liaison with a woman of ill repute named Madame Pourpe, were also dredged up in an attempt to blacken his public image. Quesnay de Beaurepaire actually admitted at one point that these questions were completely irrelevant to the official charges.[53] But he continued to elaborate on them, lacking any better means to influence the public. The only point successfully raised by the prosecution was that, both as a soldier and as a politician, Boulanger had been extremely ambitious; but this in itself was no crime.[54]

After a week-long session, the Senate found Boulanger, Dillon, and Rochefort guilty on both counts and sentenced all three to deportation to a French penal colony. In this trial without a defense, only Boulanger had been really discussed by the prosecuting attorney and the witnesses he called to the stand.[55] As soon as the verdict was published, Boulanger issued a reply which, like the accusation against him, overlooked the real charges. After calling the High Court a mere rubber stamp of a criminal cabinet, he gave an involved explanation of his use of War Ministry funds.[56] Public opinion seems to have been generally indifferent to both the accusation against the General and his petulant reply. Students of law and politics did not hesitate to say publicly that the charges were legally unsound. For most citizens, however, the points raised were too complicated to discuss in detail.[57] Even if he had failed to sway public opinion, Constans still succeeded in keeping Boulanger out of the country. For the government, that alone was a gain.

[53] France, Haute Cour de Justice, *Affaire Boulanger, Dillon, Rochefort: Procédure générale*, p. 45.

[54] Bataille, *op. cit.*, pp. 51–59.   [55] *Ibid.*, p. 73.

[56] Général Boulanger, "Au peuple, mon seul juge!" (pamphlet); cf. Henri Rochefort, *Les aventures de ma vie* (5 vols.; Paris: Dupont, 1897), V, 190–191.

[57] A.P.P., B a/973, July 18, 1889; B a/972, Aug. 17, 1889.

Far more successful in influencing public opinion was the Paris World's Fair, which opened on May 5, 1889, exactly one hundred years to the day after the convening of the Estates-General at Versailles. It was at Versailles also that the Fair was officially inaugurated by President Carnot, who called its magnificent realizations "the work of France, not of a party." The Conservatives were then invited to "take their place once more in the direction of the country's affairs." [58] This speech set the tone for the entire exposition, which celebrated the French Revolution not in a political, partisan sense, but for its economic and cultural achievements. As if to emphasize this point, the soaring Eiffel Tower reminded all Frenchmen that their country was still in the vanguard of progress.[59]

In the purely political field, the government scored its most telling blow against Boulanger on July 13 with the passage of a law forbidding candidates to run for office in more than one district in each election. Unlike previous measures against Boulanger, this one was introduced by a group of Radicals—including Clemenceau, Floquet, and Pichon. They admitted frankly that its purpose was "to thwart a plebiscite on the name of one man." The bill drew the usual criticisms from the Conservatives, who accused its authors of resorting to expedients in trying to oppose a force stronger than they. In a sarcastic vein, Le Hérissé offered a counterproposal forbidding Boulanger by name to run in any by-election! The most serious criticism of the bill, however, came from Jaurès, who noted that even if Boulanger were to win in sixty ridings, he would have to withdraw from fifty-nine. These seats would not

[58] Charles de Mazade, "Chronique de la quinzaine," *Revue des Deux Mondes,* XCIII (May 15, 1889), 468–469.
[59] Raymond Isay, *Panorama des expositions universelles* (Paris: Gallimard, 1937), pp. 178–180.

necessarily fall to Conservatives if the Republicans had genuine electoral support there. By proposing this "artificial precaution," said Jaurès, the Republicans were just admitting their own weakness before the voters.[60]

Despite the admonitions of Jaurès, a majority composed of Opportunists and Radicals was easily mustered for the bill. It is, of course, impossible to determine how the coalition of Boulangists and Conservatives would have fared if the General had been able to run wherever he liked. What is known is that when the *scrutin de liste* was abolished, Boulanger had planned to run in about one hundred districts and then withdraw in favor of loyal followers. He did foresee that a law barring plural candidacies by a single individual might be passed. In that case, he claimed, there would be no difficulty in having his followers elected on the first ballot.[61] If this were true, one might ask, why then had the General planned to run in a hundred districts in the first place? The fact remains that the Boulangist central committee had not organized itself into a true political party. Aside from its titular head and the fourteen incumbent Boulangists in the Chamber, there were few partisans of the General who were likely to be candidates in their own right. By forcing the Boulangists to improvise a party organization, the government gained a tactical advantage.

Not taking any chances, the Tirard ministry now held all civil servants to the strictest possible loyalty; anyone suspected of sympathy to Boulanger or his allies was carefully eliminated from the administration.[62] This may be one of the reasons for Boulanger's disappointing performance in the can-

[60] *J.O.C.* (1889), pp. 2002–2009.
[61] *Le Matin,* March 21, 1889; cf. A.P.P., B a/972, May 17, 1889.
[62] Charles de Mazade, "Chronique de la quinzaine," *Revue des Deux Mondes,* XCIV (Aug. 1, 1889), 710–711.

tonal elections of July 23. Disregarding the law against plural candidacies, the General asked for a write-in vote in eighty cantons—no more, no less—as a protest against this new "blow to universal suffrage." [63] In the end, Boulanger's name was presented by his organization in ninety-three cantons, and he lost in all but four. Inasmuch as the issues in these contests were primarily local, it would be unfair to call the results a crushing defeat for the General; but his national "image" was a bit tarnished thereafter.[64]

THE GENERAL ELECTIONS OF 1889

In spite of considerable adversity—Boulanger's flight to Belgium, the defection of some of his lieutenants, the changes in electoral procedure, and his defeat in the local elections— the Boulangist movement managed to hold together. Even more, it maintained its working relationship with the Conservatives. The disarray caused by the General's abrupt departure proved to be only momentary. At the first shock on hearing the news, the members of several Boulangist committees in the departments (in Bordeaux, notably) thought of resigning. On second thought, however, most of them decided to stay on.[65] Although Thiébaud never returned to the Boulangists, Michelin did; he sold his newspaper to a group of antirevisionist Radicals in June, 1889, and ran as a bona fide Boulangist in Paris three months later.

Those who returned to the Boulangist movement appear to have done so primarily because it did not collapse. Although Michelin was able to form a committee of his own in Paris, it never matched the strength of Boulanger's organization and— what is perhaps more important—had no access to royalist funds. During the period of Michelin's separation from that

[63] *L'Intransigeant*, July 21, 1889. [64] *Le Paris*, Aug. 2, 1889.
[65] A.N.F., F⁷ 12447, April 6, 1889.

229

organization, he loudly criticized it for failing to present a specific program before the general elections.[66] To this charge Mermeix replied serenely: "This concern about a program seems futile to us." To qualify as a Boulangist, each candidate was simply to promise to accept the Republic and to vote for revision if elected. Only once the constituent assembly actually met would it be necessary to draw up a program.[67] Michelin eventually accepted this formula. He knew that he had a far better chance of being elected as a Boulangist than as an independent.

Among the Conservatives, a similar reasoning seems to have prevailed. When the Duchesse d'Uzès learned that the General had fled, she stopped contributing to his cause. By early May, however, she had resumed.[68] Since no one but Boulanger seemed to her to be capable of restoring the monarchy, she really had no other choice except to continue her generous investment in his venture. If she withdrew her financial support, she would not only lose everything she had contributed previously, but would also risk becoming a political enemy if he happened to win. As the Duchesse became reconciled to Boulanger, Dillon was resuming his collection of funds from other royalists.[69] Although many individual royalists did think of leaving the coalition with Boulanger just after his flight, they apparently reconsidered following reminders by party leaders that the arrangement was designed for their benefit.[70]

As the general elections of 1889 approached, there was no hint of the theory, formulated some time later, that by leaving France, Boulanger ruined his own party and dragged the roy-

[66] *L'Action*, May 25, 1889.   [67] *La Cocarde*, May 25, 1889.
[68] A.P.P., B a/974, April 10 and May 3, 1889.
[69] *Ibid.*, April 29, 1889.   [70] *Le Gaulois*, April 16, 1889.

alists down with it.[71] This theory seems to have originated with Dillon's personal secretary, who used it to explain the coalition's defeat in the general elections of 1889. The General's flight to Brussels, he claims, was a "desertion of which we were all victims." The "we" in this case refers to the Conservatives, who were urged to draw the logical moral from their defeat and never again to have any dealings with a party of the Left.[72] Since by then the Right had already cut its ties with Boulanger, such advice hardly seems necessary. That it came from the secretary of Dillon, who had persuaded Boulanger to leave France in the first place, is ironic at the very least.

If royalist post mortems are discounted, a vastly different picture of the 1889 elections emerges. What caused the Boulangists the most difficulty was not the General's flight but the change in electoral procedure, which forced them, in effect, to create a party. The measure of their success in adapting to the change can be seen in the more than 120 Boulangist candidates in the general elections of 1889. Perhaps more indicative of the party's strength is the fact that about thirty royalists and Bonapartists added the qualification "Boulangist" to their party label in order to win more votes.[73] In Paris, the very base of the movement, Boulangist propaganda continued to win adherents after the General left the country.[74]

As for the Conservatives, some had indeed been initially dejected following Boulanger's sudden departure; but the

[71] For a clear summary of this theory, see Denis W. Brogan, *The Development of Modern France, 1870–1939* (London: Hamish Hamilton, 1959), pp. 210–213.

[72] J. Lamoureux, *Un an d'exil* (Paris: Savine, 1890), pp. 4 *et passim.*

[73] *La République Française,* Sept. 24 and Oct. 7, 1889.

[74] A.P.P., B a/969, April 17, 1889; B a/971, July 3, 1889.

party soon regained confidence and looked forward to certain victory. Paul de Cassagnac was the first to recognize that the physical absence of Boulanger might be a help to the Right, rather than a hindrance. As long as the General was in France, winning votes by the force of his personality, there was a danger that he might entice a significant number of Conservative voters into his ranks. Now that he was safely in exile, the Conservative candidates would benefit from his patronage by winning Republican votes.[75] Shortly before the elections, Cornély took up this idea and advised Boulanger not to return to France. By staying abroad, predicted the royalist journalist, "he will owe everything to the Conservatives." [76]

A manifesto from the Comte de Paris on August 28, 1889, indicates that the Conservative-Boulangist coalition was still functioning according to plan. "Wherever you have candidates," he told his followers, "support them energetically. Elsewhere, bear in mind the necessities of the contest and do not treat as enemies those who fight the same adversaries as you." [77] Thanks to the single-member constituency, the Conservatives were able to maintain their alliance with Boulanger without the risk of being drawn into his concept of a new Republic. Frary noted that Boulangism, which might have become the trade-mark of all the opposition parties under the *scrutin de liste,* was now simply the credo of a new party.[78] The Conservatives maintained their identity.

It is true that, in the general elections, "less than twenty candidates dared to run as Monarchists." [79] But this in itself does not prove that Boulanger's flight to Brussels had killed

---

[75] *L'Autorité,* April 20, 1889.   [76] *Le Gaulois,* Sept. 6, 1889.

[77] *Ibid.,* Aug. 28, 1889.

[78] Raoul Frary, "Chronique politique," *La Nouvelle Revue,* LX (Sept. 1, 1889), 197.

[79] Brogan, *op. cit.,* p. 213.

the royalist party. Those who called themselves Monarchists in this period were, in fact, Legitimists; the Orleanists and most Bonapartists used the Conservative label, which had proved so helpful in 1885. In the elections of that year, no candidates ran as Monarchists; all rightists were grouped under the Conservative banner in order to maintain discipline and benefit thereby from the *scrutin de liste*. The Right was still very well disciplined in 1889, but the new electoral law allowed each candidate to identify his individual political coloring.

With Boulanger safely out of the country and the *scrutin d'arrondissement* now in force, each Boulangist or Conservative voter could decide for himself what the issues of the campaign really were. For that devout royalist, Auguste Boucher, the question put to the electorate was simple: monarchy or republic? "In 1885," he recalled, "universal suffrage was asked to condemn only the politicians; in 1889, it is being asked to condemn both the politicians and the Constitution. . . . We shall know on the evening of September 22 whether the Republic has survived." [80] Certainly at no other time in the history of the Third Republic was the question of the regime so clearly put to the electorate. Even in 1889, however, many adversaries of the government recognized that, just as in 1885, most voters were not fundamentally hostile to the Republic. So Cassagnac sought to reassure his readers by saying, "Our concern is not with the REPUBLIC itself but with the MEN of the Republic." [81] As the elections drew closer, many Boulangists talked less about revising the constitution and more about changing "the present administration . . . the Opportunist coterie." Mermeix also tried to ally the fears of many voters, adding: "Whatever the Opportunists and

[80] Auguste Boucher, "Chronique politique," *Le Correspondant*, CLVI (Sept. 10, 1889), 985.

[81] *L'Autorité*, Sept. 20, 1889.

ex-Radicals say, the existence of the Republic is not at issue." [82]

What was at issue, in the minds of the Boulangists at least, was their own revolutionary, Jacobin conception of the Republic. A revisionist theorist who proudly identified himself as an executor of Auguste Comte's will argued in 1888 that the great Revolution of 1789 must be allowed to resume its true course.[83] Boulangist electoral propaganda in the fall of 1889 reflected such revolutionary idealism by addressing voters as *citoyen*.[84] The party's program, announced one poster, was "bequeathed to us by the FRENCH REVOLUTION." [85] Social injustice would quickly disappear, predicted another, if the principles of the great Revolution were put into practice. At the same time, however, the authors of this message, who described themselves as the "Republican Socialist Revisionist Committee of the fourteenth *arrondissement*," openly repudiated what they called "the baneful doctrine of class struggle." [86] In this, they closely followed the theories of Naquet, who maintained that more education and an equitable tax structure—not communism—would resolve the workers' problems in an industrial society.[87]

The importance of industrialization was not, however, grasped by many of the General's partisans, as indicated by the following assertion from a Boulangist weekly in Paris:

France, which is in relation to its neighbors the best endowed country, the one to which nature has been the most generous, is

[82] *La Cocarde*, Sept. 7, 1889.

[83] Georges Audiffrent, *Parlementarisme, dictature* (Paris: Welter, 1888), *passim*.

[84] A.P.P., B a/1465.   [85] *Ibid.*, B a/1468.

[86] *Ibid.*, B a/1518, Nov. 7, 1889.

[87] Alfred Naquet, *Socialisme collectiviste et socialisme libéral* (Paris: Dentu, 1890), pp. 175, 195, *et passim*.

dying. Revision of the constitution, by giving France institutions better suited to our mores and our times, along with the great scientific discoveries of our age, will allow it to regain its place in the world.[88]

In point of fact, France was better endowed as an agricultural than an industrial nation. What coal reserves it did possess were inefficiently developed by family firms operating in a protected economy hampered by lack of credit and inadequate transport facilities.[89] The country's relative industrial decline in the late nineteenth century was due less to its political institutions than to the Malthusian attitude of French entrepreneurs. Few if any of the Boulangists seem to have understood this, however. They placed all their hopes in a primarily political solution to their country's difficulties.

Boulangists and Conservatives entered the first round of the general elections on September 22 in a spirit of glowing optimism and met with bitter defeat. In a letter to Naquet that day, Boulanger predicted that the first ballot would yield 223 Boulangists and Conservatives and 138 Republicans.[90] He was to be sadly disappointed: instead of 138 Republicans, there were 203, as against 111 Conservatives and only 17 Boulangists. With a few exceptions, such as the departments of the Haute-Garonne, Meurthe-et-Moselle, and Haute-Vienne, the alliance between Boulangists and Conservatives worked perfectly. Only in these three departments did the two parties oppose one another. Thirteen out of the seventeen Boulangist victories on the first ballot were won outside of Paris in departments where there were large Conservative majorities.

[88] *Le Quinzième,* Jan. 17–23, 1889.

[89] Charles P. Kindleberger, *Economic Growth in France and Britain, 1851–1950* (Cambridge, Mass.: Harvard University Press, 1964), pp. 17–29.

[90] Bibliothèque nationale, N.A.F. 23783, no. 74.

Boulanger himself had done extremely well. In the blood-red Clignancourt district, he won on the first ballot with an official count of 8,303 votes, as against 5,500 for his leading rival, the possibilist Joffrin.[91] The government, however, ruling that the General's candidacy was illegal because he was in exile, impounded the ballot boxes and declared Joffrin the winner.[92] For the same reason, Dillon was deprived of his first-ballot victory in the Morbihan. Throughout the country, the election results had been affected in some measure by the change in voting procedure. Thanks partly to the *scrutin d'arrondissement,* the compact regions of opposition which had existed in 1885 were now fragmented. The Charentes were not as Bonapartist as formerly, while the Nord and the Finistère produced mixed delegations of Conservatives and Republicans.[93]

Even this severe setback did not cause the royalists to leave their Boulangist allies before the second ballot. They were too embroiled in the coalition to benefit from a rupture at this point. When Philippe de Grandlieu warned that the Boulangists were dragging the royalists down to defeat, Arthur Meyer called him a traitor to the party and predicted victory in *ballotage.*[94] After the second round, however, there could be no further illusions. The Boulangist total rose to 38 and that of the Conservatives to 167, but the Republicans emerged as undisputed masters of the new Chamber with a total of 363 seats.[95] A terse note from Arthur Meyer announced that since their pact with the Boulangists had not served its purpose, the royalists were now ending it.[96]

[91] A.N.F., C 5326 A 96.   [92] *Le Temps,* Sept. 24, 1889.
[93] Raoul Frary, "Chronique Politique," *La Nouvelle Revue,* LX (Oct. 1, 1889), 645–646.
[94] *Le Gaulois,* Sept. 29, 1889.
[95] *La Justice,* Oct. 7 and 8, 1889.
[96] *Le Gaulois,* Oct. 8, 1889.

In view of their late start as a political party, the Boulangists had made a respectable showing. They won 18 seats in the Seine, mostly in working-class districts, as compared to 20 for the Republicans. Only a few well-known Boulangist candidates, such as Rochefort in Paris and Koechlin-Schwartz in Lille, were defeated, while some less important figures scored impressive victories. Maurice Barrès in Nancy and Henri Aimel in Bordeaux were among the few Boulangists in the provinces who won with little or no help from the Right. In Limoges, the Boulangist candidate, who had been in third place on the first ballot, won on the second after the Radical candidate withdrew in favor of an Opportunist.[97]

On the other hand, Boulanger's previous by-election victories generally failed to help either Conservative or Boulangist candidates in the general elections. Only in the Dordogne, where the Right won four seats previously held by Republicans, did the General's earlier success seem to have aided his allies. In the Nord, however, the Republicans regained eleven seats, as against nine for the Conservatives and one Boulangist, Lalou. The victory in the Somme of the Boulangist, Millevoie, was offset by the loss of a formerly Conservative seat to a Republican. In the Charente-Inférieure, where no Boulangists were elected, the Republicans won two seats from the Right.[98] Taken across the nation, therefore, the Boulangists' failure was complete. Because their coalition with the Right had been predicated on winning an absolute majority in the new Chamber, anything less had to be a disaster.

Herein lies the justification for the extraordinary and virtually dictatorial measures employed by Tirard and Constans. They understood that Boulanger's success depended less on

[97] *La Justice,* Oct. 9, 1889.

[98] Alphonse Bertrand, *La Chambre de 1889: Biographies des 576 députés* (Paris: Michaud, 1890), *passim.*

his loyal Jacobin followers than on his alliance with the Right. All that mattered, therefore, was to prevent the Boulangist-Conservative coalition from winning a majority in the general elections of 1889. By so doing, the government split the coalition and permanently undermined the General's position.

11

The Legacy of Boulangism

~~~~~~

That the general elections of 1889 had constituted a vote of confidence in the Republic could hardly be denied, even by its most dedicated enemies. "We must recognize that universal suffrage has not favored the Conservative party," wrote Boucher candidly. "It seems that the Republic has been given a second chance." [1] That the elections did not reflect an equal amount of confidence in the incumbent Republicans is shown by the fact that only half of the Deputies elected in 1889 had served in the previous Chamber. Among the vanquished was Jules Ferry, who lost in the first round in his stronghold of Saint-Dié to a self-styled "Boulangist-Conservative." Martin-Feuillée, a former Opportunist minister known for his purges of the judiciary, lost in the same round to a Conservative in Rennes. In Amiens, René Goblet, who had been co-author of the laic school laws but was in other respects a very pale Radical, was beaten by the Boulangist Millevoie.[2] "The voters," Boucher concluded, "have expressed their desire to have, if not a new form of government, at least a better sort of Republic." [3]

[1] Auguste Boucher, "Chronique politique," *Le Correspondant*, CLVII (Oct. 10, 1889), 179.

[2] Charles de Mazade, "Chronique de la quinzaine," *Revue des Deux Mondes*, XCV (Oct. 1, 1889), 707–709.

[3] Auguste Boucher, "Chronique politique," *Le Correspondant*, CLVII (Nov. 10, 1889), 373.

Both royalists and moderate Republicans agreed that the new kind of Republic desired by the electorate was one in which extremes of Right and Left would be avoided.[4] Amidst the victory celebrations of the Opportunists, Jules Simon advised them to avoid any wholesale purge of the Conservatives in the new Chamber. The Right was now thoroughly disenchanted with the Boulangists, he noted; any use of highhanded methods would only serve to draw these strange bedfellows together again.[5] The government seems to have followed this admonition: only six royalists were deprived of their seats as Deputies; of these, three recovered them in the ensuing by-elections.[6] This policy of moderation, which had actually begun with the recall to France of the Duc d'Aumale, made the Republic even more inviting to the royalists, who by now had lost all hope of controlling the government.

A new role for the conservatives clearly had to be found. According to the Vicomte de Gontaut-Biron, the Deputies of the Right had nothing to gain by opposing the Republicans on all issues. What they should do, he said, was to form a Conservative minority and work for their own interests within the regime.[7] An open suggestion by the Marquis de Castellane that the royalists abandon all hope of a restoration and frankly accept the Republic was, however, rejected by the party's leaders.[8] At a plenary meeting of Conservative Deputies held on November 13, 1889, it was moved that the party adopt as a policy statement the declaration made by the Comte de Paris

[4] See Cornély's comment in *Le Gaulois*, Oct. 22, 1889.

[5] *Le Matin*, Nov. 13, 1889.

[6] Guy Chapman, *The Third Republic of France: The First Phase, 1871–1894* (London: Macmillan, 1962), p. 290.

[7] Vicomte de Gontaut-Biron, "La Chambre de 1889 et la droite," *Le Correspondant*, LCVII (Oct. 25, 1889), 189.

[8] *Le Gaulois*, Nov. 4, 1889.

on September 1, 1886. On that occasion, the pretender had instructed his party to avoid systematic opposition to the Republicans. The habit of two years of systematic opposition could not be broken overnight, however. In an emotionally charged atmosphere, the meeting adjourned without a vote on the motion.[9] If many Conservatives were still ideologically opposed to any form of cooperation with the Republic, they were nonetheless in no mood to rejoin Boulanger.

THE BOULANGISTS' LAST ATTEMPT

The postelection disorder among the Conservatives was more than matched by the utter chaos which shook the Boulangist camp. Immediately after the disaster, Naquet wrote to the General, suggesting that he leave as soon as possible for America. Naquet argued in a letter of October 8, 1889, that Boulanger's further separation from his native land would help his party by making it appear less personal. Once the Boulangists gained control of government, he could return.[10] This crude attempt to oust the General from his own movement failed, as did that of Laguerre to exclude Dillon and Rochefort. Laguerre's obvious wish to seize control of the Boulangist organization elicited a sharp rebuke from the General, who reaffirmed his intention to remain its leader.[11]

Along with personal rivalries, there was some disagreement among the Boulangists as to the causes of their defeat. In the first of a spate of post mortems, Déroulède blamed his party's failure on governmental pressure on the voters, as well as outright fraud. At the same time, he admitted that sincere love

[9] *Ibid.*, Nov. 14, 1889.
[10] Bibliothèque Nationale, N.A.F. 23783, no. 53.
[11] A.P.P., B a/969, Oct. 9, 1889.

for the Republic had prompted many Frenchmen to oppose Boulanger and his movement. The Opportunists had succeeded in convincing the people that a Boulangist victory would mean the destruction of the Republic.[12] The General himself explained that after his three-fold victory of August 19, 1888, both he and his followers had assumed that public opinion throughout the country was favorable to their cause. The error was in thinking that they could win a majority in the Chamber with so little advance preparation. "We were in too much of a hurry," he admitted; but he expressed confidence that by the next general elections, the Boulangists would have the votes of most French citizens.[13]

Boulanger's own analysis of the defeat provides a clue as to why Naquet wanted him to go to America. Under the mistaken impression that everyone who had voted for him was a Boulangist, the General assumed that it would be a relatively easy matter to increase this total to an absolute majority of the electorate. He accordingly issued a manifesto from Jersey, his latest refuge, promising the French people that his "National Party" would continue to work for the establishment of a republic open to everyone. A regime of this kind, he predicted, would be based on the program he had presented at Tours on March 19, 1889, and would "assure the national reconciliation of all good citizens." [14] By reiterating the proposals he had made at Tours, Boulanger failed to distinguish between the support formerly given to him by frustrated rightists and that of his own party, which leaned strongly to the Left.

What the General himself did not understand was already plain to his political lieutenants. When asked what their future course should be, Laisant replied: "The Boulangists in parliament should move to the Left in order to dispel any ambiguity

12 *La Presse,* Oct. 10, 1889.   13 *Le Matin,* Oct. 23, 1889.
14 *Ibid.,* Nov. 12, 1889.

as to their true identity." [15] Indeed they could hardly do anything else. Abandoned by their Conservative allies, the Boulangists emerged more clearly than ever as a leftist group. Only on the Left could they expect to find any possible collaborators.

Leftist collaborators now proved difficult to find. The Radicals continued to oppose the movement as they had done since 1888. Those Socialists who had collaborated with the Boulangists did so primarily because they expected the movement to help them win public office. Except for the few Socialists who were elected to the Chamber as Boulangists in 1889, that movement withdrew its already vacillating support from the General. Before the new Chamber met for its first session on November 12, 1889, some of the Boulangists decided to stage a peaceful demonstration at the Place de la Concorde to protest the government's invalidation of Boulanger's votes. Although the invalidation violated both the constitution and common democratic principles, only the Blanquists were willing to join in the demonstration. Even they were badly split over Boulanger. In the recent general elections, two Blanquist candidates who had adopted the Boulangist label—Granger and Jules Roche—won, while two who had run only as Blanquists—Chauvière and Vaillant—lost.[16] The demonstration turned out to be an utter failure, to the undisguised joy of many Conservatives.[17]

Having recently constituted a political force of national importance, the Boulangists were expected to try to regain some measure of their former strength. From December, 1889, to July, 1890, the Ministry of the Interior maintained extensive surveillance operations all along the Breton coast. It was be-

[15] *La Cocarde,* Oct. 9, 1889.
[16] *Journal des Débats,* Nov. 10, 1889.
[17] A.P.P., B a/970, Nov. 13, 1889.

lieved that Boulanger might try to land in France just as
Napoleon had done and lead his partisans in an assault on the
regime. Over a hundred surveillance reports, including several
false alarms of a landing, are filed in the Archives Nationales.[18] A few even include maps of a possible landing area
near Cancale, considered the most likely spot because the railway lines between Saint-Malo and Rennes ran nearby. On
learning of such extreme precautions, the Boulangist committee in Paris called them ridiculous and repeated its intention to
use only political means to take office.[19]

An opportunity for the Boulangists to improve their political fortunes arose in the form of elections to the Paris city
council on April 27 and May 4, 1890. Here, the party was
on its home ground and had every reason to be optimistic.
Since the Conservatives had little following in the capital, the
loss of their support did not appear very important. To win
additional votes, the Boulangists included antisemitic and
Blanquist candidates among their own. One of the latter was
Boulé, who had run against Boulanger in the by-election of
January 27, 1889. He was publicly recommended by the
General as a fellow "victim of the Opportunists." [20] In its
campaign propaganda, the Boulangist organization tried to
woo the Parisians with promises of local home rule. In the
main, however, its appeals were directed to national issues,
such as revision of the constitution and the quashing of the
High Court's verdict.[21]

Despite good organization and discipline, the Boulangists
saw only one of their candidates elected on the first ballot and
one more on the second. Even before May 4 it was clear that

[18] They are located in carton F⁷ 12447.
[19] *La Presse,* March 8, 1890.
[20] A.P.P., B a/909, bis, April 12, 1890.
[21] *La Presse,* April 9 and 13, 1890.

the party was finished; having lost on its home territory, it could hardly count on success elsewhere. Its emphasis on national, rather than local, issues may have been one of the reasons for its defeat. Just as important, however, is the fact that the public had lost hope of ever seeing the General and his partisans assume power. "Fifteen months ago," Frary observed, "General Boulanger represented a host of grievances and hopes; the grievances subsist, but the hopes have practically vanished." [22]

After the vote of April 27, some of the leading Boulangists went to Jersey, where they found the General completely demoralized over the results. Despite efforts to console him, he alternated between tears and rage at his candidates' poor performance.[23] Boulanger's behavior, plus the results of the second round, helped ruin his committee's morale. Georges Laguerre did not hesitate to declare publicly that the General was "finished, irreparably finished." Laguerre led a faction which included Naquet, Laisant, Mermeix, and Susini, all of whom favored immediate dissolution of the National Committee and the entire movement. Opposing them was a group of lesser-known members, led by Déroulède, who wanted it to continue. At the Committee's meeting in Paris on May 5, Déroulède's group accused its opponents of treason. This argument was enough to keep the Committee in being by a vote of 18 to 10. An ambiguous declaration was then issued to the effect that while "not wishing to disturb the country by temporarily sterile agitation," the Committee would maintain its program.[24] Three weeks later, however, the same Committee, pausing briefly to thank General Boulanger for his services,

[22] Raoul Frary, "Chronique politique," *La Nouvelle Revue*, LXIV (May 1, 1890), 200.
[23] A.N.F., F⁷ 12445, May 1, 1890.
[24] *Lyon Républicain*, May 7, 1890.

formally voted to disband.[25] Its treasury was now completely empty; there was not even enough money to pay off previous debts contracted during the Paris municipal election campaign.[26]

By this time, the General had apparently resigned himself to at least a temporary retirement from politics. It was he who pushed the National Committee into taking the final step of voting its own dissolution when he wrote to Laisant on May 14: "The task of the committee of which I am the president seems to me to be at an end." He went on to explain that he did not mean to withdraw permanently from the political scene. "But I want no more intermediaries between myself and universal suffrage." [27] By this act, Boulanger effectively severed relations with his former lieutenants. In the fall of 1890, the first installments of *Les Coulisses du boulangisme,* Mermeix's then startling revelations of the General's ties with the Right, began to appear in *Le Figaro.* In his own version of the affair, Boulanger accused all the members of the Committee, save Rochefort, of making deals with the reactionaries. He claimed that he never took any interest in money matters and was totally ignorant of the contributions made by the Comte de Paris. Finally, he blamed his party's defeat in the recent Paris elections on the Committee's overly warm attitude toward the Conservatives.[28]

The end of the Boulangist movement was but a prelude to the end of Boulanger himself. When Madame de Bonnemains became ill with tuberculosis, he moved with her in May, 1891, from the damp climate of Jersey to the slightly less damp climate of Brussels. Her death in July left him extremely

[25] *La Presse,* May 23, 1890.
[26] A.P.P., B a/1465, May 17, 1890.
[27] *L'Intransigeant,* May 17, 1890.
[28] *Le XIXe Siècle,* Sept. 16, 1890.

morose to the point of rarely leaving the house except to visit her grave at Ixelles. For three months longer, he continued to live modestly with two nieces and his eighty-seven-year-old mother, who was completely senile and thought that he was still War Minister.[29] Then, on September 30, he shot himself at the grave of his mistress. Although his suicide note gave grief at her death as the motive, the fact remains that Boulanger was then penniless. Having used his inheritance to pay previously incurred debts, he asked his few remaining friends for money. Some of them promised him a loan, but none kept the promise. While Madame de Bonnemains was alive, she had helped support the General. This may partly explain why he was so attentive to her. In Paris, he had known other women even when he was officially her lover.[30]

While the General was wasting away, his former partisans tried to regroup under the banner of Boulangism without Boulanger. Shortly after he left the National Committee, a group of young leftists formed an organization with the ponderous title of "Republican Socialist Revisionist Alliance." The first draft of their program was simply a repetition of old Boulangist slogans, plus a new demand for annulment of the High Court's decision. When this program was presented to members of the Committee, they judged it to be too plainly oriented toward Boulanger, the man. In the final draft, the clause on the High Court was replaced by a more general provision to eliminate all exceptional jurisdiction. Even that old favorite, abolition of the Senate, was stricken because many former Boulangists favored the American bicameral system. What emerged was nothing more or less than the current Radical program, and it was accepted by nearly all Boulangist committees in the provinces. One member of the new organization

[29] A.N.F., F⁷ 12447, Sept. 4, 1891.
[30] A.P.P., B a/969 bis, Oct. 19, 1891.

explained his position as follows: "We Boulangists were just Radicals who tried to take advantage of General Boulanger's popularity for our own purposes." [31]

While the original Boulangist program was being replaced by one of a more orthodox Republican nature, the Boulangists Deputies in the Chamber began to seek membership in some of the older, established parties. Realizing that their re-election was doubtful as long as they wore the Boulangist label, the advanced faction led by Laisant tried to join the Socialists. Their application was refused, however, as was that of the less socially conscious Boulangists who wanted to become Radicals. Only the Jeromist wing of the Bonapartists offered a haven to the few partisans of the General who sought admission to that party.[32] Thus was fulfilled, in intent at least, Frary's prediction of 1889 that most Boulangist Deputies would eventually return to the Republic.[33] That such a return was encouraged by Boulanger's suicide is beyond doubt. Shortly after the news from Ixelles had reached France, a police agent reported: "The death of General Boulanger is considered by most of his former partisans to be a fortunate occurrence from the political standpoint." With the man on horseback now gone, they might be respectable enough to enter the mainstream of French political life.[34] Within two weeks, all the so-called revisionist committees throughout the country were formally dissolved on their own initiative.[35]

With the final disintegration of their organization, the Boulangist leaders came to a parting of the ways. Their unity of purpose had been concerned more with the means of arriving

[31] *Le Matin,* May 19, 1890.

[32] A.N.F., F⁷ 12445, Feb. 23, 1891.

[33] Raoul Frary, "Chronique politique," *La Nouvelle Revue,* LX (Oct. 15, 1889), 855.

[34] A.P.P., B a/977, Oct. 2, 1891.

[35] A.N.F., F⁷ 12445, Oct. 22, 1891.

at a new constitution than with the constitution itself. Now that the means they had chosen proved to be insufficient, their former unity was destroyed. Within a few years, Naquet became a convert to anarchism, while Rochefort went off to socialism. The brilliant young Georges Laguerre sought solace in drink and eventually fell victim to alcoholism. Some of the lower-ranking Boulangists, such as Barrès, continued to stress nationalism and were drawn to the Right, which became increasingly identified with nationalistic movements after 1890. At the time of the Dreyfus affair, a large number of the old Boulangists still active in politics were anti-Dreyfusard.[36] Their later activity with the new, nationalist Right has tended to obscure the leftist character of the Boulangist movement.

WHAT BOULANGISM SIGNIFIED

Boulangism was the composite political philosophy of the leading Boulangists; that is, of the members of the National Committee. It was formed of various strands: nationalism in foreign affairs, an ill-defined desire for social progress, and the conviction that universal suffrage would let France speak with one voice were it not for the monarchist constitution of 1875. The political career of General Boulanger brought all these elements to public attention and gave them concrete expression in the form of the Boulangist movement. Yet as Naquet was only too eager to point out, they had all been present in national politics long before the General made his appearance.[37] Prior to the concerted revisionist campaign of 1888 and 1889, the Boulangists had been known as "advanced Republicans."

The origins of Boulangism can be traced to the moderate

[36] John Roberts, "General Boulanger, 1837–1891," *History Today,* V (Oct., 1955), 668–669.

[37] *La Presse,* April 19, 1890.

Republicans' great victories of 1879 and 1881, by which they definitely took control of the regime away from the monarchists. At the same time, the return to France of the Communards injected into the party system an extreme leftist element, which demanded that the work of the French Revolution be continued. For the ex-Communards and their sympathizers, the very word Republic meant continued revolution —continued progress toward the Left, not a stable, bourgeois regime. These Jacobin leftists became the stalwarts of the Boulangist party. They pressed their demands all the harder because they knew that, since 1881 at least, there was no serious danger of a monarchist restoration.

By continuing the work of the Revolution, these "advanced Republicans" meant using 1793 as a base and proceeding from there. To arrive at the form of government in use at that time, it would first be necessary to revise extensively the Orleanist constitution of 1875. The far Left was ideologically committed to the unicameral legislature as the sole possibility of allowing the voice of the people to be heard in government. Although the majority of these Jacobins had few notions of economics, they were convinced that no economic or social reforms could be passed under the present regime. They also believed that reforms of an ideological nature, such as the separation of church and state, depended on a more genuinely Republican form of government than the one established in 1875.

Since these general principles were also shared by the Radicals, that party formed common lists with the far Left in the general elections of 1885. Indeed, the very presence of the far Left seems to have incited the Radicals to be (or at least to act) even more progressive than they might otherwise have been. Certainly the diatribes against the Opportunists from Clemenceau and Pelletan during the campaign of 1885 were every bit as harsh as those from Rochefort. Once the Radicals were asked into the new government, however, both they and the far Left ceased to demand revision of the constitution. They enjoyed the immediate benefits of having three of their number in the cabinet, including General Boulanger.

As War Minister, Boulanger tried his best to be the very incarnation of Jacobin republicanism. He excluded royalists from important military positions, made life a little more bearable for enlisted men, spoke sympathetically about the strikers at Decazeville, and above all, adopted a militant stance toward Germany. Although there was no lack of patriotism on the Right, the Conservatives of this period were extremely prudent, since they believed that the Republic was incapable of successfully waging war. On the militant Left, however, it was not forgotten that the first real military victories of the French Revolution had been won only after the establishment of a republic. The Radicals and former Communards were certain that a truly progressive republic would release the natural *élan* of the French people, thereby allowing the nation to repel aggression with as much success as in 1793. The Commune itself was another such manifestation of vigorous nationalism on the part of the Left.

During the entire period of Radical participation in government, the question of constitutional revision remained dormant. Only Henri Michelin felt strongly enough about revision to call for discussion of the question during the ministerial crisis of December, 1886. He was quickly voted down, however, by his own leftist colleagues, whose immediate concern was not the constitution but re-entering the government. Even after the Goblet ministry had been overthrown, neither the Radicals nor the men of the far Left extended their protests over the ensuing entente between Opportunists and Conservatives, into the constitutional sphere. In fact, the issue of

251

revision was reintroduced not by the "advanced" Republicans, but by the Comte de Paris, whose surprise manifesto of September 15, 1887, announced his intention to oppose the very regime that his followers had established. After the Rouvier cabinet had fallen in November, the question of revision began to be taken seriously in the Chamber. A motion by Jolibois to have it discussed won the votes of Conservative Deputies, while that of Michelin was endorsed by both the Radicals and the far Left.

It was not until more than four months after revision had been approved in principle by nearly two-thirds of the Deputies that Boulanger adopted it publicly as an article of faith. His first declaration in favor of revision came on March 30, 1888, just after his tremendous success in the Aisne against opposition from all parties. Although the vast majority of his votes appear to have come from Radicals, he had presented no program and was officially not even a candidate. The only common denominator of his victory was protest—against his forced retirement from active service, against the present government, against current economic and social conditions. To engaged in a sustained campaign, however, the General needed a more positive message. His declaration in favor of revision served first of all as a tactical measure which prepared the way for an alliance with the Right on the sole issue common to both the Conservatives and his own partisans. Revision also provided the ex-Communards and dissident Radicals with a banner behind which they could assemble their own grievances.

The creation of a specifically Boulangist movement in favor of revision antagonized the Radicals, who could not be a party to a plebiscite on the name of one man. They therefore opposed Boulanger while at the same time working for revision with new-found determination. Radical promises of a new constitution did not receive the same enthusiastic popular response as did those from Boulanger, because the Radicals were identified—correctly so—with the government. By standing outside the government, the Boulangists seemed to offer a true alternative to the present state of political affairs.

That alternative was never explained in detail, because the Boulangists, while united in their opposition to the constitution of 1875, could not fully agree on a new one. They generally preferred a unicameral legislature, but could not decide among themselves as to what form the executive should take. On the one hand, there were Michelin and his friends, who had inherited the Left's old ideological hatred of a strong executive. So they proposed an agent or *commis,* whose function would be merely to carry out the popular will as expressed in the legislature. Naquet, on the other hand, perceived that a strong executive was needed if reforms were to be accomplished. In this respect, Naquet was ages ahead of most other French leftists, who were too blinded by ideological prejudice to understand that authority is as necessary for progress as for reaction. He recognized, however, that the Jacobin Left would not tolerate a strong executive concentrated in the hands of one person; so he suggested a directory, presumably with Boulanger at its head.[38] All these conflicts of principle were present in Boulanger's speech to the Chamber of June 4, 1888, in which the General attempted to give an outline of a new constitution.

Regardless of their differences on the finer points of constitutional theory, the Boulangists were generally agreed on their

[38] To the French, Naquet does not seem to have revealed his plans for Boulanger. In an article addressed to Englishmen, however, he predicted that the General would be "elected chief of the Executive power" ("General Boulanger: His Case," *New Review,* I [June, 1889], 14).

final goal: the establishment of a more democratic republic. Boulangism was not, as later claimed, a form of latent Caesarism, endemic to the French people. This particular explanation of the movement seems to have originated with its moderate critics, who refused to admit that it could have rational causes. Even as objective a commentator as Gabriel Monod fell victim to this temptation. At the height of the Boulanger affair early in 1889, he offered this analysis:

The truth is that the temperament of the majority of the French nation—a temperament at once military and democratic—a leveling, but not a liberal spirit—is a Caesarian temperament; and our administrative organization, centralized to excess, is also favorable to Caesarian government.[39]

In 1890, now that the worst was over, Monod changed his mind.

There is a solid stratum of Republicanism in the country, and the Boulangist movement was not, like the Bonapartist movement of 1848–1851, a general and spontaneous impulse in favor of Caesarism.[40]

The reason why Monod and other sincere but bewildered French moderates equated Boulangism with Caesarism is that they took the former to include all the various parties, even royalists and Bonapartists, that at one time or another favored the General. In fact, Boulangism was the overall political philosophy of the leftist members—the majority—of his committee.

From this reasoning, it follows that not everyone who voted

[39] Gabriel Monod, "The Political Situation in France," *Contemporary Review*, LV (April, 1889), 494.

[40] Gabriel Monod, "French Affairs,'" *Contemporary Review*, LVIII (July, 1890), 20.

for Boulanger was necessarily a Boulangist. In an attempt to group under a single heading, "Boulangism," the many different elements which composed the General's electoral majorities, one writer has referred to "the multiplication of Boulangisms." [41] Far more precise is the analysis offered by André Siegfried:

In the Boulangist coalition, we must distinguish two heterogeneous elements: on the one hand, the Boulangists of the first period and, one might say, of the first inspiration, who were the only authentic Boulangists and the only ones of Republican origin; on the other hand, those of the anti-Republican coalition, who, while associating with the first for reasons of political tactics, did not cease for all that to be what they had been previously: pure royalists and genuine Bonapartists. [42]

These differences were temporarily obscured during Boulanger's by-election campaigns of 1888. In provincial by-elections, the General received more votes from Conservatives than from leftists. This alone does not signify, however, that the Conservative voters had become Boulangists. They harbored many grievances against the government and even—in some cases—against the regime, but these grievances could not find true expression in a party of the extreme Left. The Conservatives who voted for Boulanger did so because there was no rightist candidate present and because he offered them an excellent opportunity to heap still more discredit on the government. They most certainly did not vote for him in order to see him and his leftist collaborators establish a more democratic republic.

[41] Adrien Dansette, *Le boulangisme* (Paris: Fayard, 1946), pp. 143 ff.
[42] André Siegfried, *Tableau politique de la France de l'ouest sous la Troisième République* (Paris: Colin, 1913), p. 488.

Boulanger's own claim that he had won large numbers of royalists and Bonapartists over the Republic was belied by the results of the cantonal and general elections of 1889. In the former, his votes came chiefly from urban, industrial centers with a previous Jacobin tradition. Conservative voters continued to vote Conservative.[43] The General elections produced two clearly defined blocs of Conservative and Boulangist Deputies at opposite ends of the political spectrum. In western France, no Boulangist was elected in a district which was dominated either by the nobles or the clergy. On the other hand, in the leftist areas where Boulangist candidates did win, Conservative votes often gave these candidates the margin of victory over their Republican opponents.[44]

In Paris, the very home of the Boulangist movement and the scene of its greatest victories, Conservative strength was very low. The Boulangist Deputies elected from the capital in 1889 appealed to the same downtrodden elements which had voted for leftist candidates in the past. In fact, many of these Deputies had served in the Chamber previously as Radicals or intransigent leftists. It is to this older loyalty to the Left that Séverine referred when she called Boulangism as phenomenon existing prior to Boulanger. Addressing herself to the Opportunist leader, Ranc, she explained: "Boulangism is disgust, not with the Republic, good Lord! but with 'your' republic, the one your friends have made." By failing to provide for the needs of the poor, she argued, the Opportunists had created a reservoir of discontent which Boulanger exploited with considerable success.[45]

[43] Raoul Frary, "Chronique politique," *La Nouvelle Revue,* LIX (Aug. 15, 1889), 844–845.

[44] Siegfried, *op. cit.,* pp. 488–491.

[45] Séverine [Caroline Rémy Guebhard], *Notes d'une frondeuse de la boulange au Panama* (Paris: Empis, 1894), p. 18.

The Legacy of Boulangism

Contemporary observers of the Boulanger affair realized that economic discontent was directed against the government. In those regions with a previous leftist tradition, such discontent normally favored the Boulangists; elsewhere, it helped the Conservatives.[46] More recently, a French scholar has sought to explain the entire affair in terms of the economic crisis which affected France during the 1880's.[47] Yet Boulangism itself was directed more at ideological issues than at those in the purely economic sphere. For the Boulangists, church-state separation and elimination of the Senate took precedence over workmen's compensation and the graduated income tax. In other words, they brought an ideological solution to material problems. Only several years later, when ideological questions were settled or otherwise disposed of, did French politics offer a material response.

THE AFFAIR'S ROLE IN HISTORY

The Boulanger affair did not result from any chronic weakness in the Republic, but was instead a sign of the regime's growing strength. It was because the Republic was no longer in serious danger that the Radicals and other leftist groups felt free to attack the Opportunists with such ferocity in 1885. The impressive gains registered by the Conservatives that year indicated dissatisfaction primarily with the government, rather than with the Republic itself. In his manifesto of September, 1887, the Comte de Paris acknowledged in effect that the Republic was too firmly entrenched to be dislodged by ordi-

[46] Gabriel Monod, "The French Elections," *The Contemporary Review*, LVI (Nov., 1889), 634–635; cf. Frederick Turner, *General Boulanger* (London: Swan, Sonnenschein, 1888), p. 9.

[47] Jacques Néré, "La crise industrielle de 1882 et le mouvement boulangiste" (2 vols.; unpub. principal thesis, Doctorat ès lettres, University of Paris, 1959), *passim*.

nary, parliamentary means. So he hit on the device of a plebiscite, but even this scheme was never put to the test. Instead, the royalist leaders decided to use Boulanger as the means to bring about a restoration. The mere fact that they intended to have the General run in about a hundred *arrondissements* and then try to push through Conservative candidates in the wake of his victories is an obvious admission of their own weakness. If the royalists or the Conservatives generally had enjoyed a genuine popular following throughout the country, they would not have needed Boulanger.

Controversely, Boulanger and his party would not have been considered a threat to the regime without the generous and well-organized support of the Conservatives. In his memoirs, which he wrote in 1890, the General admitted having received about six million francs from the royalists.[48] Another estimate places the total at eight million. Of this sum, about three million came from the Duchesse d'Uzès, who lost interest in politics after the General's defeat. The Comte de Paris contributed two and a half million francs, while other royalists contributed among them an equal amount.[49] Just as important as the royalists' financial aid is the support they gave Boulanger electorally. Although the General did receive many votes from the Left, all his victories in provincial by-elections, except in the Aisne, were in departments where the Conservatives had been the leading party in 1885. Boulanger's needs and those of the royalists complemented one another: Conservative votes gave him the margin of victory in most by-elections, while his own followers on the Left were expected to put Conservatives in office in the general elections of 1889.

[48] *Mémoires du général Boulanger* (Paris: Edinger, 1890), pp. 153–154.
[49] Adolphe Cohn, "Boulangism and the Republic," *Atlantic Monthly*, LXVII (Jan., 1891), 95.

Because the Tirard government understood the nature of the Boulangist-Conservative alliance, it was able to halt the General's offensive against the regime. Under the Floquet ministry, the Radicals were preoccupied with Boulangism and tried to eliminate its cause by proposing revision of the constitution. Some economic and social reforms were also suggested, but they fared even worse than revision. The Opportunists ignored both questions and concentrated all their efforts on preventing a Boulangist-Conservative victory in the general elections of 1889. By their success in this endeavor, they reduced Boulanger almost overnight to a political nonentity. The disbanding of his electoral organization a year later gave further justification to their tactics.

Although the Opportunists succeeded in defeating General Boulanger and his party, they did not end the economic misery upon which Boulangism fed. From 1889 to 1893, a total of fifteen social laws were passed by Opportunist governments. This unprecedented burst of activity in a normally stagnant area seems to have been the Center politicians' reaction to the popular revolt which had erupted in 1888. As social, rather than economic measures, however, these laws simply ended some of the more flagrant abuses in French industry.[50] The core of the problem remained.

In France, the industrial workers' standard of living remained dismally low for decades, the result of inefficient industries whose productivity was so low as to allow only a handful of capitalists to skim off the meager profits. Slow industrialization prevented the urban proletariat from rising perceptibly above its continual misery or from becoming suffi-

[50] Jacques Néré, "The French Republic," *The New Cambridge Modern History,* Vol. XI: *Material Progress and World-Wide Problems, 1870–1898,* ed. F. H. Hinsley (Cambridge: The University Press, 1962), pp. 312–314.

ciently numerous to exercise a decisive influence in national politics. As Georges Sorel noted in 1908, the workers would benefit from efficient factories, but France had few of these in the late nineteenth century.[51] Thus was engendered the chronic discontent which Professor Fox of Cornell University has called "Boulangitis," the disease of the protest vote. Although not fatal, this malady required the Republican politicians to spend far too much time defending the Republic rather than governing. They therefore neglected the deeper causes of popular discontent, from which more protest votes were to spring.[52]

Government inaction was also maintained by that typically French phenomenon known as *le parlementarisme,* which does not mean parliamentary government as such, but rather its abuse.[53] As Belleval remarked in 1888, a true parliamentary system works best when there are two parties to alternate in governing. France, however, really had nothing but a one-party system, in which all power gravitated to the sluggish Opportunists, who refused to enact needed reforms.[54] Yet the ultimate blame for monopoly of power by the Center must fall on the royalists, whose systematic opposition to the government on all questions effectively paralyzed the workings of parliament. In the absence of a loyal opposition, the Opportunists had no choice but to hoard all governmental authority. Since this prevented popular discontent from finding an outlet

[51] Georges Sorel, *Les illusions du progrès* (Paris: Rivière, 1908), pp. 267–268.

[52] Edward Whiting Fox, "An Estimate of the Character and Extent of Anti-parliamentarism in France, 1887–1914" (unpub. Ph.D. diss., Harvard University, 1941), p. 17n.

[53] Marquis de Castellane, "Les cahiers conservateurs en 1889," *La Nouvelle Revue,* LX (Sept. 1, 1889), 23.

[54] Louis de Belleval, *Sommes-nous en république?* (Paris: Rousseau, 1888), pp. 274–275.

within the government itself, the discontented turned to Boulanger.[55] Royalist intransigence in 1888 made *le parlementarisme* especially acute and thereby contributed greatly to the General's success.

Intransigence of both Right and Left reached its zenith on the question of constitutional revision. When the Comte de Paris abandoned the Orleanist constitution of 1875, he encouraged the leftist Deputies to revive their dormant opposition to it. Boulanger's own public declaration in favor of revision helped focus all political and economic grievances on the regime. Yet the critics on France's existing constitution could not agree on a replacement. The various suggestions for a new constitution, as reported by Révillon to the Chamber on February 9, 1889, were even more vague and self-contradictory than was Boulanger's.[56] So the Tirard ministry wisely avoided discussing the constitutional problem, which largely settled itself after Boulanger's political defeat. Not until 1940 was the nature of the regime seriously called into question. Because it brought the issue to a head, the Boulanger affair can be seen as a *crise de croissance*—the Republic's growing pains.

---

[55] Marquis de Castellane, "1789–1889: Les conservateurs." *La Nouvelle Revue,* LVI (Jan. 1, 1889), 17–18; for a similar view, see P. G. Hamerton, "The Political Situation in France," *Contemporary Review,* LV (April, 1889), 501.

[56] *J.O.C.* (1889), pp. 357–358.

Bibliography

PUBLIC DOCUMENTS

France. *Journal officiel de la République française: Débats parlementaires, Chambre des Députés,* 1886–1889. (Cited in the footnotes as *J.O.C.*)

———. Haute Cour de Justice. *Affaire Boulanger, Dillon, Rochefort: Procédure générale, réquisitoire,* 1889.

———. Ministère des Affaires Etrangères. *Documents diplomatiques français, 1871–1914.* 1ère série, Vol. VI. Paris: Imprimerie Nationale, 1934. (Cited in footnotes as *D.D.F.*)

Germany. *Stenographische Berichte über die Verhandlungen des Reichstags,* 1886–1887. (Cited in footnotes as *Verhandlungen.*)

———. Auswärtiges Amt. *Die Grosse Politik der Europäischen Kabinette.* Edited by Johannes Lepsius, Albrecht Mendelssohn Bartholdy, and Friedrich Thimme. Vol. VI. Berlin: Deutsche Verlagsgesellschaft für Politik und Geschichte, 1924. (Cited in footnotes as *Grosse Politik.*)

BOOKS

Acomb, Evelyn Martha. *The French Laic Laws, 1879–1889: The First Anti-clerical Campaign of the Third French Republic.* New York: Columbia University Press, 1941.

Adam, Paul. *Le mystère des foules.* Paris: Ollendorff, 1895.

Andrieux, Louis. *La révision.* Paris: Librairie de la *Nouvelle Revue,* 1889.

Bibliography

Audiffrent, Georges. *Parlementarisme, dictature.* Paris: Welter, 1888.

Barbou, Alfred. *Le général Boulanger.* Paris: Perrin, 1887.

Barrès, Maurice. *L'appel au soldat.* Paris: Juven, 1911.

Bataille, Albert. *Causes criminelles et mondaines de 1889.* Paris: Dentu, 1890.

Beau de Loménie, E. *Les responsabilités des dynasties bourgeoises.* Vol. II: *De MacMahon à Poincaré.* Paris: Denoël, 1963.

Belleval, Louis de. *Le complot contre le suffrage universel.* Paris: Rousseau, 1888.

——. *La politique opportuniste: Colonies et pots-de-vin.* Paris: Rousseau, 1888.

——. *Sommes-nous en république?* Paris: Rousseau, 1888.

Bertrand, Alphonse. *La Chambre de 1889: Biographies des 576 députés.* Paris: Michaud, 1890.

Blunt, Wilfred S. *My Diaries.* 2 vols. New York: Knopf, 1921.

Bodley, J. E. C. *France.* 2 vols. New York: Macmillan, 1898.

Bonjean, François. *Dix ans de dictature opportuniste.* Avignon: Imprimerie spéciale du *Réveil du Midi,* n.d. [1888].

Boulanger, Georges. *Les discours du général Boulanger depuis le 4 août 1881 jusqu'au 4 septembre 1887.* Paris: Périnet, 1888.

——. *Mémoires du général Boulanger.* Paris: Edinger, 1890.

Bourgeois, Emile. *Manuel historique de politique étrangère.* 4 vols. Paris: Belin, 1926.

Bourgeois, Emile, and Georges Pagès. *Les origines et les responsabilités de la Grande Guerre.* Paris: Hachette, 1921.

Brogan, Denis W. *The Development of Modern France, 1870–1939.* London: Hamish Hamilton, 1959.

Brulat, Paul. *Lumières et grandes ombres.* Paris: Grasset, 1930.

Bryce, James. *Modern Democracies.* 2 vols. New York: Macmillan, 1921.

Buisson, Georges and A. Henri Canu. *M. Paul Déroulède et sa Ligue des patriotes: La vérité.* Paris: Savine, 1889.

Buthman, William Curt. *The Rise of Integral Nationalism in France.* New York: Columbia University Press, 1939.

Bibliography

Byrnes, Robert F. *Antisemitism in Modern France.* New Brunswick, N.J.: Rutgers University Press, 1950.

Cambon, Paul. *Correspondance, 1870–1914.* 2 vols. Paris: Grasset, 1940.

Carette, Albert. *La République et le régime parlementaire.* Paris: Dentu, 1887.

Cavailhon, Edouard. *La France ferrycide.* Paris: Balitout, 1888.

Chapman, Guy. *The Third Republic of France: The First Phase, 1871–1894.* London: Macmillan, 1962.

Chastenet, Jacques. *Histoire de la Troisième République.* Vol. II: *La République des républicains, 1879–1893.* Paris: Hachette, 1954.

Chaudordy, Jean-Baptiste-Alexandre Damas, comte de. *La France en 1889.* Paris: Plon, n.d. [1890].

Chevalier, J.-J. *Histoire des institutions politiques de la France moderne, 1789–1945.* Paris: Dalloz, 1958.

Chincholle, Charles. *Le général Boulanger.* Paris: Savine, 1889.

Chirac, Auguste. *L'agiotage sous la Troisième République, 1870–1887.* 2 vols. Paris: Savine, 1889.

Clapham, John H. *The Economic Development of France and Germany, 1815–1914.* Cambridge: The University Press, 1955.

——. *Histoire religieuse de la France contemporaine.* 2 vols. Paris: Flammarion, 1951.

Clough, Shepard B. *France: A History of National Economics, 1789–1939.* New York: Scribner's, 1939.

Corpechot, Lucien. *Souvenirs d'un journaliste.* Paris: Plon, 1936.

Coubertin, Pierre de. *L'évolution française sous la Troisième République.* Paris: Plon-Nourrit, 1896.

Da Costa, Charles. *Les blanquistes.* Paris: Rivière, 1912.

Daniel, André. *L'année politique.* Vols. XII–XVI (1885–1889). Paris: Charpentier, 1886–1890.

Dansette, Adrien. *L'affaire Wilson et la chute du président Grévy.* Paris: Perrin, 1936.

——. *Le boulangisme.* Paris: Fayard, 1946.

Daudet, Léon. *Devant la douleur.* Paris: Nouvelle Librairie Nationale, 1915.

Débidour, Antonin. *L'Eglise et l'Etat en France sous la Troisième République, 1870–1906.* 3 vols. Paris: Alcan, 1906.

Denis, Pierre. *Le mémorial de Saint-Brelade.* Paris: Ollendorff, 1894.

Digeon, Claude. *La crise allemande de la pensée française, 1870–1914.* Paris: Presses Universitaires de France, 1959.

Dommanget, Maurice. *Edouard Vaillant: Un grand socialiste.* Paris: La Table Ronde, 1956.

Drumont, Edouard. *La dernière bataille.* Paris: Dentu, 1890.

——. *La fin d'un monde.* Paris: Savine, 1889.

Ducray, Camille. *Paul Déroulède, 1846–1914.* Paris: Ambert, 1914.

Dutilh, Clodomir. *Opportunistes et radicaux.* Bordeaux: Bellier, 1882.

——. *La souveraineté du peuple.* Bordeaux: Rapin, 1885.

Engels, Friedrich, and Paul and Laura Lafargue. *Correspondance.* 3 vols. Paris: Editions Sociales, 1956.

Eyck, Erich. *Bismarck and the German Empire.* 2nd ed. London: Allen & Unwin, 1958.

Ferry, Jules. *Discours et opinions.* 7 vols. Ed. Paul Robiquet. Paris: Colin, 1893–1901.

——. *Lettres.* Paris: Calmann-Lévy, 1914.

Frank, Walter. *Nationalismus und Demokratie im Frankreich der Dritten Republik, 1871 bis 1918.* 2nd ed. Hamburg: Hanseatische Verlagsanstalt, 1941.

Freycinet, Charles de. *Souvenirs, 1878–1893.* Paris: Delagrave, 1913.

Galli [Gallichet], Henri. *Paul Déroulède: Raconté par lui-même.* Paris: Plon, 1900.

Gay [Garennes], Ernest. *Dernière défaite.* Paris: Savine, 1891.

Girardet, Raoul. *La société militaire dans la France contemporaine, 1815–1939.* Paris: Plon, 1953.

Goguel, François. *La politique des partis sous la Troisième République.* Paris: Editions du Seuil, 1958.

Goncourt, Edmond and Jules de. *Journal: Mémoires de la vie littéraire.* 22 vols. Monaco: Imprimerie Nationale, 1956–1958.

Goulette, Léon. *Avant, pendant et après l'affaire Schnaebelé.* Paris: Bayle, n.d. [1887].

Grammont, M. de M. *Rouvier et le général Boulanger devant le pays.* Paris: Dentu, 1887.

Grison, Georges. *Le général Boulanger jugé par ses partisans et ses adversaires.* Paris: Librairie Illustrée, 1889.

Hanotaux, Gabriel. *Mon temps.* 4 vols. Paris: Plon, 1947.

Impartialis [Poinsard, Léon]. *Les Français sont-ils en état de vivre sous le régime parlementaire?* Paris: Louis Alexander, 1889.

Isay, Raymond. *Panorama des expositions universelles.* Paris: Gallimard, 1937.

Jackson, J. Hampden. *Clemenceau and the Third Republic.* New York: Collier Books, 1962.

Joughin, Jean T. *The Paris Commune in French Politics, 1871–1880.* 2 vols. Baltimore: Johns Hopkins University Press, 1955.

Kayser, Jacques. *Les grandes batailles du radicalisme, 1820–1901.* Paris: Rivière, 1962.

Kindleberger, Charles P. *Economic Growth in France and Britain, 1851–1950.* Cambridge, Mass.: Harvard University Press, 1964.

Kühn, Joachim, *et al. Der Nationalismus im Leben der Dritten Republik.* Berlin: Paetel, 1920.

Laisant, Charles-Ange. *A mes électeurs: Pourquoi et comment je suis boulangiste.* Paris: Mayer, 1887.

———. *L'anarchie bourgeoise.* Paris: Flammarion, 1887.

Lalance, Auguste. *Mes souvenirs, 1830–1914.* Paris: Berger-Levrault, 1914.

Lamoureux, J. *Un an d'exil.* Paris: Savine, 1890.

Lanessan, J.-L. de. *La république démocratique.* Paris: Colin, 1897.

Laur, Francis. *L'époque boulangiste.* 2 vols. Paris: Le Livre à l'Auteur, 1912–1914.

Lecomte, Maxime. *Le boulangisme dans le Nord: Histoire de l'élection du 15 avril.* Paris: Librairie Illustrée, 1888.

———. *Les ralliés: Histoire d'un parti, 1886–1898.* Paris: Flammarion, 1898.

Bibliography

Lépine, Louis. *Mes Souvenirs*. Paris: Payot, 1929.

Ligneau, Jean de [François Bournand]. *Juifs et antisémites en Europe*. Paris: Tolra, 1891.

Louis, Paul. *Histoire du socialisme en France de la Révolution à nos jours*. 3rd ed. Paris: Rivière, 1936.

Magué, André. *Le proscrit de Jersey: Etat actuel de la France*. Neuilly: Marceau, 1890.

Matter, Florent. *Paul Déroulède*. Paris: Sansot, 1919.

Maury, Louis. *M. Boulanger devant l'opinion publique*. Poitiers: Millet, Descoust & Pain, 1888.

Mermeix [Gabriel Terrail]. *Les antisémites en France*. Paris: Dentu, 1892.

——. *Les coulisses du boulangisme*. Paris: Cerf, 1890.

——. *La France socialiste: Notes d'histoire contemporaine*. Paris: Fetscherin et Chuit, 1886.

Meyer, Arthur. *Ce que mes yeux ont vu*. Paris: Plon, 1911.

Millaud, Edouard. *Le journal d'un parlementaire*. 4 vols. Paris: Oudin, 1914–1925.

Naquet, Alfred. *Questions constitutionnelles*. Paris: Dentu, 1883.

——. *La république radicale*. Paris: Germer-Baillière, 1873.

——. *Socialisme collectiviste et socialisme libéral*. Paris: Dentu, 1890.

Néré, Jacques. *Le boulangisme et la presse*. Paris: Colin, 1964.

Newton, Thomas W. L., ed. *Lord Lyons: A Record of British Diplomacy*. 2 vols. London: Arnold, 1913.

Nicot, Lucien. *L'Allemagne à Paris*. Paris: Dentu, 1887.

Pecheux, Théodule. *Les élections générales de 1889*. Paris: Baudu, n.d.

Pottecher, Maurice. *Jules Ferry*. Paris: Gallimard, 1930.

Power, Thomas F., Jr. *Jules Ferry and the Renaissance of French Imperialism*. New York: King's Crown, 1944.

Rambaud, Alfred. *Jules Ferry*. Paris: Plon-Nourrit, 1903.

Reinach, Joseph. *Les petites catilinaires*. Vol. I: *La foire Boulangiste*. Vol. II: *Le cheval noir*. Vol. III: *Bruno-le-Fileur*. Paris: Victor-Havard, 1889.

Rémond, René. *La droite en France de 1815 à nos jours.* Paris: Aubier, 1954.

Robert, Adolphe, Edgar Bourloton, and Gaston Cougny. *Dictionnaire des parlementaires français.* 5 vols. Paris: Bourloton, 1890.

Rochefort, Henri. *Les aventures de ma vie.* 5 vols. Paris: Dupont, 1897.

Rolland, Romain. *Le cloître de la rue d'Ulm.* Paris: Albin Michel, 1952.

Ruhemann, Alfred. *General Boulanger, "der Reformator des französischen Armee": Lebensbild des französischen Kriegsministers.* Berlin: Walther und Aplant, 1887.

Sée, Henri. *Histoire économique de la France.* 2 vols. Paris: Colin, 1951.

Seignobos, Charles. *L'évolution de la Troisième République, 1875–1914.* Vol. VIII of *Histoire de France contemporaine,* ed. Ernest Lavisse. 10 vols. Paris: Hachette, 1921.

Séverine [Caroline Rémy Guebhard]. *Notes d'une frondeuse de la boulange au Panama.* Paris: Empis, 1894.

Siegfried, André. *Tableau politique de la France de l'ouest sous la Troisième République.* Paris: Colin, 1913.

Simon, Jules. *Souviens-toi du Deux-décembre.* Paris: Victor-Havard, 1889.

Sorel, Georges. *Les illusions du progrès.* Paris: Rivière, 1908.

Soulier, Auguste. *L'instabilité ministérielle sous la Troisième République, 1871–1938.* Paris: Sirey, 1939.

Sybil [Charles Benoist]. *Croquis parlementaires.* Paris: Perrin, 1891.

Szajkowski, Zosa. *Anti-Semitism in the French Labor Movement.* New York: S. Frydman, 1948.

Taylor, A. J. P. *The Struggle for Mastery in Europe, 1848–1918.* Oxford: Clarendon Press, 1954.

Tenot, Eugène. *La vérité sur M. Boulanger militaire.* Paris: Alcan-Lévy, 1888.

Testis [Gabriel Hanotaux]. *Les hommes de 1889.* Bordeaux: Gounouilhou, 1893.

Bibliography

Tharaud, Jean and Jérôme. *Paul Déroulède*. Paris: Emile-Paul, 1914.

———. *La vie et la mort de Déroulède*. Paris: Plon, 1925.

Thomson, David. *Democracy in France: The Third and Fourth Republics*. London: Oxford University Press, 1958.

Turner, Frederick. *General Boulanger*. London: Swan, Sonnenschein, 1888.

Uzès, Anne de Mortemart, duchesse d'. *Souvenirs de la duchesse d'Uzès*. Paris: Plon, 1939.

Verly, Albert. *Le général Boulanger et la conspiration monarchique*. Paris: Ollendorff, 1893.

Viau, Raphaël. *Vingt ans d'antisémitisme, 1889–1909*. Paris: Charpentier, 1910.

Weill, Georges. *Histoire du mouvement social en France, 1852–1924*. 3rd ed. Paris: Alcan, 1924.

Weygand, Maxime. *Mémoires*. 3 vols. Paris: Flammarion, 1953.

Zévaès, Alexandre. *Au temps du boulangisme*. Paris: Gallimard, 1930.

Ziekursch, Johannes. *Politische Geschichte des neuen deutschen Kaiserreiches*. 3 vols. Frankfurt: Societäts Drückerei, 1927.

ARTICLES AND PERIODICALS

L'Action. 1886–1889.

L'Autorité. 1886–1891.

Barrès, Maurice. "M. le général Boulanger et la nouvelle génération," *Revue Indépendante,* VII (April, 1888), 55–63.

La Cocarde. 1888–1891.

Cohn, Adolphe. "Boulangism and the Republic," *Atlantic Monthly,* LXVII (Jan., 1891), 92–98.

The Contemporary Review. 1885–1891.

Le Correspondant. 1885–1891.

Le Cri du Peuple. 1886–1889.

Dietz, Jean. "Jules Ferry: Sa seconde présidence du Conseil, II," *Revue Politique et Parlementaire,* CLXIV (Nov. 10, 1935), 288–311.

———. "Jules Ferry: Sa seconde présidence du Conseil, III". *Revue*

Bibliography

Politique et Parlementaire, CLXIV (Dec. 10, 1935), 500–518.

——. "Jules Ferry: La révision de la Constitution et le scrutin de liste, I," *Revue Politique et Parlementaire,* CLXVI (March 10, 1936), 515–532.

Le Drapeau. 1885–1889.

Le Figaro. 1885–1891.

Fox, Edward Whiting. "The Third Force, 1897–1939," in Edward Mead Earle, ed., *Modern France* (Princeton, N.J.: Princeton University Press, 1951), pp. 124–136.

La France. 1886–1889.

Le Gaulois, 1885–1891.

Girardet, Raoul. "La Ligue des patriotes dans l'histoire du nationalisme français (1882–1888)," *Bulletin de la Société d'Histoire Moderne,* 12ème série, no. 6 (1958), pp. 3–6.

Goblet, René. "Souvenirs de ma vie politique," *Revue Politique et Parlementaire,* CXLI (Oct. 10, 1929), 3–24.

Hoffman, Stanley. "Protest in Modern France," in Morton A. Kaplan, ed., *The Revolution in World Politics* (New York: Wiley, 1962), pp. 69–91.

L'Intransigeant. 1885–1891.

La Justice. 1885–1891.

La Lanterne. 1886–1889.

Malon, Benoît, and Eugène Fournière. "Physiologie du boulangisme," *Revue Socialiste,* VII (May, 1888), 507–521.

Le Matin. 1885–1891.

Naquet, Alfred. "General Boulanger: His Case," *New Review,* I (June, 1889), 1–15.

Néré, Jacques. "The French Republic," in F. H. Hinsley, ed., *Material Progress and World-wide Problems, 1870–1898,* Vol. XI of *The New Cambridge Modern History* (Cambridge: The University Press, 1962), pp. 300–322.

New York Herald. 1888–1889.

La Nouvelle Revue. 1885–1891.

Le Pays. 1885–1886.

Pelletan, Camille. "General Boulanger: His Impeachment," *New Review,* I (June, 1889), 16–29.

Bibliography

Piou, Jacques. "Le boulangisme," *Revue de Paris,* XXXIX (March 15, 1932), 301–320.

La Presse. 1888–1891.

La République Française. 1885–1891.

Revue Politique et Littéraire (Revue Bleue). 1885–1891.

Roberts, John. "General Boulanger, 1837–1891," *History Today,* V (Oct., 1955), 657–669.

Le Temps. 1885–1891.

Watson, D. R. "The Nationalist Movement in Paris, 1900–1906," in David Shapiro, ed., *The Right in France, 1890–1919* (London: Chatto & Windus, 1962).

Weber, Eugen. "The Right in France: A Working Hypothesis," *American Historical Review,* LXV (April, 1960), 554–568.

ARCHIVES

France. Archives nationales françaises. C5300 A 70 through C5327 A 97; F⁷ 12445 through F⁷ 12448; F⁷ 12549. (Cited in footnotes as A.N.F.)

——. Archives de la Préfecture de Police. B a/497; B a/906; B a/969 through B a/977; B a/1337; B a/1465 through B a/1467; B a/1496; B a/1515 B a/1518. (Cited in the footnotes as A.P.P.)

——. Bibliothèque nationale. N.A.F. 23783.

UNPUBLISHED MATERIAL

Carnes, Jess Gale. "The French Army Officers and the Establishment of the Republic." Unpublished Ph.D. dissertation, Department of History, Cornell University, 1949.

Fox, Edward Whiting. "An Estimate of the Character and Extent of Anti-parliamentarism in France, 1887–1914." Unpublished Ph.D. dissertation, Department of History, Harvard University, 1941.

Néré, Jacques. "La crise industrielle de 1882 et le mouvement boulangiste." Unpublished principal thesis, Doctorat ès lettres, University of Paris, 1959.

———. "Les élections Boulanger dans le département du Nord." Unpublished complementary thesis, Doctorat ès lettres, University of Paris, 1959.

———. "Le vrai visage du boulangisme." Unpublished manuscript, Paris, 1961.

Index

Index

Index

Michelin, Henri, 58, 67, 99, 102, 191, 208, 251; proposes revision, 44, 89-90; differs with Boulanger over revision, 136-138; leaves Boulangist movement, 223-224; returns to movement, 229-230
Millerand, Alexandre, 58, 130, 164, 197-198
Monod, Gabriel, 65, 186, 254
Moreau, Emile, 127-130, 155-156
Münster, Count, 47, 51-52, 55, 60, 212
Mun, Albert de, 36

Naquet, Alfred, 105, 135-136, 142, 146, 176, 180, 182, 189, 191, 193-194, 208, 234, 245, 253; political philosophy, 73-76; early political career, 99-101; Tours speech, 217; tries to oust Boulanger, 241-242; converts to anarchism, 249
Nationalism, French: associated with Left, 28, 48, 100, 175, 201; during war scare, 58; and Boulanger's fall from office, 66-68; exploited by Boulangist propaganda, 108-109; shifts to Right, 249
National Republican Committee, 99-100, 103, 105, 142, 147, 175-176, 195, 223, 245-247

Opportunists, 8-21, 23-25, 27, 34-35, 92, 96-97, 103, 106, 121, 124-126, 146, 151, 153, 159-160, 162, 179, 200, 242, 250-251, 259-260; hostile to Boulanger, 45, 61-62; collaborate with Right, 63-64, 77; move against Boulanger, 211-213, 218, 228
Orleanists, 6, 13, 131, 153, 166, 191-192; embarrassed by pretender's manifesto, 82-84; collaborate with Boulanger, 106, 115-116, 122-123

Paris, Comte de, 6, 35, 37, 43, 63, 90, 106, 108, 114-115, 165, 240, 252, 257, 261; issues manifesto, 80-84; confirms Orleanist-Boulangist alliance, 131-132, 200, 232
Parliamentary government, 3-4, 23, 260

Patriotism, French, 9, 47-48; contributes to Boulanger's popularity, 54, 93, 95-96, 127, 251
Peasants, 6, 17, 123-124
Pelletan, Camille, 12, 17, 20, 64, 88, 97, 112-113, 121, 158, 199, 213, 217, 219, 225, 250
Piou, Jacques, 36
Poincaré, Raymond, 164
Protest vote, 3, 96-97, 108-109, 125, 252, 260
Pyat, Félix, 111

Quesnay de Beaurepaire, Jules, 222, 225-226

Radicals, 1-2, 7, 14-16, 19-21, 23-24, 30-31, 61, 68-69, 76, 82, 103, 106-107, 110-112, 118-119, 121, 125-126, 141, 151, 153, 159-160, 162, 179, 188, 198, 212-213, 219, 225, 228, 248, 250-252, 256; bring Boulanger into government, 25-26; overthrow Rouvier ministry, 87-90; propose revision, 113-114
Raoul-Duval, Edgard, 39-43, 63
Reinach, Joseph, 50, 214
Revision of constitution, 11-12, 75-76, 92, 104-105, 115, 117-119, 127, 132ff, 163-166, 173-174, 182-185, 247, 251-253, 259, 261; in Radical program, 7; rejected by Radicals, 44; accepted by Deputies of Right and Left, 89-90; accepted by Boulanger, 113; accepted by Floquet, 114; rejected by Chamber, 213-214
Rochefort, Henri, 8, 16, 46, 54, 61-62, 70, 99, 129, 173, 182, 188-189, 206-207, 237, 241, 246, 249
Rolland, Romain, 204-205
Rouvier, Maurice, 59-60, 64, 69, 72, 82, 86-87, 89-90, 205, 213

Saint-Cyr military academy, 31-32, 78, 102
Say, Léon, 40
Schnaebelé affair, 57-60, 77
Scrutin d'arrondissement, 17-18, 212-214, 233, 236